P9-BIJ-830

"*Unless the trend is sharply reversed . . . by the end of the decade anyone who punches a time clock or inhabits an executive suite from San Diego to Penobscot will have to get the nod from the personality tester before exercising the atrophying privilege of working,*" writes MARTIN L. GROSS in this acid analysis of brain watching—the multi-million-dollar business that stands between you . . . and your future.

READ WHAT THE CRITICS HAVE TO SAY ABOUT HIS TIMELY AND CHALLENGING BOOK:

"The American public has been in need of a blast against the use of invalid personality tests, and this is provided, in fact with a vengeance, by this angry journalist."
—NEW YORK TIMES BOOK REVIEW

"Mr. Gross has exposed their racket in a book that could hardly be bettered. He combines full knowledge with acute analysis, sound organization and caustic style."
— —SATURDAY REVIEW

"If Martin L. Gross's *The Brain Watchers* is even 50% true, there is no reason to look any further for the causes of the stock market decline. For what this book charges, in effect, is that there is nothing so stupid or so easily gulled as a great corporation."
—WALL STREET JOURNAL

"*The Brain Watchers* is an important book. It is a responsible book. It is a perceptive book."
—NEW YORK HERALD TRIBUNE

MENTOR Books of Related Interest

THE FOLKLORE OF MANAGEMENT *by Clarence Randall*
A provocative study of modern business methods and
of the misconceptions which threaten good management. By the retired president of Inland Steel and
former special adviser on Foreign Economic Study to
President Eisenhower.   (#MP443—60¢)

TOWARD THE LIBERALLY EDUCATED EXECUTIVE
            edited by R. A. Goldwin and C. A. Nelson
Top men in the fields of industry and education
analyze the type of leadership needed in business.
                                         (#MD299—50¢)

AUTOMATION: Its Impact on Business and People
            by Walter Buckingham
An incisive analysis of the most important economic
and social consequences of automation in industry.
                                         (#MP525—60¢)

THE AFFLUENT SOCIETY *by John Kenneth Galbraith*
A cogent argument for a re-adaptation of economic
ideas and attitudes to the society of affluence in which
we now live. By the distinguished Harvard economist
and economic advisor to President Kennedy.
                                         (#MT534—75¢)

TO OUR READERS: If your dealer does not have the
SIGNET and MENTOR books you want, you may order
them by mail, enclosing the list price plus 5¢ a copy to
cover mailing. If you would like our free catalog, please
request it by postcard. The New American Library of
World Literature, Inc., P. O. Box 2310, Grand Central
Station, New York, New York, 10017.

The Brain Watchers

by
MARTIN L. GROSS

A SIGNET BOOK
PUBLISHED BY THE NEW AMERICAN LIBRARY

© COPYRIGHT, 1962, BY MARTIN L. GROSS

All rights reserved under International and Pan-American Copyright Conventions. No part of this book may be reproduced without permission. For information address Random House, Inc., 457 Madison Avenue, New York 22, New York.

Published as a SIGNET BOOK
by arrangement with Random House, Inc.,
who have authorized this softcover edition.
A hardcover edition is available from Random House, Inc.

FIRST PRINTING, OCTOBER, 1963

SIGNET TRADEMARK REG. U.S. PAT. OFF. AND FOREIGN COUNTRIES
REGISTERED TRADEMARK—MARCA REGISTRADA
HECHO EN CHICAGO, U.S.A.

SIGNET BOOKS are published by
The New American Library of World Literature, Inc.
501 Madison Avenue, New York 22, New York

PRINTED IN THE UNITED STATES OF AMERICA

To my wife, Anita

Sincere acknowledgment to those members of the psychological community who read and offered their comments and suggestions on this volume prior to publication.

Contents

PROBING THE BRAIN WATCHER

PART ONE

Your Psyche For Hire

1 THE PERSONALITY COLOSSUS

This book is about brain watching, the art, its practitioners, and its subjects, some 50,000,000 hapless Americans.

Brain watching is a vital twentieth-century sociological phenomenon that has made your mind, inner thoughts, political opinions, frustrations (including the sexual), aspirations—what we commonly call *personality*—the raw material of a humming, seemingly insatiable American industry.

The importance of a man's or woman's personality has undoubtedly reached the zenith in this "swell guy" era and its premium on quiet adjustment. Intelligence, competence, sweat, and ability are becoming mere base requirements for the chance to show your true mettle, through your personality. Schools, corporations, government—anyone who hires, fires, promotes, selects, or chooses—have long sought the psychologist's touchstone: "How can I measure the *real* man?"

The psychoanalyst attempts a measurement whose overhead runs into years and thousands of dollars. The brain watcher, or personality tester, as we shall see, claims that he can measure this same elusive human imponderable as easily and as accurately as counting compact cars off a Detroit assembly line. He can, he says, measure the psyche for anyone who wants to know, in as little time as five minutes, and as cheaply as $20 a head, less normal business discounts.

The brain watcher has many profiles. He may be an industrial psychologist, a university professor of psychology, the personnel director of a large corporation, a self-employed small factory owner, a $4,700-a-year academic Ph.D. turned $12,000-a-year commercial tester. He is often a government agency supervisor, the operator of an employment agency, a management consultant, an executive locator, a school psychologist or guidance counselor, a military psychologist, the admissions officer of a university or professional school. Or, he may merely be an enterprising entrepreneur whose only academic qualification as a brain watcher is last month's rent receipt on an elaborate suite of offices whose full-length plate glass door reflects the unlikely name: "Personality Research and Development Institute, Inc."

He has tackled his work with typical Yankee fervor, and, rather than an infant psychological toy, brain watching today is a more than $50,000,000-a-year business that has become one of the main determinants of your career, your job, your very place in society. With his tools, the question-and-answer tests (How many people do you hate very much? None? Over 50?), inkblots, other paper scalpels, and an extraordinary quantity of huckster bravado often unbecoming to his profession, he has convinced those who will pay for psychological information about their fellow man that he can reduce a man's "yes" and "no" answers and other test responses to the measurement of such human traits as radicalism, extroversion, aggressiveness, happiness, and even latent homosexuality and a craving for early-morning Martinis.

A test subject is likely to be quizzed on hundreds of intimate questions (including such impertinent ones as "Does some particularly useless thought keep coming into your mind to bother you?"), asked to draw pictures of nude women, supply the punch lines to outdated dialect gags, create "imaginative" stories from cartoon situations, and complete such sentences as "My father. . . ." He may even be asked to submit a handwriting sample and, to the dismay of more reputable testers, sit while his facial bulges are analyzed. From these the tester claims that he can predict, with uncanny accuracy far surpassing human intuition or experience, who is a candidate for the psychological slag heap and who will succeed at a specific job—whether a copywriter for Kenyon & Eckhardt; an engineer at Westinghouse; a middle management man at Sears, Roebuck; a wholesale salesman for Exquisite Form Brassieres; a secretary in any one of hundreds of firms; or a prospective clergyman in the Presbyterian Church.

The brain watcher is not to be underestimated. He is versatile, adaptable, and enveloping—difficult for the unsophisticated or untutored to beat, and almost impossible for anyone but the most professionally secure to evade. In industry, where he is paid handsomely (one firm, Worthington Associates, recently paid $100,000 for a psychological audit of its managerial staff), he tries to separate the crabgrass from the Merion Blue in any given group of employees.

He screens would-be employees from milk routemen to senior vice presidents; tests men already on the job and recommends promoting, demoting, firing, or shelving; helps choose thousands of executive trainees from the legions of annual college graduates seeking to make the corporation their career; and even participates in the selection of successors to company presidents. In our schools (see Chapter VII: The Three R's through Graduate School) he tests junior high and high school youngsters for clues to their future professions, and weeds out the ostensibly psychologically unsound from students applying to many professional schools, including several sizable medical colleges. In 1960, half a million high school youngsters took a battery of tests—including personality inventories—the results of which will go to their schools as part of "Project Talent," sponsored by the U. S. Department of Health, Education and Welfare. Both the College Boards and the National Merit Scholarship Corporation have announced their quest of a personality selector to isolate the psychologically qualified (or unfit) among our superior college-age youngsters.

The brain watcher screens out casualty-prone servicemen, and even tests wives for corporate compatibility. He virtually hand-picks policemen in such cities as Los Angeles. In some corporations he may permanently attach himself to an executive, probing him at least once a month—at dinner or on the golf course—for potential advancement or discarding. At Columbia University, researchers are experimenting with a personality test designed to be given to driver applicants, to refuse licenses to the "accident-prone" in advance. One insurance firm recently initiated a testing program which requires youthful drivers under twenty-five to pass a personality quiz or pay a penalty. The New York City Youth

Board intends to use related techniques to predict which of a given group of school children will ultimately become juvenile menaces.

"It's only a passing fad," hopefully says a top official of the Standards Division of the U. S. Civil Service Commission. The facts, however, refute his optimism. From all indications, the number of firms using brain-watching services is increasing significantly, especially among smaller companies anxious to emulate those already using "scientific selection." A recent nationwide survey of 852 companies, made by the Bureau of Business Research of the University of Texas, showed that of those firms answering this query, 56 percent are using personality and "interest" tests. Of 58 companies polled by *American Business* magazine, 30 were using these techniques. The now-famed *Fortune* poll indicated that 60 percent of 63 firms surveyed were using personality tests for selection or upgrading. A leading testing company, Science Research Associates of Chicago, much of whose business includes personality testing, now has 11,000 industrial clients, three times as many as in 1957.

The roster of firms that attempt to peek into the mind, and soul, of applicants or employees reads like a Dun & Bradstreet register: Westinghouse; Sears, Roebuck; Pan American World Airways; Johnson & Johnson; Tidewater Oil, Long Island Lighting; Standard Oil of New Jersey; Benton & Bowles advertising; U. S. Rubber; American Machine & Foundry; Republic Steel; IBM; ITT; Borden Company; Lever Brothers; Carnation Company; Burlington Industries; Hartford Fire Insurance; and hundreds more of their size. Thousands of smaller firms are also among the brain watcher's best customers, including representatives in every field from Fanny Farmer Candy Shops to Western Airlines.

Estimates are difficult but—aside from millions in the military and schools—it appears that more than 10,000,000 Americans have already had their psyches probed by prospective and current employers, and more than a million more are being tested each year. One successful firm, Activity Vector Analysis of Providence, Rhode Island, expects that its lay analysts in hundreds of firms throughout the country will test over 300,000 workers and executives this year.

The growth is accelerating, especially in "human inventory," the testing of men already on the payroll, and in the so-called creative industries once considered off limits to overzealous brain watchers. It is becoming increasingly com-

mon for newspaper reporters and editors, writers, radio or
TV network personnel, public relations executives or advertising agency account men and copywriters to have their
already delicate future hinge on a tester's swift evaluation.

Unless the trend is sharply reversed by some now unknown, immutable business law, by the end of the decade
anyone who punches a time clock or inhabits an executive
suite from San Diego to Penobscot will have to get the nod
from the personality tester before exercising the atrophying
privilege of working.

Modern man in the sixties is seated indecorously on the
prongs of a dilemma. Words such as "motivational research," "human relations," and other psychological jargon
titillate his upcoming twenty-first-century consciousness and
he applauds any probes into the mind, or soul, of man. Yet
with vestigial pride of the declining Protestant ethic, he
nourishes his own little-remaining privacy. The brain watcher,
who views suspiciously anyone who is not publicly voluble
about himself, has no such anxiety. Individual man, he
says, was meant to be probed, for the corporation, society,
and profit.

The psychological theory which sustains the brain watcher
is that every job, from salesgirl to board chairman, has an
ideal personality description, or type, for which he hopes to
find the right mate among men. He is convinced and, more
important, has convinced many others that human personality is sufficiently simple and static that it can usually
be measured in minutes (or hours) and projected ahead to
predict a man's behavior in any given job or professional
situation. By merging the two, the round hole warmly nest-
ling its round peg, he has reincarnated the old saw as the
modern tester's *semper psychologicus.*

The tester's success has been born out of prosperity and
frustration—actually out of the managerial revolution and
its hordes of executives and allied "creative" workers and
salesmen. According to Dr. Frederick Harbison of Princeton, since 1947 there has been an average increase of 32 percent in the number of executives in the large majority of
firms he studied. At the same time, there has been a significant decrease in the self-employed, and in the single-
entrepreneur-owned company, whose boss intimately knew
every man and job and did not require pseudoclinical advice
to tell him whom to pick as his next foreman.

With the new opportunity, there has been a talent ex-
plosion of college-trained men anxious to join the corpora-

tion, almost all of whom meet the normal employment requirements of a decade ago—education, appearance, ability, proper voice and manner. In the new anonymity of the mammoth firm and its imitators, owned by everyone and by no one, how do you choose among them? How do you pick foremen, supervisors, even vice presidents, that may be personally unknown to the top echelon?

The generic category of "psychological testing" is not new to industry. Management has had reasonable success with such tests as those that measure manual dexterity of workers assembling miniature electronic parts, and has attempted to learn something about a man's mental acuity from instruments such as the Otis Intelligence Test.

The next step, personality testing, was not only inevitable, but too attractive to reject despite common-sense doubts. Not only does it offer itself as a cut-off selection tool for the overworked, often undertrained company personnel man, but also as an irresistible chance to slice away a man's mind for a peek at his corporate loyalty, potential paranoia, or whichever of his supposed weaknesses intrigues his employers. It is also the "scientific" answer to management's unverbalized but ardent hope that man can be reduced to statistics like the tester's norms and percentiles, as easily manipulated as marketing and production figures.

Personality testing has been bought unemotionally by some, while others, especially personnel men, have seized it with a blind enthusiasm bordering on the semireligious. Even the testers themselves are surprised at their acceptance. "Indeed," says Lyle N. Spencer, president of Science Research Associates of Chicago, a giant testing firm and test distributor, "the psychologists who developed these tests in their laboratories never expected the science to be embraced so ardently by businessmen." A psychologist at Sears, Roebuck, which requires all management men to take a full battery of personality tests, claims that they can correctly predict whom to promote 67 percent of the time. Says another one of the faithful, a Diamond Hosiery executive: "We don't hire any salesmen who aren't recommended by our testing firm. Forty percent of our applicants are turned down because they fail the personality tests."

Despite this tide of cultism, there are serious and sober academic doubts as to the accuracy of the personality tests (see Chapter XI: Brain Watching: Science or Cult?). Other aroused critics attack what they consider its intrinsic immorality. "Individuals cannot be classified into neat little bundles and judged wholly on their capacity for adjustment," Crawford H. Greenewalt, president of Du Pont and a vociferous holdout against the testing trend, stated recently in a speech. "The other day I took one of the standard psychological testing sheets used so widely now in personnel work and applied it to a rare and highly individualistic American—Benjamin Franklin. Based on what we know of Franklin's character, I could only conclude that he would have had bad luck winning a place for himself today if he were judged on these standards."

The obvious contest—man versus the testers—may be shaping up as the battle of the century in which, as preliminary armament, we may have to relearn entirely the rules of the job of getting a job—to find the soft underbelly of what may be the most successfully promoted challenge to modern man's individuality. This struggle between privacy, exceptional worth, and the thesis that forty hours a week is only a down payment on modern man's indebtedness may well be a decisive one.

A Park Avenue tester throws out the challenge: "We often don't bother checking references or past work experience," he says. "We learn more about a man from his personality tests."

To everyone to whom this clinical comment has shuddering overtones, and who would do battle—Keokuk salesman, unsuspecting student, or Madison Avenue copywriter—this investigation of the brain watcher and his extraordinary operations is dedicated.

2 THE BIG QUIZ: THE SEARCH FOR THE SQUARE AMERICAN

A youthful Master of Psychology, who may once have dreamt of vital research, leaned back to the limits of his six feet by six feet chest-high partitioned office and explained the psychological limitations of the man whose personality profile dangled in his hand. "To the untrained eye, these scores might seem quite sufficient. He scored at a high ninety-first percentile in intelligence, the seventy-fifth percentile in both emotional stability and extroversion, an average fiftieth percentile in self-confidence and a high ninety-sixth percentile in sociability. But for the job he has applied for, a salesman for a consulting service to lawyers, he just won't do," the young tester explained patiently.

"His scores indicate that he is a leaner. He is not a forceful person and likes to be led. There are also hints of neuroticism. He is friendly, wants recognition quickly, and must have a warm congenial work atmosphere. He seems to have a basic inability to make decisions. He is obviously not the man for the job. He would have to come up against some tough attorneys and sell them. He's smart enough, but I'm afraid he just doesn't have the drive."

This spokesman for the brain-watching community was a confirmed "assembly-line" quiz tester, an advocate of the principle that your adjustment for life—or more important, a job—can be determined solely with a statistical evaluation of your answers to impertinent personality quizzes. As a staff member of The Personnel Institute, a psychological testing house on New York's East Side, he and his colleagues indict (or acquit) the psyches of hundreds of job applicants a day. At any one time, the futures of a mass of unknowing men lie stacked alongside the confident young tester awaiting his near-literary attention. "We operate purely on a statistical basis," he explained about the operation. "Once we grade the quizzes, we can compare a man's raw scores at a glance with the general population, with people in the same field, and often with men in the very same company he is applying for."

The personality quizzes and the versatile percentiles which damned the hopeful young salesman are the backbone (a sizable 60 percent or more) of the brain-watching industry, and the type of personality obstacle the job-seeker is most apt to encounter, at least on his first joust. Typically, the assembly-line testing Goliath distributes hundreds of sets of its "battery" of quiz tests to its clients, who give them to their applicants or employees to fill out, and then return the completed forms to the testing company. There your psyche is approved, condemned, or relegated to psychological purgatory in an impersonal automated atmosphere in which the tester never sees, touches, or smells his quarry.

Most of the assembly-line firms are basically mail-order psychological factories which operate courtesy of the U. S. mail. A graphite-seeking IBM machine turns out yards of personality scores, which the enthusiastic psychologists juggle into imaginative one-page profiles of their subjects, to which they add the real currency of the business—the verdict that the man is a "good," "fair," or "poor" hiring risk. Clients are promised results within forty-eight hours, and for the personnel man impatient to learn what his own considered judgment on a man is going to be, the tester will telegraph or phone the answer—collect—within twenty-four hours. With this esoteric dollar-and-cents game, known in the trade as "blind evaluation," a San Francisco executive's personality can be probed for a Chicago manufacturer by a testing company in New York without the man ever leaving home, except partially in spirit.

The brain watcher is universal, but much of this activity is centered in a narrow belt, a psychological rain forest running between 32nd Street and 59th Street in Manhattan whose geographic center is somewhat east of Madison Avenue and closer to Park. More often than not, the tester who inhabits this area occupies a pastel office in a new birthday-cake or curtain-wall building as modern as his "science."

The mammoth of the assembly-line testers is The Klein Institute, a million-dollar-a-year organization located on New York's Third Avenue, which tests approximately 35,000 job applicants a year for 1,100 clients, including executives, foremen, and salesmen for such diverse firms as Borden's, U. S. Rubber, Revlon, Warner Brothers, and hundreds of other prominent corporations. Their price tag per psyche is flexible and varies anywhere from $20 for routemen (all Borden's wholesale ice-cream salesmen must sample the Klein battery) to $150 for a full-scale executive probe. Not many blocks away, the competing Personnel Institute has funneled some 100,000 executives, engineers, and salesmen through its operation over the years under the guidance of its head —fatherly, talkative Morris Pickus, an old-time sales consultant and Chicago advertising man. His excursion into a complex field for which he has no academic background has grossed upwards of $385,000 a year through an impressive list of 1,600 industrial clients who have included Westinghouse, Cities Service, Stop and Shop Stores, The Toni Company, Pabst Brewing, Bristol-Myers, and even Philip Morris cigarettes.

These and other mass testers have stealthily accomplished a hiring revolution—who is to be permitted to work where, and how—that has callously undone our traditional ritual of getting a job. Ever since junior high school days and its clumsy introduction to "business letter writing" and admonitions to sit up straight and to wear a clean white shirt at interviews, the prospective employee has been thoroughly conditioned in the acceptable in approaching a job. The ceremony has been updated and now includes such additional traditions as the well-written résumé (usually ghosted by a $20 service), a flattering, five-year-old photo, and an aggressive yet tactful letter outlining the applicant's superiority.

But, unfortunately, as we are first beginning to understand, the entire meticulous performance has generally become a wasted effort, a vestigial sun dance meant to mesmerize management and personnel men who have already abdicated much of their hire-fire decision-making to the brain watcher. Rather than rehearse outdated job-getting ceremonies, the prospective workingman (and even the junior-high student) would do better to understand the machinations of his new working Sovereign—the tester—

who, incidentally, is unimpressed by any rituals except those of his own making.

The ritual he most admires is ensnaring a subject into his testing mill. The trap usually begins with a help-wanted ad in the morning newspaper, which includes all pertinent job particulars except that the applicant will soon have a personality quiz thrust under his nose as a rude introduction to modern measurement.

> Young executive trainee. $8000 per annum. Sizable firm seeks college graduate with at least one year experience in sales promotion. Must be intelligent, resourceful, creative.

The ad drew hundreds of replies which were winnowed to a dozen candidates, each of whom was given an assembly-line tester's battery, including a popular yellow four-page form known as "The Personality Inventory," a 125-question instrument developed by Dr. (Ph.D.) Robert G. Bernreuter and published by the Stanford University Press. Personality quizzes are produced by the sheaves by prolific psychologists, as if off some endless paper belt, but not all will do for mass testing. The question-and-answer brain-watching establishments have specific requirements: a test must be inexpensive, easy to take, be graded readily, and be purely statistical, for at $25–$40 a head, there is little time to waste on painstaking introspection. Bernreuter's quiz scrupulously fills this neo-Freudian bill of particulars.

Like most others in the field, it was originally designed as a counseling aid, but it has made the transition into the brain-watching business smoothly, without any academic or financial regrets. In fact, today it is the mainstay of many personnel-testing operations. "The Bernreuter," as it is always folksily called—with a wince of envy by psychologists who marvel at the comparatively incredible income it has made for its creator—reportedly sells over a million copies a year. At 40¢ for the set (with scoring keys), and additional sets at only 6¢ in volume of 500 or more, the Bernreuter has a substantial yearly gross, yet it provides the raw material for brain watching us at an uncommonly insulting few cents a head.

The hopeful executive trainee's first sight of the Bernreuter was, like most subjects' initial view of personality tests, an annoying one. The Bernreuter and its cousin quizzes are big, brash, and impertinent, and unashamedly probe for confessions about your anxiety and emotional stability, your sex life and ideals, work attitudes, health, phobias, social attitudes, religious values, and other personal matters. All quizzes capitalize on the thesis that most people are naïve about tests and that an individual's potential maladjustment can be measured simply by asking him to answer "Yes" or "No" to queries on how sick emotionally (and even physically) he actually is. In this contemporary question-and-answer game, the contestant is not encouraged to cheat, but the wrong answers—as many of the "trainees" painfully learned—can mean ostracization as a corporate leper.

What does the Bernreuter look like to an anxious, unsuspecting job seeker being measured for corporate size?

Do you daydream frequently?

Do you prefer to associate with people who are younger than you?

Are you troubled with the idea that people on the street are watching you?

Have books been more entertaining to you than companions?

Do you usually prefer spending an evening alone?

Are you usually considered to be indifferent to the opposite sex?

Do you often feel just miserable?

The right answers on this sample are all emphatically "No." Even a minor admission that you occasionally prefer reading—and have been known to do it in solitude—can lose you irreplaceable personality points. The Bernreuter is not a very deep scalpel but it can bloodily slash you up, if you are not careful. The man who confesses that he daydreams, for example (Einstein's mainstay during his clerkship in the Swiss patent office when he gave birth to Relativity), is heavily penalized. And even though you now *know* that someone is watching you, and feel just miserable about it all, it is unwise to admit it to Mr. Bernreuter, or his $35-a-head confreres.

The Bernreuter, like almost all personality quizzes, is based on the psychological thesis that the human personality is actually a humble pie composed of many "traits" such as "neuroticism," or "sociability," which the tester can slice up and sample with a series of questions and their answers. (The Bernreuter sees your personality as being composed of six distinct parts: neurotic tendency, self-sufficiency, introversion-extroversion, dominance-submission, self-confidence, and sociability.) When placed back together he is convinced that it represents the "whole man."

The tester has a virtually unlimited inventory of traits to choose from among published personality tests—each author of which is convinced that in his five or ten traits he has magically isolated the true amalgam of human personality. The author of the Washburne S-A Inventory, for example, views human personality as a rewarding blend of happiness, alienation, sympathy, purpose, impulse judgment, and self-control. The Thurstone Temperament Schedule, however, a popular quiz which has been used by Chicago testers Science Research Associates, and test-oriented Sears, Roebuck & Company, divides the psyche somewhat differently into seven traits—including "active," "reflective," "vigorous," and "impulsive."

The Klein Institute, like many commercial testers, synthesizes such diverse views by grading each subject on a gargantuan scoring sheet which lists some thirty-three traits, from "tact" to "sense of humor," taken from several tests. The tester's real art is the handsome manipulation of these traits into personality profiles and working opinions on which collection of them (organized as a man) best fits a particular job slot.

To learn which traits are currently fashionable in industrial circles, a visit to a large testing company seemed in order. The psychologist (this time, a Ph.D.), was happy to elaborate. "What do most of our clients want in a man?" he asked rhetorically. "Well, I would say they are looking for long-range men with low alienation, good adjustment, and a lack of resentment—a man who psychologically identifies with the company. We don't want a person saddled with personal problems, and the higher he scores on tests like the Bernreuter, the better. We measure his tact and diplomacy on the George Washington Social Intelligence Test, and we expect that he would score well on this too."

As you may have already realized, you don't just pass a personality test; you must conquer it. Even though the trait names and approach may occasionally vary a shade, the uniform shallowness of what the tester believes should be socially acceptable in our society underlies his entire theory, and molds all the "right" answers he demands before permitting anyone to cross the corporate threshold. Basically the quiz tester is searching for the Square American: the non-neurotic, reasonably hard-driving, cooperative, anti-cultural, self-confident, loyal, conservative, healthy employee. And conversely—as we shall see throughout—he hopes to smoke out what he believes is the worried, cultured, nervous, autonomous, hypochondriacal, liberal, artistic, sympathetic, impulsive, unworthy psychological mess. No matter what he calls his scales, this bias permeates all his little quizzes.

One trait the quiz tester is most adamant about is "neuroticism." The contracting businessman has left its definition entirely to the brain watcher, but has indicated with plain language that he wants no part of such people in his company. The usual view of the neurotic is a shattered soul infecting society with his tension. But the world of the neurotic, as the safe-playing tester sees it, is a giant one populated by three out of every four of us.

To the tester, a neurotic is simply anyone who doesn't score at the seventy-fifth percentile, or above, on any one of his many neurotic scales. By this monstrous twist of statistical logic, the brain watcher has decreed that only the least neurotic fourth of the population—as measured by his tests —is employable. In fact, many firms hire only those who score in the top ten-fifteen percentiles under the happy impression that they have, at a few bucks per, somehow magically tapped the most stable seventh of humanity for their payroll.

The percentile is the quiz tester's crest, a symbol of the statistical affair that he is having with the "norm" or "average" personality. On the Bernreuter, for example, you are often judged on how well you do in comparison with the original norm of 656 college men and 544 college women in 1938, whoever they are. A man who scores in the sixtieth percentile in "self-confidence" today supposedly has more moxie than three-fifths of these aging college kids.

Earning the quiz tester's appellation of "neurotic" is simpler than rolling off a psychiatrist's couch. On the Bernreuter, for example, a confession of common tensions, such as stage fright or worrying over misfortunes, can plummet you into the below-seventy-five danger zone. The Bernreuter neurotic scale is so sweeping in its *Gestalt,* in fact, that an admission that you prefer "a play" to "a dance" is interpreted as an anti-social neurotic tendency that could drop your percentile into lowly, unrewarding regions.

In probing your neuroticism, the quiz man often relies on such semi-ridiculous queries. [The Thurstone Temperament Schedule "neurotic" scale—called "Stability"—reads like a tour de force in quiz psychology nonsense. For example:

Are your hands and feet often cold? (No, not even in winter); Does it irritate you to be interrupted when you are concentrating? (Never. You welcome all coffee breaks); Can you relax in a noisy room? (A simple task for a generation raised doing homework inches from the radio speaker); Can you study with the radio on? (They actually asked the question).]

Some quiz testers, however, desperately seek originality and enjoy experimenting with new techniques for gauging our neuroticism. One of them, the Washburne S-A Inventory, developed by Dr. Samuel Washburne of Syracuse University and much used by assembly-liners, probes your stability—what he calls "Alienation"—partly in terms of its volume. For example:

About how many people have you disliked (or hated) very much? (a) none (b) 1 to 3 (c) 4 to 10 (d) 11 to 50 (e) over 50.

How many times in the last year have you ever wanted to run away from home or your present circumstances? (a) none (b) 1 to 5 (c) 6 to 15 (d) 16 to 100 (e) over 100.

The man who hates four or more people and who hoped to get away from it all more than five times (an especially liberal allowance for a tester) is the least employable.

Knowing the tester's mental processes—actually brain watching him in self-defense—is essential to job survival in many firms. Bright young men, like the would-be consulting firm salesman who didn't have the "drive," generally are not as unsuited as the tester would have us believe. More likely, they are untutored or instinctively unknowing about tests. By failing to put his best psyche forward on the test (cheating), he scored only as much self-confidence as the next guy. Many an applicant who has brought even a shred of self-flagellation or introspection to the quizzes has been trapped in much the same way.

The job seeker must remember that he is being compared statistically to others whose positively oriented answers have made the norms themselves *slanted* statistics. Survival depends upon grasping the simple key that separates the successful modern from those destined for the psychological slag heap; the tester's Mad-Hatter questions are meant to be *handled* rather than answered (see Chapter VII).

The tester has limitations, but with the prize of the potential evaluation of all men and its resultant power, prestige, and income, at stake, he has not been asleep against the threat. In fact, his first line of defense is usually a lie inserted right in the test introduction, a fillip that can impress, and then devastate, a tyro test-taker. The typical quiz opens with a sly comment something like this:

This is not a test in the conventional sense. There are no right or wrong answers, and one answer can be just as good as another. Be sure to answer all the questions honestly, otherwise the test will be of no benefit to you.

(One outstanding psychologist, associated with a large test distributor, finds this amusing. "Anyone who has two brains to rub together knows it is not true," he says, pointing out that the "non-existent" right answers are usually printed on cut-out stencil forms and included in the package sold to testers.)

For the less gullible, many tests have incorporated special "lie" scales to flush out cheaters. The Washburne has an ingenious "Truthfulness" scale based on a set of "ever-never" questions sprinkled throughout the test to trip men so involved in "image-building" that they fail to admit personality flaws common to us all.

"Did you *ever* tell a lie?" "Did you *ever* take anything, even a pin or a button that belonged to someone else?" The key word is, of course, "ever," and the right answers are "Yes." Failing to give it costs approximately four points each. "If a man gets a 'T' score higher than fifteen, his test bears watching," says one tester. "If it goes over thirty, it proves he's faking and we throw the whole test out."

Despite their defense (we will examine many others), this propensity to play with the tester—and incidentally make the ninetieth to ninety-fifth percentile the most oversized hunk of humanity—is irresistible. That it can, and is being, done successfully, is demonstrated by a case history of a young executive—now the European head of a large advertising agency—who dramatically bested his tester.

As a young copywriter looking for a job, he visited a placement service, which recommended him to Sears, Roebuck & Company, who happened to be looking for three experienced, but youthful copywriters. The ad man recalls the incident vividly. "I went to their New York headquarters, where the personnel man explained that three men would be chosen from among hundreds of applicants for an important job. He outlined my whole future, including raises, and discussed my promotion to divisional manager almost as a certainty if I were one of those finally chosen. He asked me: 'Would you mind taking some tests?' I had some experience with personality tests as a volunteer in the psychological testing laboratory at Syracuse University, where I went to school, so I went along.

"He explained that Sears had used a battery of personality tests on their executives and had developed an 'Ideal Success Pattern' or 'corporate profile.' By comparing my scores with that, he said, the tests would show how closely I would fit into the company. At this point I knew that Sears was not for me, but I decided to go through with it just to see how well I could do. A week later, I spent an entire day taking an interest test—I think it was the Kuder Preference—a motivational study, a personality inventory, and other tests. I took them as if I were a Sears, Roebuck executive, whom, for test purposes, I imagined to be a stuffed shirt. I gave the stuffy answers to all questions. A few days later they called me in. I was one of twelve left from an original field of three hundred. I was tested again with the same tests and some new ones, interviewed, then told that I was one of the finalists.

"The day I was asked to report for a final interview, I was ushered into the largest conference room I had ever seen. Ankle-deep in rug, I was led up to an officious-looking fellow, who offered his hand: 'Welcome to Sears. You are now a member of the team,' he said. I looked straight at him and told him that I was sorry—that I had taken a job with a small advertising agency just the day before, which was the truth. He paled and could hardly talk. 'But you can't,' he stammered. 'Your personality profile shows that you wouldn't be happy in such a place—in fact, you wouldn't be happy anywhere except in a firm like ours. Besides, don't you realize how much money we have already spent testing you?' I had no answer, so I just said goodbye, headed toward the door, and out."

To thwart such cavalier behavior by job-seekers and employees and to unmask potential corporate security risks, quiz testers have developed disguised techniques which avoid the simplistic, often transparent "yes" and "no" questions. The "word game" is one novel neurotic-hunter the tester hopes will confuse his subjects. It is used in the Personal Audit, a circumspect test which has been part of the battery at General Aniline and Armstrong Tire and Rubber,

and other sizable companies. The P-A tries to feign its
punches by avoiding the direct "Are you a sick boy?" question. Instead it poses its Steadiness-Emotionality scale in
the form of an innocent-appearing game in which the testee
is asked to circle one of four choices that goes most "naturally" with the capitalized word, a few of which are surprisingly spicy:

NUDE	naked	unclothed	immodest	shameless
DEBT	obligated	weight	necessary	nightmare
RAPE	attack	assault	ruin	temptation
SMOOTH	level	soft	flat	touch

The correct answers are the obvious prosaic responses in
the column nearest the capitalized words, and each answer
going toward the right is penalized proportionately. The
words in the far right column are the most damaging, undoubtedly because, to the quiz tester, they are indications
of verbal artistry or atypical sexual interest, both unaccept-
able responses.

According to this quiz master, the virile male who believes
that *smooth* goes with *touch*, the young virginal saleslady
who associates *rape* with *ruin*, are just as unemployable as
the young suburbanite who might not be able to resist choosing *nightmare* as the word that goes most naturally with
debt. The applicant who chooses the unlikely words is, says
the tester, in bad shape. The diagnosis: "Unusually sensitive,
feelings are volatile and deep-seated, intense and usually
not too well adjusted, marriage may not prove satisfactory.
Repressions and sexual conflicts are not uncommon."

This insistence on the prosaic is the clue that reveals the
tester's subconscious as being even more simplistic than the
mores of the corporations he slavishly serves. The Washburne, for example, has a scale to measure your "Purpose"
in life, and the tester's unrealistic prejudices are as obvious
as television situation comedy. The test device is a list of
twenty-four life purposes, from which the subject is supposed to pick ten which appeal to him. More than half of
them, including most in this sample, are traps for the "he-
donist" who hopes to get more than a fifty-year watch in
return for the gift of life:

> To have interesting and important work
> To inherit a million dollars
> To be brave, truthful, loyal, and kind

To travel widely

To have good looks and personality

With the Square American as your guide, the "right" life choices are self-evident. Washburne grants salvation to men who want to do important work and have taken the Scout pledge to heart, but heavily penalizes the candid person who shares the common craving for a large inheritance or travel. Ironically, "personality" is also unwanted in this limited world.

Successfully anticipating the tester's bias is generally good insurance, but the statistical tester has one reservation: he fears the overzealous man who scores in the zenith one percent (rather than the safer top 5 or 10 percent) as a nerveless and pushy Samson who may one day shake the foundations of his adopted corporation. A case history of such an absolute soul (at least on his quizzes) was described by a New York tester, who felt obligated to warn management about the man's prowess. A recent applicant for a job at the Wheeling Corrugating Company, a bright college graduate in his twenties, took a test battery which included the Bernreuter. When scored, it showed him to be at the ninety-nine-plus percentile in the positive traits of dominance, emotional stability, and self-confidence. The unsure quiz man felt compelled to recommend him, but added this ominous warning just for the record: "Management will have to beware of his talent, drive, and possible impatience. Unless he can move at his own pace, there may be trouble."

The assembly-line tester is not the only quiz man who stands between a man and his future; in fact, other members of the national brain-watching fraternity, which numbers in the thousands, can be even more formidable opponents. Increasingly, for example, job seekers are being put through the test mill at the offices of one-man testing operations set up by individual psychologists, who have thus boosted themselves near the financial pinnacle of their profession. At such a shop, like one in Port Washington, Long Island, run by a psychologist who calls himself a "Personal Personnel Consultant," executives (at $75 to $150 per evaluation) can expect not only a sizable battery of tests, but an hour, or longer, personal interview. The same is true of the psychological divisions of the prestigious management consultant firms such as Stevenson, Jordan & Harrison, who charge considerably higher fees ($100 to $250) than a blind

operation, and insist on seeing and interviewing the man
they are evaluating.

The quiz tester is becoming more versatile every day.
Some universities, such as Rensselaer Polytechnic of Troy,
New York, have set up testing units that not only do research, but also pick up spare income testing for corporations in their area. Occasionally, a non-psychologist will
label himself a "free-lance tester," and go through all the
required motions of the work, including the collection of
fees. One did just that at the Underwood Corporation for
two years recently, testing almost all levels of management.
(The Olivetti people, who have taken over Underwood, have
since thrown the tests and testers out.)

Several large executive locators and recruiters have also
picked up the brain-watcher's quiz mantle (see Chapter
VIII). Even the Forty-Plus Club of New York, a non-profit
group devoted to getting jobs for unemployed management
men over forty, insists on giving personality quiz tests before agreeing to help a middle-ager who may have been
pressured out of his job by fast-paced younger bloods. Every
man who seeks the aid of Forty-Plus must, in addition to
being interviewed and carefully checked, first submit to the
Thurstone Temperament Schedule and the Kuder Preference
Record, the results of which, says a spokesman, are "available to prospective employers." The importance of this post-
forty joust is indicated by the discouraging figures: of every
hundred men who apply for help, only eight are chosen,
greatly on the basis of their quiz scores.

To the man who must suffer the tests, each minute variance in operation of his brain watch is important. The mail-
order testers, for all their shortcomings, do their job quickly
and remotely. The entire operation takes an hour or less of
your time, and you are either rewarded or derided within a
day or two. Other operations take up to three or four hours
of an applicant's time, and testers like Richardson, Bellows,
Henry & Company may spend two days administering a
series of interviews and ten or more tests.

Harassed job seekers have even been thrown from norm
to percentile during an inconclusive lost week, or two. A
personnel man from Ohio recently recounted such a testing
ordeal that he will not soon forget. A man in his mid-
thirties who has been employed by the same company for
ten years, he answered an ad in the *Wall Street Journal* for
a personnel job on the West Coast. The job involved manag-

ing the personnel administration of two plants of a $100,-000,000 food processing company in California.

He received a call from the West Coast informing him that of more than 500 men who answered the ad, he was one of 110 being contacted. A company representative visiting the Midwest would soon be in touch with him. Shortly after, he was called to Chicago, where he was interviewed and personality-tested late into the day. In fact, he was forced to remain in Chicago an extra day when he missed his return plane. A few days later he was notified that further testing and screening would be necessary—this time at a testing company in Milwaukee. He made the trip, and almost immediately after this "last" travail he received a call from the Coast to fly out there immediately. The personnel man himself recounts the later chapters of his testing odyssey.

"With some trouble, I arranged for a four-day vacation from my job and flew out to Los Angeles," he recalls painfully. "Then at 8 A.M., a young lady called at the hotel and told me to get ready. We were driving out to one of the plants. When we got there, I waited an hour, then was transferred to another building, where I waited another hour. Eventually the testing psychologist showed up and we went to lunch, then made a tour of the suburbs by car while he pumped me with questions. Later that afternoon, I took a series of personality tests, and as late as 6 P.M., I was taking an I.Q. test. That night we drove back to Los Angeles and I returned to my hotel, expecting that it was finally all over.

"Then suddenly the next morning, I was told to pack and fly up to San Francisco immediately. I did, and there I met one of the firm's V.P.'s. They insisted that I take some more tests, including one of the 'daydream' neurotic ones, for which I knew all the answers. By this time I had serious doubts whether I wanted the job at all, but I continued because I had already invested so much time. My last meeting was with the personnel chief, who was shocked at the company's attitude of urgency. He said that the job might not even open up for a while. In fact, I got a strong impression that it had already been sewed up by someone else before I was even contacted and forced to travel half around the country to be tested a half dozen times. I flew home, disgusted. A month later, I received a letter that 'despite my unique qualifications' they had picked another man, and my application was being put 'on file.' I am convinced that there must be an easier way to get a job."

One of the most intriguing brain watches extant, and one which the savvy workingman should be conversant with, is *empirical* personality testing. Empirical testing simply means that the tester has eliminated all theories on job criteria—what makes a good anything—and has decided simply to compare an applicant's test scores with "key" successful men in a given company. When dealing with test-experienced men this can mean checking how well a subject lies on quizzes in relation to a long line of liars preceding him. Apparently this does not ruffle the culture-conditioned brain watcher, who merely assumes the corporation wants men who lie.

The National Cash Register Company operates a tight empirical test system, in which its hired testing company zeros-in on NCR's "ideal" salesman—as measured by his test scores—and tries to duplicate him wholesale, like so many decalcomanias. Its New York tester has tabulated the personality scores of a thousand NCR men, the most successful of whom have been immortalized as the company scoring key. The closer an NCR job applicant's neuroticism and self-confidence match up with this punch-card model, the better his chances.

Empirical testing has been bought most enthusiastically by our giant corporations, many of whom—IBM, Lever, Sears, Standard Oil of New Jersey, and others—have courted Ph.D. psychologists with five-figure salaries and have set up their own elaborate empirical personality-testing empires, giving the corporation what they believe is a better-vested and individually mind-tailored operation than they could buy at $50 a head on the outside. Although barely visible to the outside world (except to those applying there for jobs), personality testing is thriving within the curtain-wall innards of many of our largest corporations, many of whom are convinced that only a company-directed program can achieve the proper level of Bourbonic inbreeding.

At the behemoth International Business Machines, whose name has become the symbol of the whole field of supra measurement—electoral, human, and otherwise—a staff psychologist swiveled in his near-bare IBM-modern office and explained that IBM had turned its back on testing companies to do its brain watching in the privacy and control of its World Headquarters office—on an empirical basis.

In corporate empirical testing, much effort is spent trying

to isolate "significant items" in the make-up of successful men that can then be searched for elsewhere. For example, if a head count of a corporation shows that while only 60 percent of its executive population are Protestant, 85 percent of its *successful executives* are also Protestant, then "Protestantism" becomes an empirically significant item that can be determined and looked for. The empirical company tester doesn't know why, or how it works, or if it has any true relation to job performance, as long as he can correlate it. IBM, for example, is undergoing an experimental study with a relatively new personality quiz and, in talking about it, their psychologist sums up the empirical man's philosophy: "If it comes out that our good men are all five feet three with green eyes, and that's what we're supposed to look for, it's okay with me." (It's highly unlikely. It would clash with IBM's modern graphic image.)

In the extreme, this kind of company testing compares with this author's own "Black Shoe–Brown Shoe Test," which costs nothing and requires no forms or training. It works like this: a simple count is made of the color of the shoes worn by male executives rated "good," and a similar count of those who left, were discharged, or are in disfavor. If a shoe color has a higher percentage among one group than another (therefore better than .00 correlation, or chance) then the winning shade becomes the new hiring, firing, and promotion key. A wing-tip-brown-shoe man, for example, might just have to find his own level, or quickly update himself to black military style. If shoes do not work, the same test can be used on gloves or galoshes in winter, seersucker or Dacron in summer, hats or hatless year-round, or in certain dire circumstances, brands of cigarettes or Scotch— with or without chaser.

Surprisingly, the well-scrubbed IBM junior executive noted for his uniform jib and his conservative no-nonsense Ivy League–Harvard Business School demeanor is chosen by means of an almost equally irrelevant test system. Since almost all future IBM management men are originally hired as data processing (computer) salesmen and carefully IBM-honed in a $10,000 year-and-a-half apprenticeship, the next generation's board chairman is being selected today with considerable attention to how well he does on its single-shot personality screen.

The test, which is given to 5,000 hopefuls each year at IBM's 200 global offices, is the Strong Vocational Interest Blank, a thirty-three-year-old questionnaire originally designed for high school vocational guidance work. Developed by Stanford University psychologist E. K. Strong, Jr., the test operates on a curious premise: you are suited for a job or profession only if your prejudices mesh smoothly with those of the "typical" man in the same field.

Strong analyzes an applicant by his likes and dislikes in a 400-question inventory of his hobbies, racial and ethnic biases (Do you like foreigners, people with hooked noses?), political and economic preferences (Do you like conservatives, socialists, people who made fortunes in business?), reading habits (*Time, New Republic, National Geographic*), etc. In creating his test, he tried out this potpourri on "successful" men in forty-five occupations, and even women in twenty-five different jobs. After statistically averaging out the responses, he psychologically deified the results as the "norm" advertising man, engineer, accountant, physician, who heretofore had existed only in Strong's imagination and in cliché conversation.

Strong too is an admirer of the Square American. He offers handsome rewards for conformity, and holds little brief for the man who believes occupations can accommodate more than one cast of practitioner, as say journalism's Lippmann and Pegler, or industry's Wolfson and Watson, Jr. An A on the Strong means you scored higher than the sixty-ninth percentile in agreeing with the homogeneous crowd, while the D is the sign of a maverick who rejects the shopworn prejudices of most of his colleagues. Strong enthusiasts are among the least lenient in brain watching. "We like to see a man score an A in the job slot he is looking for," one tester stated while watching a Strong scoring sheet (this author's) burr swiftly through an IBM machine. "We will accept a B plus if he measures up well on other tests, but seldom lower."

The IBM hopeful meets the Strong as a forest-green-covered twelve-page booklet specially printed for the company. It opens with an introduction that ominously hints that this is the moment of business-machine truth. It reads:

This test has been developed to measure your interest because past experience has shown that men with certain interest patterns are more successful in some types of work than others. For this reason it has been included as one of the steps in our selection procedure designed to evaluate the probability of your success at IBM. You are required to respond to the various items in as frank and objective a manner as possible. In this way, you will be benefiting both yourself and IBM since a more reliable estimate of your potential with IBM can be made.

What does the Strong look like to the young Ivy Leaguer out to conquer the IBM, or other industrial giant? Basically it is a list of activities and attitudes, next to which he is asked to mark an L (Like), I (Indifferent), or D (Dislike). For example:

army officer
bookkeeping
hunting
taking long walks
snakes

American Magazine
New Republic
rough-house initiations
foreigners
conservative people

The would-be executive is also asked to study a list of ten famous men—from Henry Ford to Enrico Caruso—and check those he would "most like" to have been, and those "least."

The Strong has a "salesman" key, but IBM shrugs this off as a sophomoric screen easily pierced by their high-caliber applicants. "It's worthless for us," says a company spokesman. "Almost all IBM men score A on it. But we have constructed our own empirical key on the Strong based on the responses of our successful men—those who stayed with us and have met their dollar sales quotas. A candidate must score an A or B on our scale to be acceptable. If not, he cannot be hired without the approval of the district manager."

What is IBM's private-stock Strong key? "I don't know why," says the company psychologist, "but a lot of good IBM men come out on the Strong looking like mining engineers." Mining engineers on Madison Avenue? Actually, IBM's prospectors are more likely to be the regimental striped-tied than the Montana jack-booted variety. But what they do obviously have in common are high scores on business detail and the traditionally conservative, management-oriented attitude of the mining profession.

IBM has invested a considerable fortune in purveying a liberal, cultured image, but like its external publication *Think,* the image is strictly reserved for outside consumption. Internally, IBM appears more at home with the uncultured young man of acceptable cubish proportions. The savvy IBM executive-trainee applicant doesn't help himself by checking that he prefers orchestra conducting to bookkeeping or being an army officer. He likes hunting, snakes, and rough-house initiations and dislikes long walks, art galleries, and tennis; and, of course, couldn't care less about people with gold teeth, people who talk loudly, or progressive people, let alone socialists. He prefers to be reincarnated as John Wanamaker rather than Booth Tarkington. He enjoys his monthly copy of the defunct *American* Magazine, even if he must rummage in the public library stacks to find it, and has never even heard of the *New Republic*. (In fact,. this last question is used by some testers as a sly indication of a misguided liberal bent. "I sometimes take a quick peek at a man's response to the *New Republic*," confides one Strong tester. "It tells me a lot about him.")

Interest tests like the Strong and, another popular one, the Kuder Preference Record, are common in let's-test-themourselves corporations. One survey by the Bureau of National Affairs showed that they were used in selection by 21 percent of the companies polled. The Kuder is more direct than the Strong and, with a long needle (backed up by a soft board to cushion aggression), the testee jabs those on a list of activities that he likes "least" or "most," as on this Kuder triplet:

> Visit a museum.
> Visit an advertising agency.
> Visit a factory in which typewriters are made.

Stabbing the first item, says the tester, is naturally a sign of "scientific interest," while trips to the ad agency and factory are respectively signs of "persuasive" and "mechanical" bents.

Among its devout, the Kuder graph is taken quite seriously, even though company testers wrangle continuously over the graph shape that represents the best interests of the corporation. The ideal General Motors–Fisher Body foreman, for example, as described in an American Management Association volume, has a Kuder chart that shows him to be terribly mechanically-minded, anti-outdoorsy, and with a reasonably high scientific bent. At Kenwood Mills, however, the proper foreman is lower scientifically and considerably more social-service, or fellow-man oriented. The Owens-Illinois people eschew completely the scientific foreman, and in selecting theirs with the Kuder, look for a "negative" correlation between a scientific interest and being a glass-making supervisor.

It is of course distinctly possible that "interests" checked on paper forms may not jibe with the job performance of mature people. The thought has been investigated by a New York Telephone Company personnel man, with hopeful results. (The Kuder, however, is still used in other areas of the Bell system.) "We had been considering using the Kuder for selection of girls in the business office," says phone company executive David Neville. "As an experiment, we first gave it to girls who had been promoted to business office supervisor. I was surprised that one of the supervisor's Kuder scores showed that she actually disliked arithmetic and computational work, and I asked her about it. 'You must have done your arithmetic well on the job to be promoted. How come?' Her answer was simple: 'I had to do it. It was part of the job.' Obviously, her so-called interest had little to do with her efficiency. We decided against the test."

In his search for the Square American, the brain watcher —and his sidekick personnel manager—occasionally uses the Kuder as a culture-spotter in the hope of revealing the surreptitiously well-rounded man whose excess culture might debilitate the management soul. Such suspicions almost injured the career of a thirty-year-old electrical engineer who had applied for a job at a large defense plant on Long Island. He was given the Kuder test, on which he foolishly divulged not only a strong interest in literature but, as an amateur saxophonist, in music as well. When the Kuder was scored the tester was plainly worried, but he gave the engineer the benefit of the doubt because of a very high mechanical interest and a low artistic score. The engineer is now a senior supervisor in charge of hundreds of men at the same plant, but a grand slam in all three "cultures" would probably have aborted a brilliant career.

This mistrust of the cultured man, and with it an admission that the corporate tester cannot comprehend the processes of the more than two-dimensional mentality, has driven some testers, and corporations, to worshiping wispy business-oriented, antilife images that they have hopefully labeled as "executive values."

The most enthusiastic proponent of testing for anticultural business values is probably Sears, Roebuck and Company, one of the shy industrial giants that talks and publishes little about its personality apparatus, yet retains one of the nation's strongest internal testing systems. Sears's testing program, administered by staff psychologists in both Chicago and New York, is older than IBM's, but much like it in that since

1942 they have painstakingly constructed a statistical wax-work of the model Sears man. They ask only that applicants and employees interested in going upwards look, at the very least, like its fraternal twin.

More than 20,000 applicants have taken the four-hour battery, and none of Sears's 11,000 management men has been promoted without first hurdling it. In addition to the Thurstone Temperament quiz and a Kuder-like test, Sears's forte is a near-duplicate of the "Study of Values," a forty-five-question test which plumbs six facets of man: the economic, theoretical, aesthetic, social, political, and religious. (Considered a "sophisticated" instrument by testers, the SOV is heavily used in executive evaluation, occasionally even by the conservative Psychological Corporation.)

Basically, the test, and Sears, want to know: Are you motivated toward or against the corporate environment? To find out, it probes your "executive values" as follows:

(1) Are our modern industrial and scientific developments a sign of a greater degree of civilization than those attained by any previous society, the Greeks, for example?

(2) If you had sufficient leisure and money, would you prefer to:
    A—Make a collection of fine sculpture or paintings?
    B—Establish a center for the care and training of the feeble-minded?
    C—Aim at a Senatorship or a seat in the Cabinet?
    D—Establish a business or financial enterprise of your own?

(3) To what extent do the following famous persons interest you:
    A—Florence Nightingale
    B—Napoleon
    C—Henry Ford
    D—Galileo

The clue to the right answers is in the profile of the "ideal" Sears man who has but two outstanding motivations, as measured by the SOV. He seeks, craves, and respects money above all, and is not only without a trace of culture, but has developed an active distaste for it. According to one report, the proper Sears executive's "economic" values soar past the eightieth percentile, while the "aesthetic" flounders not far from zero. The man in the bottom quarter culturally, who would be an obnoxious bore elsewhere, could be considered a misplaced aesthete at Sears.

The conflict that Sears has set up between culture and the buck makes the right answers on the SOV obvious. Modern industrial society is the zenith of mankind. Despite your riches and leisure, the call to accumulate money you no longer need is so compelling that you must start the chase all over again. As final proof of your economic drives, you prefer Henry Ford, the most.

Sears has obviously not built such a successful operation with a management of distorted personalities (of course, other giants such as Du Pont do equally well without personality testing.) Therefore, either Sears's management men have actually conformed their personalities in order to advance) or, more likely, competent Sears executives have been playing tag with the company psychologist, with the poor tester being "it." In fact, a confidential study on 200 New York Telephone executives showed that middle-management men—when the prod of a job or promotion was removed—looked much like everybody else on the Study of Values.

Corporations that do their own testing are constantly searching for new faddist testing ideas, hoping to concoct an unbeatable psychological potion for which the workingman has no antidote. One of the most current is the Edwards Personal Preference Schedule, a "forced choice" test that is supposedly less fakeable than the typical personality quiz. The Edwards is, or has been, used in dozens of corporate testing systems including Kenyon & Eckhardt advertising, Allied Chemical, on certain executive trainees at Westinghouse, for upgrading at ITT, and at the green glass giant on Park Avenue, Lever Brothers.

With the aid of four staff psychologists, the Edwards is given to all applicants for sales jobs and some 600 other key positions at Lever. Developed by University of Washington psychologists, it sets up 225 pairs of statements, each half of which is supposed to hit the testee as being equally socially desirable or undesirable. By forcing you to choose either A or B—to differentiate without knowing what the tester is looking for—Lever Brothers hopes that the "true you," like some of its preparations, will be literally squeezed out into the open. For example, it asks you to choose A or B:

A. I would like to be a recognized authority in some job,
profession, or field of specialization.
B. I feel guilty whenever I have done something wrong.

A is the correct choice, for it adds to your score in
"Achievement," while B represents "Abasement," which is
better in the corporate make-up in considerably smaller doses.

A. I get so angry that I feel like throwing things.
B. I like to avoid responsibilities and obligations.

Confessing to A is a sign of unwelcome "Aggression," but
B is even more uninviting. It is a tip-off to your "Autonomy."
Once an expression of independent strength of purpose, the
latter is now the Edwards' odd-ball and nonconformist category in which are lumped together the desire to "criticize
those in positions of authority" and the desire to "avoid responsibilities and obligations." With the help of the Edwards, such folk are excluded from the management of many
firms, including the soapy giant.

Several companies and testers have become enthusiastic
about another fashionable test, the biographical index—one
of the most awesome challenges to the sanctity of both individual privacy and worth. This personality version of Mid-
dletown, U. S. A., is fast becoming one of their favorite veri-
fiers of acceptable squareness.

The relatively new technique statistically rates your life
history (often with the help of a computer) by comparing
your biographical facts with "successful" men in the same
firm for telltale life experiences that may be out of line. If
your firm's typically good management man, for example, is
by and large small-town Americana, one of a brood of three
sired by a skilled blue-collar worker, and one who had to
work his way through college, where he was president of the
junior class, this is the life history the tester enforces to
make the corporation a homogeneous fraternal order.

For some brain watchers, biography tests seem more "realistic" and less offensive than queries on bowel movements.
But to the job seeker, or job holder, it requires not just the
molding or slanting of attitudes, but a hard look at the actual
facts of your life that may now be an unchanging, and unjust,
yoke around the executive neck. The biography method has
been used by several firms: the U. S. Chamber of Commerce
(see Chapter VIII: So You Want To Be an Executive?),
management consultants Richardson, Bellows, Henry & Com-

pany to test their clients' personnel, the Life Insurance Agency Management Association for screening insurance agents, and both Standard Oil of Indiana and Standard Oil of New Jersey, among many others.

Testers at Standard of New Jersey have only recently won the right to put their management through the psychometric paces with this and other quiz tests. Standard of Indiana, however, has used the biographical index for some time, extracting life histories with, of all things, multiple-choice questions. This is a sample of its eighty-nine question "biography":

What is your weight?
1. Under 150 pounds.
2. 150 to 170 pounds.
3. 171 to 185 pounds.
4. 186 to 200 pounds.
5. Over 200 pounds.

If you graduated from high school, how did you rank scholastically in your graduating class?
1. Did not graduate.
2. Lower third of the class.
3. Middle third.
4. Upper third.

Which of the occupational groups would you say include most of your friends?
1. Salesmen.
2. Professionals, executives, and business managers.
3. White-collar workers.
4. Craftsmen, tradesmen, and artisans.
5. Others.

Standard Oil of Indiana has not released its key, but it is reasonably safe to assume that you associate with fellow executives and finished in the upper third of your high school class. It is more difficult to hazard a guess at the weight of the "norm" SOI man, but "over 200" pounds surely sounds like an ominous personality item.

Standard Oil of New Jersey is not advertising its new executive key either. However, they have indicated that a man with advanced degrees, especially technical ones, will gain statistically on the management biographical index. This is interesting considering that 31 percent of SONJ's top 587 managers never went to college and some 3 percent never even got past grammar school. In fact, the present board chairman—who holds a meager nontechnical A.B. from the University of Rochester—might well gird himself before sampling what his own tester has served up.

The classic test in this biographical field is the Life Insurance Agency Management Association test, developed in 1932 and since then taken by over 1,000,000 men who have applied for life insurance agent jobs at 291 companies, including the giants—Metropolitan, Prudential, etc. For years, the LIAMA psychologists in Hartford, Connecticut have attempted to develop a conventional personality quiz, but despite premature comments that it "worked," today LIAMA admits that none of the personality standards have predicted anything for some time. "We are pleased with our biographical index, however," states a spokesman, "and we think it is a better way to gauge personality." For better or worse, the LIAMA test has had a strong hand in shaping the psychological outlines of our persistent army of hard-soliciting insurance agents.

The ideal insurance agent, as LIAMA's biography sees him, is a most admirable male—a stanchion of society, and unemployed. Specifically, he is an executive who has been out of work one month or less; was with his last employer ten years; has a net worth of $40,000; carries $40,000 or more in life insurance; has at least one college degree; has three or four dependents (not less or more); belongs to four or more organizations; and has held office in at least two of them. "I have never met such a man and I don't think I'd hire him if I did," says the New York franchised general agent for a large eastern insurance firm. "Every man we hire represents a cash investment by the company and myself of three to four thousand dollars. I wouldn't trust this test with that kind of money. The LIAMA test cost me nothing and that's exactly what I think it's worth. I've been in the business fourteen years and I know that if I had taken the test myself I would have failed it. If I gave it to everyone beforehand like I am supposed to, I would have lost many good agents."

The general agent admits to "helping along" the grades of low-scorers who his intuition tells him have the makings of insurance salesmen. Unfortunately, LIAMA recently decided to call back all scoring keys to Hartford to thwart, as they say, "managers who cheat."

The advantage of tests like LIAMA's, which can be

scored by laymen, has not been lost on employment managers who have long hankered for a cheap, hard-to-beat five-minute tourist guide to anybody's head—a test that could be given without the costly interference of a high-priced psychologist. The answer, AVA or Activity Vector Analysis, has become a boomlet of significant proportions that evaluates over 300,000 Americans a year in over 1,000 firms, including such bellwethers as Western Union, Hanover Bank, The Toni Company, Continental Can, Liggett Drug, P. Lorillard Company, Chas. Pfizer, Long Island Lighting, Chirurg & Cairns, advertising, Pan American World Airways, R. J. Reynolds Tobacco, and even Campbell Soup.

An eighty-one-adjective word game developed by Walter V. Clarke Associates of Providence, Rhode Island, the AVA has assumed near-cult proportions through undoubtedly the most successful promotional scheme in testdom. Firstly, it is cheap: AVA clients pay a set annual fee averaging $1,000 (up to $3,500 for giants, like Campbell Soup) for the right to test as many applicants and employees as they want as long as AVA test blanks—at a few cents each—hold out. In most instances, AVA clients can probe you at unbeatable petty cash prices—perhaps as low as 50¢ a head.

Even more important, AVA has converted hundreds of plodding personnel directors—usually fourth-rung managers fighting a holding operation in the typical company—into "Certified AVA Analysts," colorful near-psychologists, disciples who can offer up to management the incense of "human relations." The AVA test has received unmuffled guffaws from several critical psychologists (see Chapter XI: Brain Watching: Science or Cult?) but many company personnel men welcome it as warmly as the three-for-one stock split.

The transformation from personnel man to "analyst" (at approximately $1,500 per man) takes three weeks and is done either at the main AVA office in Providence, Rhode Island, or, for the more fortunate, at a luxurious hotel at Fort Lauderdale, Florida, where the trainee (and often his wife) attend a sunny seminar, all expenses paid by his firm. The personnel men return to their offices with a sun tan, a diploma, and abiding faith in a technique capable, they say, of picking anyone from "president to janitor." The blue-ribboned diploma lovingly nailed to the paneled office walls of personnel managers across the nation is a masterful merchandising gimmick that insures the personnel man's vested interest in AVA, for there is nothing as psychologically inactive as a nonpracticing AVA Analyst.

The powerful AVA test is physically unassuming, a single sheet of paper containing eighty-one adjectives such as "cool, scairdy cat, persuasive, considerate." The testee is merely asked to place an "X" before words that have ever been used by anyone to describe him, then go back and check, in a second column, those words that he personally believes describe him. AVA has four vectors, which the analyst scores from the checked adjectives with a stencil card, then connects on a graph into an insect-like four-legged profile. Your profile is one of myriads of these little personality constellations printed on an "AVA Pattern Universe," a sort of stellar chart to the analyst's Milky Way.

Vector I, Aggressiveness, or Do-ability, is high in those people who check off adjectives like "persistent" or "go-getter." Vector II, Social-ability, the salesman's mark, has a list of adjectives including "enthusiastic" and "attractive." People who score high on Vector III, Emotional Stability or Sit-ability, are the "mild" and "complacent" type, while a high Vector IV, Flex-ability (traditionalism versus independence), would be found in conforming persons who check off words like "harmonious."

The shapes created by connecting these vectors are what AVA calls "standard job patterns," developed from sampling a handful of people in various occupations. The AVA "company president," for example—a moderate man who is reasonably aggressive, moderately social and independent, and has low Sit-ability—was created from an AVA sample of only 30 men, a Gallup-like miniaturization if there ever was one.

There are an almost infinite number of AVA doodles for everything from a social worker to a hardy Vermont farmer —whose AVA graph, incidentally, looks like a backward "Z." Playing with AVA doodles can be fun, especially if you are not involved as a job applicant or employee. The AVA accountant (sample of 20) is rather personalityless: mildly unaggressive, unsociable, reasonably controlled, and moderately conforming. Their "outside salesmen" show more dash: aggressive, extremely sociable, with low emotional control, and a reasonably independent chap. The machine operator (sample of 78) shows only one stand-out trait: he has Sit-ability.

Because of its low cost, AVA Analysts usually succeed in ensnaring everyone within their grasp, including management, factory help, and even secretaries. How the AVA secretary profile, for instance, is converted into actual hire-fire decisions for many thousands of young women, was explained by an analyst at drug manufacturers Chas. Pfizer & Company. "A typical secretary should show up on the AVA as relatively introverted, not very aggressive, with a high Sitability, and high conforming tendencies which would make it easy for her to follow the company's rules," the Pfizer man explained. "Of course if she were working for a vice president, we would want her to be more self-assertive and independent." Without meaning to, AVA has hypothesized a new personality norm for American secretaries: those who take dictation for anyone below a V.P. must be distinguished by dullness.

The AVA has another popular measure, a fifth scale called "Activity Level," or "Life Force," which tries to screen out sluggards likely to deliver less, and excessively vital employees whose compulsion to give more than a day's work for a day's pay might upset corporate equanimity. Activity Level is calculated merely by counting the number of adjectives a man has checked, whether they are contradictory or not.

Apparently the tireless figure who built American industry is virtually unemployable in the vast AVA empire. "We prefer not to hire a man who scores over 80 in activity level," candidly admits a Celanese Corporation spokesman, an AVA user. "Beyond that they get into everybody's hair and don't get along with associates."

Not even an employee's exceptional money-making talents can balance this AVA longing for corporate adjustment, as a fairly recent case history demonstrates. A publishing firm which had AVA-tested all applicants and almost all of its 800 employees reluctantly hired a highly recommended advertising space salesman. "We like a reasonably high activity level in a space salesman's job," the AVA Analyst recounted. "But this salesman's AVA activity level indicated to me that he was too dynamic. I watched him closely because I knew there would be trouble. Just as I expected, he blew up not long ago and had a fight with his immediate supervisor. In fact he almost backed him up against the wall. The only reason we keep him on is that he does such a good selling job, one of the very best in our company."

Violent arguments about AVA, its claims, its obvious popularity, and whether or not it works, resound throughout the brain-watching community and even in the more sober confines of the American Psychological Association. ("Psychologists are naturally peeved at us because we were the first to take their tools and put them into the hands of laymen," says an AVA account executive.)

But the AVA worshipful praise it extravagantly. At the Long Island Lighting Company in Hicksville, three staff AVA Analysts have been happily juggling AVA doodles since 1957 to select all new employees—including engineers, linemen, clerical workers, accountants. In fact, they confidently enter a man's AVA score as a permanent guide to his LILCO future. Others, however, like the chic New York department stores B. Altman (which had used it to screen salesladies) and Consolidated Edison of New York, who used it for six years before dropping it, have become equally disenchanted with AVA.

Despite such instances of doubt, impressionable businessmen have been transfixed by the brain watcher's hard sell, a merchandising masterpiece reminiscent of the best of Barnum. Unlike psychiatrists and attorneys who enforce professional codes that prohibit soliciting, many testers also double as adroit salesmen. (The American Psychological Association has conducted at least one investigation of unethical claims by testing companies.)

One New York City psychologist (a local M.A. graduate), employed by a large testing house, speaks freely about his "sales pitch" to company personnel men on the rewards of "scientific selection." "I generally call them up cold," he explains. "I concentrate on small firms who can use our services and can't afford staff psychologists. Most of them have never heard of us, but I deliver the pitch, stressing the idea that we can improve the caliber of their staff and reduce turnover. I ask for thirty minutes of their time—perhaps the most important half hour of their business career. Generally, they ask me to drop in to see them."

This gullibility of personnel men is a near-wonder of an otherwise pragmatic commercial community. It is actually the strongest stanchion supporting the brain-watching industry. One vice president of a large milk foods products company is typical of this naïveté. Although he uses personality tests to select advertising and public relations people for the company, he recently confessed that he had no idea what the tests were all about. He assumed that his testers knew what they were doing.

Just how far this innocence can go was illustrated by an experiment conducted by Dr. Ross Stagner of Wayne State

University on sixty-eight personnel men attending a conference. Dr. Stagner administered a common personality test to the personnel men, but instead of the true results, each man was handed back a trumped-up "Personality Analysis Report." It was composed of statements taken from hack astrology charts, including such banalities as: "Your sexual adjustment has presented problems to you." Each man's report was *identical,* but the individual personnel man's name was typed in to maintain the illusion.

When asked to evaluate the phony test's "validity," nine out of every ten personnel men bit and agreed that their reports were "good" or "amazingly accurate" descriptions of their personality. In fact, college students—without a day's corporate log time—proved considerably less gullible on the same experiment.

This grasping, religious faith of industry is not pleasant to contemplate, but it has its humorous attributes, as a recent testing tale illustrates. A New York paper wholesaler, representing more than ninety paper mills, went searching for a top-notch, high-salaried salesman. After extensive personality testing of applicants, an inexperienced young man was taken on despite company policy to hire only veteran paper sellers. The company could not resist the tester's praise. "This man is a natural born salesman," the quiz tester trumpeted.

The paper firm eagerly awaited realization of the promise. They waited one, two, then three years without any sign of results. "He has been here almost five years and hasn't produced for us yet," the firm's personnel man confided recently. "We'll string along a little more. He may still be what the test predicted. After all, we've invested so much in him now that we're reluctant to let him go."

Although the brain watcher's merchandising has been monumental, it is less significant than his genius in aborting opposition from the men and women whose lives he toys with daily. For an industry that is responsible for the rejection of hundreds of thousands of people each year, there is a shocking lack of resentment against the tester from the public. The reason is simply this: most testers have covered themselves by lying. The man who may never be a vice president because he failed a battery of personality tests is never told the real reason. He is given any one of a dozen vapid excuses and smilingly leaves the office of the tester with his ego intact. "I wouldn't be doing my job if they left angry at me or the company," says a prominent testing consultant.

In fact, an alarming document in this campaign to keep the public innocent and disarmed has actually been published by a Park Avenue tester for all its clients. It is a "pony" entitled "How To Turn Down A Job Applicant," part of which reads:

> Don't let yourself be trapped by the applicant who asks "How did I do on those tests?" . . . It's best not to volunteer any information about test results. If he brings the subject up you can say something to the effect that he "did very well" and add that your decision had nothing to do with test results. A white lie? Of course, but it's the kind of harmless deception that all of us have occasion to resort to without suffering any pangs of conscience.

Despite the magnificent flimflam, faith in the big quiz is not absolute. Some clients pay and leave, shifting to other testing techniques, and some eventually desert personality testing altogether. One such young entrepreneur, the head of a Wall Street brokerage firm, called in a quiz tester to evaluate applicants for the job of cashier-trainee, a $75-a-week starting position. "The fellow seemed all right to me, but the tester gave him a horrible report," he relates. "Then I sent another, and another, and finally six different applicants, all of whom were reported back as 'poor' hiring risks. I decided to stop the personality testing altogether and hire the next man that seemed good to me. That was five years ago and he is now our cashier at a five-figure salary. I sometimes wonder if the tester would ever have sent me a good report. After all, that would have been the end of his thirty-five-dollar tests."

His reaction is encouraging. However, it should not be prematurely interpreted as a solid ground swell. For every hardheaded businessman determined to maintain his prerogatives, there are twenty other employers anxious to hire their own testers or to lay $35 on the line for the quiz man's neo-Freudian high-sign and the opportunity to give a prospective employee pencil and paper with which he can incriminate himself psychologically.

3

THE CLINICAL TESTERS:
INKBLOTS, NUDES,
AND THE UNCONSCIOUS

A thirty-two-year-old wholesale salesman with strong experience in the soap and cigarette line applied for a job as a salesman for a nationally advertised brand of brassieres. The firm's sales manager sent him to a New York testing company, where the surprised applicant faced a battery of tests unlike any he had ever seen before. For more than an hour, he worked conscientiously to concoct a story from a crudely drawn wash sketch, finish such leading sentences as "I worry about . . ." and strain his pitiful art talent to draw first a nude woman, then a fully clothed man.

Shortly after the testing report was complete, he was informed his was not the proper psychological fit for a bra salesman. "Selling women's girdles and bras is an extremely competitive and tough racket with an income up to $20,000 a year if the man is damn good," says his tester. "We often have to recommend against men with successful experience in the same line if they don't measure up on our tests.

"What are we looking for? The right man is energetic, restless, and wants money, power, and fame. He is informal and talks a blue streak. He is affable on the surface, and knows how to ingratiate himself. He doesn't really like people, but likes to use them. He is dominating, stubborn, insistent, demanding. He is mildly unscrupulous, a bit of a pirate. He is shrewd and conniving, and can change tactics at will. He is basically insecure and doesn't like intimate relationships. He hates supervision and thinks his boss is stupid. He likes to be his own boss, and eventually will go into his own business. He is often a ladies' man, conceited on the surface. Way down though he is insecure, but only his wife knows it. He is competing all the time with his father."

This unusual dissertation on the subconscious motivations of bra peddling—which the applicant didn't measure up to —is the trademark of a new and more fearsome breed of tester, to whom the statistical juggling of the quiz man is early paleolithic.

The quiz men have built a multimillion-dollar industry by slyly tricking job seekers into answering incriminating questions about themselves. The technique is still a best-seller, but the fact that the more sophisticated can sometimes guess their way to position and stock options has been pricking away at some managements. Not only doesn't the corporation enjoy being trifled with, but the whole blasphemous idea of test-faking had even begun to deflate some of their faith in the commercial art of mind-measuring. What the corporation really needed, its pious personnel men decided, was a truly "cheat-proof" test that could trip the interloper not far from the reception desk.

Their answer is the clinical tester, fresh out of the mental hospital, from whose underpaid clinics he has nimbly transplanted himself to the lush corporate field at two to three times the going wage. He has brought his black bag with him, overflowing with inkblots, free-association techniques, uncaptioned cartoons, and nude drawings—"projective" tests originally designed to plummet paranoiacs and schizophrenics. They are more likely to feature a quickie psychoanalysis than a direct question about a man's bowel movements.

He has convinced test buyers—from Borden's to Republic Steel—that the method can just as easily be used to probe normal men, whether bra salesmen or those at the top level of management. With his cheat-proofs, he claims, he can strip away anyone's defenses in an hour or less and force him to reveal his naked drives and *true* personality. One New York client has bought the technique so wholly that it soberly enters the clinical tester's direst predictions on the man's confidential *medical record*.

Like the medical men they ape, testers would like to have a solid front of professional agreement to impress their customers and the public. Actually, though, they are involved in an almost comical fratricidal war between the psychometrist and his norms and the clinical man with his projective insights.

The theory tenuously holding up the whole projective industry is that the quiz tester and his norms are hopelessly jabbing at the surface of personality, while the projective tester probes underneath for the subconscious of the *whole* man. Human personality, says the clinical brain watcher, is like a giant North Atlantic iceberg with only a fraction of its mass piercing the surface. When an applicant is given an unstructured stimulus—anything from an inkblot to a piece of a shoelace—he supposedly projects himself into the situation to make sense out of it, and unwittingly reveals his unconscious thoughts and motivations to the tester, whether he wants to hold back or not.

Despite many academic warnings that the use of projectives in industry is an "experiment" (see Chapter XI: Brain Watching: Science or Cult?) or perhaps only a modern parlor game played with inkblots instead of a ouija board, its obvious snob value and supposed relation to Freudian technique, although cousins removed, have created a sensational boom in projective testing. Its popularity is especially strong among "human relations" oriented managements, who take consolation from the idea that projectives seem less depersonalized than the statistical tests.

The clinical tester comes in many forms. Dr. Theodore Jackson, chief psychologist for Stevenson, Jordan & Harrison, a large management consulting firm which tests over 1,000 executives a year, states that he strongly "prefers" projectives, although he insists on double-checking his results with an interview. The consulting giant of Richardson, Bellows, Henry & Company has different psychologists give at least two projectives including the inkblots plus a psychological interview as part of its $250-per-man assessment. Several corporate testers including the Atlantic Refining Company have adopted projectives for their internal testing systems, and even the test-happy Lever Brothers has almost completely phased out the Q & A tests for the more fashionable clinical ones.

Some cheat-proof testers, however, have appropriated a wrinkle virtually unknown behind the mental hospital's red brick walls. They have borrowed the profitable assembly-line technique and its blind analysis that insists that it's not necessary to personally confront a man, or even his unconscious, to probe him. "The contact in an employment interview is superficial," claims one "blind" clinical Ph.D. "The applicant puts on a façade and the result is more a projection of the tester's own personality."

Blind clinical analysis costs anywhere between $30 and $85 a shot, more than most Q & A probes, but less than those by testers who insist on meeting their subjects in the flesh. Surprisingly many companies are satisfied with these cheaper clinical shots in the dark. Without any obvious complaints, the blind system has been or is being used to select salesmen for Schenley whiskey; personnel workers for ITT; technical, advertising, and public relations help for Borden's; chemists and foremen for Shulton toiletries; insurance agents for Maryland Casualty; drug detail men for Ciba and other pharmaceutical houses; and mechanical employees for the New York *Daily News*. Even Scott's garden-supply house puts all its executives through the clinical hoop before they are considered for promotion.

One of the giants of the clinical field is The Personnel Laboratory, Inc., located in the testing belt near New York's Park Avenue. The company trademark, a laboratory microscope, is prominently displayed on its promotional literature, possibly as a reminder of its "scientific," all-seeing prowess. A member of its staff, a young Ph.D., bubbles with the enthusiasm of the projective men, who consider themselves the upper-class "U's" of the brain-watching world. "We have applied clinical psychology to job selection, mainly because we can learn much more about a man with this technique," he says. "The average college graduate can cheat on statistical tests, but it's almost impossible on our projectives. He doesn't know how we are going to interpret his responses."

Personnel Lab avoids the confusion of meeting its subjects, even in the hallway, by analyzing a job seeker solely on his responses to a twenty-two-page testing booklet, "Survey of Personal Resources," filled out without the help, or the presence, of the test psychologist. To record his unconscious on paper, the job seeker spends an hour or more "creating." He invents dramatic tales from a crudely drawn cartoon, sketches artless pictures, and completes such loaded teasers as "My worst . . ." The clinical sleuth dissects each line and nuance for "significant" responses, then collates the clues into a short—often half a page—personality portrait with his recommendation as a *good, fair,* or *poor* hiring risk. For those who can't make it in to New York, the firm maintains an ingenious testing network throughout the country. For $10 to $15 a head, local psychologists administer the battery in the nearest city, then send the completed projective form, instead of the flesh-and-mind man, back to the testing house for analysis.

The heavier price tag on projectives once restricted its use to high-salary, high-bonus employees whose unsatisfied needs could supposedly affect the corporate balance sheet. Today many companies are becoming equally interested in the hidden motivations of second- and third-string management and some are even paying to study their blue-collar men, more and more of whom are getting the clinical nod.

One young married fellow of twenty-four who had a small child applied for a job as a $70-a-week-plus-commission milk routeman for a dairy that believed in the subconscious aspects of milk delivery in suburbia. The applicant, who had been a truck driver, laborer, assembly-line worker, and a recently discharged Navy petty officer, was told that he would have to take a projective battery, which he graciously did.

"We had to turn him down," says the tester sorrowfully. "On the Thematic Apperception Test, he told a crime-and-punishment story involving a parent and child, in which he was the child. In the sentence completion, he answered: 'Most women . . . are very smart.' 'My ambition is . . . to go to heaven.' His drawing of the human figure was elemental. He is obviously a meek, submissive, mousy fellow defeated at twenty-four—henpecked with a wife who probably tells him what to do. This job requires a mature outgoing man who can make a good impression on housewives."

Clinical testers are, by and large, a jaundiced lot. After years of working with mental patients, many clinical men see the world through Freudian cataracts—as a place populated by hordes of near-psychotics who belong behind strong custodial walls instead of in the warm protective bosom of the Corporation. A New York firm, for example, recently advertised for a $12,000-to-$15,000 "systems man," a type of efficiency expert. The ad received three hundred answers which were studied for experience and references. Forty of the best men were called in for personal interviews, which narrowed the field down to eleven superior candidates, all of whom were then sent to a blind clinical house for evaluation. Of these eleven remnants of an original three hundred, the cynical testers rated only three as "good." The other eight, they said, showed disturbing psychological wounds in varying degree.

One "unsatisfactory," whom the testers acknowledged in their report as being an "intelligent, highly verbal, and

gifted" executive, was rejected because of a "strong underlying depression." Said the tester's report: "He has no understanding of the problems that normally arise in the
mid-forties and therefore has no means of resolving them."
Without meaning to, the tester had introduced him to one
crushing problem of modern middle-aged executives: the
clinical personality tests.

In the same batch, another man was clairvoyantly rejected
because of the sick implications of his *appearance*, even
though the tester had never seen him. The report boldly
states: "He tries to impress others with his appearance—as a
means of manipulating them."

The clinical man publicly exudes tremendous confidence.
A promotion sheet from one firm, which tested men for
radio station KHQ in Spokane, makes this typical boast: "On
the basis of this documented study KHQ can safely assume
that when ———— considers an applicant a good risk, he will
work out satisfactorily in virtually nine cases out of ten."

However, some of the more competent clinical testers—
when caught off guard and not pointed toward a cash register—candidly confess the trepidation that goes with their
job. "This is not a science. The data is always incomplete,"
admits one tester. "It is the sign of a mature clinician that he
doesn't believe he has all the answers. I sometimes stay up
nights worrying when a case is borderline. To achieve real
accuracy and depth would require a lot of time and talent—
at least seventy hours of testing and interviewing and thousands of dollars. This is out of the range of most corporations."

The testers' doubts are admirable, but they have scrupulously been kept from the customers. As a result, their admittedly money-making compromise has become a cult among
many naïve personnel men. One disciple, who uses clinical
tests to screen labor relations executives, finance men, and
production experts in a New York firm, is so wrapped up in
the dogma of the one-hour paper-and-pencil analysis that it
has even strongly affected his personal life.

"I was the first one tested in this company," he explains.
"Even though I was already employed here at the time, the
results were very penetrating and upsetting for me. It was
about as much as I could take. But once I recovered from the
shock, I got interested in the tests. The experience, and thinking about it, has now revolutionized my whole life—my attitude toward myself, my wife, my kids. If my predecessor
had used this kind of testing, I probably wouldn't have got-

ten my present job. But in certain areas, mankind has to push forward even though it is upsetting. One of these is testing in employment." The personnel manager's supine worship of the art seems amazing when he admits that he has never bothered to read outside material on the projectives. His only knowledge of the career-making (or breaking) technique came from the tester himself.

The origin of projective tests is in the nineteenth-century research on free association. In free association, the person expresses the thoughts as they form in his mind, regardless of form or content. When properly done, it requires a great deal of time, the skillful hand and evaluation of a psychiatrist, and is not readily adaptable as a commercial brain watcher's gambit.

The closest to it for testing purposes, to explore what psychologists call the "daytime fantasies," is the Thematic Apperception Test, or TAT, developed in 1935 by Dr. Henry A. Murray of Harvard. The subject is shown nineteen vague black-and-white illustrations, including one of a nude man climbing up or down a rope and one completely blank card, and is asked to make up a story to describe what is taking place in each one. The tester expects that unconsciously the testee will "project" himself into the role of the leading character and pull out the stopper on his unresolved frustrations.

The original TAT is usually given orally. The subject does the test in two steps, a day or more apart. The first day he verbally creates stories from ten cards, then he returns the second day and is given these instructions: *"Your first ten stories were excellent, but you confined yourself pretty much to the facts of everyday life. Now I would like to see what you can do when you disregard the commonplace realities and let your imagination have its way, as in a myth, story, or allegory."*

According to TATers, the hero of these little fables is actually the test subject himself, and the tester listens carefully as the man fends his way through his own Land of Oz. "How much force does the hero manifest?" asks a discourse on TAT scoring. "Does the hero make things happen or do they happen to him? Is the hero's path of achievement difficult or easy?" The good executive (or what have you) is Jason gaining the golden fleece, St. George slaying the dragon, Lancelot or D'Artagnan gaily manipulating his environment, overcoming fierce obstacles, winning the princess or the throne, carrying off mountainous pots of treasure every time.

There is no room in TAT mythology for Sisyphus and his eternally uncompleted job of rolling a stone uphill.

On the more mundane TAT cards, and *whenever* not accompanied by instructions to create myths, the good applicant is the one who invents uncreative, traditional stories that give away little of himself and show only such conventional motivations as hard work, discipline, cooperativeness, and optimism. In *Personnel* Magazine, published by the American Management Association, the author of an article entitled "The Executive Personality" illustrates what management looks for in TAT responses.

The test was given to a twenty-nine-year-old sales manager, described as a man of "median" intelligence for an executive, clinically normal, with a college degree in marketing." The unabridged version of this executive's successful response to TAT Card No. 1 (which shows a violin and a young man) is one of three reprinted in the article. It reads as follows:

TAT CARD 1:

"Well this reminds me of a—this is the story about a boy who has some musical talent. He's young but his parents have recognized this talent and have started him playing the violin. First of all he had a rather cheap inexpensive violin and recently this past Christmas he was given a rather fine instrument and he's looking at this particular instrument with a feeling of oh—awe perhaps visualizing the day that he might become quite a famous concert master. Is that enough ending or—

Interviewer: As you see it.

That's—that's about the way I stand.

Interviewer: Do you think he will achieve this success? Yes, I think the guy, the kid looks like a fellow that has talent. It would be my guess that he, through hard study and hard work, that he will go on to become a successful musician, perhaps not a concert master but the type of musician who should play with symphonies and that sort of operation.

In another card he told of a young man bringing bad news to a woman, but he assured the tester that since "these people both look like mature people that are facing their responsibilities," he was convinced that "Everything will turn out all right."

The sales manager's warmed-over soap operas are good indications that the TAT tester actually rewards *lack of* introspection and originality. Says the article's author about the subject's fatuous TAT responses: "The striving for achievement, optimism, positive attitude towards others, and admiration of authority in these stories hardly need to be pointed out. *They show no particular originality, no individual quirks. Rather they are pervaded throughout by the standard executive philosophy.*" (Italics mine.)

Dozens of royalty-free tests "adapted" from Dr. Murray's famous little TAT pictures are in circulation. One clinical firm uses a single blue-and-white water-color drawing, in which two men with indistinguishable features are facing each other across a set of desks. One is seated, and the other is standing and gesturing. To drop the victim's psychic guard, the test's author capitalizes on the frustrated storyteller in us all. He also adds an old testing standby: a simple lie.

"This is a test for imagination," the test introduction prevaricates. "Use the situation pictured above to make up as dramatic a story as you can. Tell what led up to the event shown in the picture, what the characters are thinking and feeling, and then give the outcome. Write your thoughts freely as they come into your mind. USE INK." Following this type of instruction in the TAT can be a disaster. Instead of receiving good ratings for "imagination" and "dramatic" story-telling, which the tester doesn't give a damn about, the subject is providing rich grist for his projective mill.

A ten-picture version of the TAT is the backbone of an entire testing giant, Social Research, Inc. of Chicago, headed by anthropologist-turned-tester Dr. Burleigh Gardner, whose firm also competes with Dr. Dichter in the motivational research business. Gardner uses his TAT cards as the major part of a $125 executive-assessment program, another blind testing operation. "We don't use the personal interview as part of evaluation," says Gardner. "We must read a man from the record, not face interactions."

From the TAT record of one hundred executives Gardner claims to have distilled the twelve factors that make a good business leader. Since clinicians are more concerned with unresolved Oedipus complexes than simple traits such as "self-confidence," it is no surprise that one of the twelve is a man's "attitude toward parents."

The man who wants to maintain close relations with Mom and Pop is skating on thin executive ice. The excessive parent-lover, he warns, will suicidally expose himself for the kid he is in his TAT stories. "In a sense, the successful executive is a 'man who has left home," Gardner writes in *Advanced Management*. "He feels and acts as though he were on his own, as though his emotional ties and obligations to his parents were severed . . ."

Mama, whose self-sacrifice and self-effacement are revered in American folk culture, is the more dangerous of the two. In fact, her strangling umbilical hold can throttle a potential vice president. "The men who still feel a strong emotional tie—far more than mere affection—to the mother have systematically had difficulty in the business situation," Gardner warns ominously. His hypothesis is interesting, especially to the hundreds of discards who never knew enough to blame Mama, and to the many successful men who have worshiped her. Andrew Carnegie built a half-billion-dollar steel empire despite the fact that his mother (after whom he named the Margaret Morrison Women's College at Carnegie Tech) was the emotional focus of his life. Franklin Roosevelt, up to his death, never quite broke his strong emotional ties to his mother, stern-willed Sara Roosevelt.

An SRI psychologist explains how the parent-loving executive is easily spotted in the Thematic cards. "Two of our ten cards have both older and younger people as characters," he explains. "The dependent executive usually tells a story that sets up the younger person in a subordinate role. For example, one subject recently told a story in which the young man was bickering with the older woman—obviously his mother—over minor household duties. They were arguing about who should open the door, etc. It definitely showed acceptance of a mother-son relationship that apparently was continuing. The person who tells this kind of story may well be married with children of his own. He may have left his childhood home in fact, but not emotionally."

Just as too much parental fealty is dangerous, rebellion—against the father—is a red flag for the TAT man. To the clinical prober, the father represents not just the male begetter, but also the Corporation—as a substitute father image. He is convinced that rebellion against one will inevitably lead to trouble in the other, and he scours the TAT captions to find the father-fighter and his corporate disloyalty, the mortal sin in the brain watcher's commandments. The testers have, in effect, set up a psychological tightrope. The executive must walk gingerly between the two bottomless pits of dependence on his father and rebellion against him.

SRI states its unlikely father-rebellion theory matter-of-factly, like an established homily. "A happy relationship with the father makes it easier for the executive to work within the framework of a large organization with its already established and operative set of over-all goals and procedures," says a staff-authored pamphlet. "Those executives whose self-assertion is stronger and who unconsciously yearn for complete independence—that is, are still fighting the father—will find it impossible to work within a framework of company policy established by superiors. Their feelings of loyalty are to themselves rather than to company policy which is the impersonal counterpart of the father-image."

Gardner describes a case of just such a father-battling troublemaker. An ex-Army officer with "outstanding abilities" and "excellent recommendations" applied for a civilian executive job and was TAT-tested at Social Research, Inc. The veteran was turned down as a potential troublemaker when the tests supposedly revealed a "dislike of cooperative action," all relating back to an unresolved childhood psychological struggle with his father. "Unconsciously," says the tester, "he viewed himself as a lone wolf operating aggressively on his own behalf."

The aggressive projective tester is constantly searching for new ways to trigger frank comments from workers without their knowledge. One of his best tools for this is the Sentence Completion Test, which is often used in the same battery as the TAT. Because it looks less complex than other projectives, it has even been picked up by some O & A testers in a harried attempt to psychologically beef-up their operation.

One popular version, the Rotter Incomplete Sentence Blank (Adult Form), used at Lever Brothers and other firms, lists forty partial statements which the testee is supposed to complete. The tester hopes that the phrases will release an unconscious confession to a usually well-camouflaged attitude, and will force the applicant to compulsively tell the truth about himself. The test operates on the premise that it is harder to lie when writing a sentence than when answering a simple "yes" or "no" question.

Some of the sentences are adroit traps for the uncautious:

My greatest fear . . .

I can't . . .

I am best when . . .

What pains me . . .

Some incomplete-sentence tests give the applicant a more definitive idea, such as these on the Hopkinson Test: "My family thought I was . . ."; "I don't like people who . . ."; "I am sometimes dominated by . . ." Others give considerably less to bite into, making the remainder of the sentence ostensibly that much more "projective" and subject to a tester's imaginative scoring. One test, developed by the Personnel Institute, has a number of questions that simply state: "Money . . . ; Religion . . . ; Death . . ."; and, of course, "Sex . . ."

Sentence Completion comes closest to being a model for the gag line about the psychologist who, when greeted with a cheery "Hello," pondered: "I wonder what he meant by that?" The clinical tester wonders about everything, and attacks a sentence like a modern coroner a corpse, poring microscopically for telltale psychological markings including the cliché "Freudian slip."

In a recent case, a testee completed the sentence "I would like to be like . . ." with the phrase: "myself, only better*s*." The tester brightened at the answer, and threw himself enthusiastically into an attack on the extra *s*. "That type of response is usually not accidental," he expounded. "It could mean just what it says, that he considers himself inferior, in a social or other sense, and would like to be like those he considers superior to himself—his *betters*."

Incomplete sentences are a volcanic game and the safest way of handling them is with conventional, optimistic, socially-acceptable answers liberally sprinkled with management clichés. The completions should not give the clinical man enough stimulus to bite his ego into, but they should give the illusion that you are answering in full and sincerely. The danger of appearing "shallow" is not considerable, and, in fact, lack of insight is considered a plus rather than a liability among many testers. Completing sentences is an art that requires thought or, at least, the intuitive talent that prompts one executive at a company conference to make a remark that brings a proud grin to the chairman's face, while another impulsive man—too eager to express himself—flubs.

One case, described in *Personnel* Magazine, shows how a stand-out man handles his incomplete sentences—with an array of corporate platitudes. The responses, done on a

Richardson, Bellows, Henry Sentence Completion Test, were made by an artful thirty-eight-year-old branch manager, who even cleverly twisted one of the tester's sentences around to mean what *he* wanted it to. The man, of "higher intelligence than the median executive," who had only a high school education, was judged "markedly normal but not-insightful" and of "high-future potentiality."

His masterful, executive-like answers were:

Working alone is . . . just that, lonely.

When I make a mistake, I . . . try to find out why and correct it.

When someone gets the better of me, I . . . am irritated but plan for the next time.

In getting to know people, I . . . believe all people have some assets.

Working with others makes me . . . feel responsible for their growth.

When they said I couldn't do it, I . . . stated that it should be tried.

I often wished . . . to do a great job.

I feel that people . . . are essentially sound and good.

When everything goes wrong, I . . . try to isolate the cause and create order.

The tester virtually cheered. "In these completions, the characteristics of extroversion, meeting frustrations by redoubling one's efforts, positive attitude to people, paternalism toward others, need for group acceptance, identification with the job, and practicality are very marked. Most striking perhaps is the way this executive completed the sentence, '*In getting to know people, I . . .*' So strong is his positive attitude toward others that he responds with 'I . . . believe all people have some assets,' though his statement of faith is, in the context, entirely irrelevant."

Intertwining the results of several projectives into one salable profile is the clinical tester's art. It is best visualized by listening to the tester who turned down the thirty-two-year-old applicant for the brassiere salesman job—an outside, hard-slugging job with completely different "clinical" requirements from those of the typical executive. "On the

Thematic Apperception Test, he told a story about two people who get together to solve a problem by cooperating," the tester explained about the bra company reject. "In the Sentence Completion, he gave logical, profound and sensible answers. He has no strong likes or dislikes and appears in harmony with himself. He looks before he leaps, and delays action.

"He is obviously not the man for the job. The *good* prospect for this job would tell a brief, poorly organized story on the TAT, a story in which the protagonist—himself—succeeds over another person. In the Sentence Completion, the *good* man would have contempt for the test—or any control or supervision. But because he doesn't want to offend, he would finish a sentence like 'I worry about . . .' with the phrase "absolutely nothing.' In the drawing of the human figure, the applicant did a careful and detailed drawing, while the good prospect for this job would do a poor drawing with the minimum requirements."

(The clinical mystique is infectious, and even the client, a vice president of the brassiere company, talks with the professional aplomb of his hired testers. "A good brassiere salesman's basic motivation should be money, either as a symbol of respect and status from his family or bank, or for money per se," he says. "Those of our salesmen who handle department stores should be more like the executive type and be able, for example, to talk management and stocks to his customers. The right man for this job should have a mailed fist in a velvet glove and be a person who has no trouble with the punishing-father symbol. I personally became interested in projective testing after I took the tests myself. They came up with a perfect portrait of me.")

The idea of testing a man by examining his feeble pencil sketches is a comparatively new and controversial clinical innovation. The concept appears ridiculous at first and, as we shall see, even at later sober sight. But ridiculous or not, it bedevils the men who developed a distaste for art in grammar school and never appreciated the dollars-and-cents significance of drawing a figure so that it looked more human than anthropoid.

But the way we draw the human figure—from the size of its ears to whether we put clothes on a female or leave her *au* birthday—intrigues the testers. They claim it is a reasonably accurate portrayal of the way we envision ourselves and our fellow men. They swear that the ability to sketch like Daumier, or hardly at all, has nothing to do with their evaluations.

Fascination with drawings as clues to man's personality is as ancient as handwriting reading. Anthropologists have attempted to re-create aspects of the Cro-Magnon man from cave etchings in Spain, and even the examination of doodles of the great, retrieved from conference wastebaskets, has been a popular game with some psychologists. One of the first drawing tests to be used as a clinical tool was probably the Goodenough Draw-A-Man Test, now used mainly in child guidance work. For adults, the Buck House-Tree-Person Test and the Machover Figure Drawing Test began as guidance and mental hospital diagnostic instruments which —like other unproven experiments—have since been expropriated by the brain watchers.

The Buck Test is divided into sections, each of which supposedly relates to a different area of life. The drawing of the house represents a person's home and family; the tree is his "life role" and general environment; the human figure, his attitude toward himself and people in general. The Machover Test, developed by Dr. Karen Machover, senior psychologist at Kings County Hospital in Brooklyn, has been used experimentally in many divergent situations—testing candidates for officer training, on Marine boots at Parris Island, and in many personnel situations. "Unfortunately," states Dr. Machover, "not as many people are as well trained in its use as they should be."

The drawing tests in commercial batteries are usually bastardizations of others. One popular one begins with these instructions: "On this page draw a picture of a man. This is not a test for art or drawing ability. It is important, however, that you try to do the best you can. Draw the WHOLE person. Do not TRACE or in any way COPY from an illustration. Your rendition should be a product of your own imagination. PLEASE USE PENCIL."

To the tester, every line, shading, and human part is fraught with meaning. He probes the untalented, distorted sketches with the intensity of an appraiser examining an old master. "A drawing can show up psychotic tendencies," explained a tester while fondling a crudely drawn sketch of a male figure. "An organized drawing, on the other hand, shows a restrained, careful person. He is decent, civilized, and the respect and opinion of others is important to him. He is not power-mad, and does not consider himself better than others. A big drawing in the center of the paper, in which the figure is looking forward, is typical of the outgoing personality. The restrained individual who wants to present less of himself often draws the figure in profile."

Many draw-a-man *aficionados* disagree on details. ("I don't believe the theory that grapelike fingers indicate a kind, gentle person," boldly states one tester.) But over-all, the following compendium is a reasonable guide to what is and what is not—in the trade—a "sick" human drawing.

1. A ground line drawn as a horizon to support your sketch is a sign of insecurity.

2. It is perfectly normal to put clothes on the male figure, but the female should be nude, complete with ample bosom. Putting clothes on a female drawing might indicate an abnormal sex attitude.

3. The omission of a part of the body means that you are somehow repelled by it. Lack of hands, or trying to hide them behind the little drawing's back, might indicate that you are fearful of their power, or what they have already done. The absence of ears is a sign that you are worried about what they will hear: you dislike criticism.

4. The drawing should be in the center of the page and reasonably large.

5. Aggressiveness and power drives are shown in the strength and quality of the lines.

6. Small parts have grave import. A button nose, once popular in Sunday comics, is a tip-off to immaturity. Emphasized nostrils indicate "temper."

7. The facial expression on your drawing's face is a reflection of your outlook on life.

8. Crude drawings may be a sign of repressed strong physical desires. In extreme cases, they are a clue to psychopathology.

9. Limply hanging arms indicate a Hamlet-like personality. Arms that go out, then come back in, and feet pointed in opposite directions may mean you are afraid to tangle with life as it is.

10. Buttons drawn on a garment are warning spots of an inadequate, dependent personality who lacked affec-

tion from his mother, and possibly hopes to compensate for it by tightly garbing his unloved body.

11. Overdressed drawings are a sign of vanity.

12. Of the two drawings, the sex granted the larger head is the one considered superior.

13. Disproportionately larger heads will be drawn by individuals suffering from organic brain disease.

The abracadabra aspects of these interpretations strike cold terror in the employee heart, especially the men who as youngsters learned to draw Dick Tracy-like characters, with their disproportionately larger heads. Fortunately the use of the draw-a-man in job selection has received heavy academic criticism (see Chapter XI: Brain Watching: Science or Cult?). Critics are also suspicious that despite the testers' disclaimers, drawing skill is important—that a well-sketched and reasonably rounded female figure shows better adjustment than a scrawny matchstick girl.

One classic experiment substantiated all the guffaws leveled at the drawing tests. Dr. John W. Whitmyre, of the Veterans Administration, asked fifty patients in a VA hospital to draw a human figure, then asked fifty normal veterans to do the same. The drawings were given to a psychologist conversant in the technique to rate them on personality. He was also to separate the psychotics from the normals. As a clever control, Dr. Whitmyre asked an artist to rate the drawings on sketching skill. The outcome was predictable: the psychologist did *not* distinguish the sick from the well drawings with any reliability. He labeled sane men psychotic, and vice versa. Amusingly, his psychological ratings were suspiciously similar to the ratings made by the artist for "drawing skill."

Every clinical technique has its special advocates, but the *grande dame* of the projective world is the little set of ten inkblots, the Rorschach, whose psychological reputation is exceeded only by the black leather couch. It has become as closely identified with the clinical psychologist, and as treasured by him, as the stethoscope with the physician. Because the inventor, Hermann Rorschach, and his later disciples, plainly intended it as a diagnostic aid in work with psychotics and severe neurotics, its entrance into the brain-watching world of normal men has been gradual. Recently, however, it has been increasing alarmingly.

Actually, there are strong doubts whether the famed inkblots work at all in personnel selection. Can they be taken out of the mental clinic and pressed into service in the corporation to pick one normal man over another for a particular job slot? One of the many doubters, Dr. Henry Dyer, vice president of the respected nonprofit Educational Testing Service of Princeton, New Jersey, chuckles at their inclusion in the brain-watcher's portfolio. (ETS officials have a refreshing tendency to be frank about testing. They are one of the few nonuniversity groups that hesitate to commercialize their research in the personality testing field.) "I don't think the use of the Rorschach as a personality test in industry is much a cut above numerology," he states candidly.

The Rorschach is complex, time-consuming, expensive, and should—say psychologists—be administered only by inkblot "experts," of whom there are reportedly not more than a few score in the country. But despite these obstacles, the glamour of the little inkblots developed by the Swiss psychologist in 1921 and still printed in Berne by Hans Huber is irresistible to many testers and corporations. Its pull on the testing industry is natural, for the Rorschach has become the caduceus of professional prestige. It distinguishes the simple personnel man with his paltry credits in undergraduate psychology from the professional psychologists, more and more of whom are taking higher-paid jobs as personnel managers.

Even after exchanging clinical white for corporate gray, some of these personnel men try to maintain the illusion of the doctor-patient relationship, which *subconsciously* they know can never exist in the brain-watcher's world. Nothing keeps this work-wish alive for convert personnel men better than keeping their inkblot cards dry and stacked for a "psychological emergency." Says the psychologist-personnel manager of Kenyon & Eckhardt advertising: "I still keep the Rorschach cards here in my desk drawer. I use them about a dozen times a year, whenever there is a good possibility that the person I am interviewing is neurotically ill."

One of the first companies to use the Rorschach was the Eagle Pencil Company, which has for years inkblotted its entire executive staff and all applicants for executive-level jobs with the aid of Kings County and Bellevue Hospital psychologists. The technique has been so "successful," according to the company personnel manager, that in the near future all employees will have their company future determined by what, besides butterflies, they see in the amorphous blots.

A larger sprinkling of men come in contact with the Rorschach through testing programs at the level of testers like Richardson, Bellows, Henry & Company, which employs local college psychology teachers on a per diem basis ($50) to administer the test. Even assembly-line quiz firms fall back on the inkblots when they feel the need for a psychological Big Bertha. One of them, in fact, called in a Bellevue expert as part of a hassle with a client who stubbornly disagreed with its opinion of a key executive. The testers wanted to downgrade the man because of "deep" emotional disturbances, but the chairman backed him up and angrily informed the testers: "I know this man thoroughly." The undaunted quiz man called in a Bellevue Hospital staff man to administer the Rorschach. "The inkblots proved he was disturbed," the tester recalls proudly. "The company finally admitted we were right, but they said the man was too valuable to let go—he knew how to make a good deal."

The ten controversial dabs of India ink finally chosen by Rorschach after experimenting with hundreds of preliminary ones are standard throughout the world. Five of the cards are shades of gray and black, two are partially red, and three contain varied colors. During an actual Rorschach session, the subject is seated in a chair with his back to the tester, who can advantageously see over the subject's shoulder to the cards in his hand, and write his own observations in secrecy. Some testers use inkblot slides ($11 a set of Kodaslides, The Psychological Corporation, N. Y. C.) to project them, like monster insects, onto a movie screen.

The psychologist introduces the test with an explanatory statement intended to reduce the subject's apprehension: "I am going to show a series of inkblots. They were made by dropping India ink on a piece of paper and folding it to make some kind of pattern. I want you to tell me what you can see in them. You may turn the card any way you like. Tell me as many things as you can make out, and when you cannot see any more, hand the card back to me." The subject is handed Card No. 1, and to head off such usual queries as "Do the white spaces count?" the psychologist has a standard monotone response: "Just tell me anything you see."

What people "see," the infinite images conjured up from the blobs of ink—a Disney-like face of a dog, human skeletons, a coat of arms, the reflection of a windmill in a pond—

and how psychologists have interpreted them for a generation have filled hundreds of volumes. The scoring of the Rorschach is a convoluted system, based on the form, color, detail, movement, the time before the first response, etc., that almost defies description. As a statistical nightmare it compares with the quiz tester's best.

A psychologist at BFS Psychological Associates, a New York clinical outfit that uses the Rorschach routinely in executive selection for its clients, tried to cut through the complex lore. "We can spot pathology in the Rorschach, but even if we find, say, paranoia—we have to balance it against the fact that the man is obviously functioning," he explained. "We wouldn't put it in the report directly but might say that the fellow should not be in a position to manage men. He might be better isolated in a technical job. The psychologist who does my Rorschach testing, like almost all of them, has a clinical background. I had to retain him in its use for normal people."

What does the normal, well-adjusted management man see in the inkblots? According to the BFS spokesman he sees a lot of things, each image of which is a significant clue to his "self-concept," which is in turn the Rorschachian tip-off to success. "The Rorschach is much deeper than the usual self-confidence scales," the psychologist claimed. "It shows what you think of yourself way down, how you handle yourself under pressure and whether there are any strong defenses preventing you from using your full capacity."

Each Rorschachian has a slightly different interpretation of what we see, but according to this devoted inkblotter, a man's aggressiveness can be determined by the type of animals he sees in the blots: small animals for the timid man, and courageous, roaring bears and lions for the fearless executive. Human images are a very strong sign of maturity, and the more the maturer, especially if they are in active, extended motion—pushing, pulling, jumping, or working. Human figures just contentedly smiling, or animals walking or kissing are kindly visions, but a sure clue to the man who really doesn't like himself—way down deep.

The Rorschach tester has even set up executive criteria, which are admittedly his own, drawn from experience and judgment, and he checks the inkblots against them to see if a client's man measures up. Here are the major executive points and, where possible, how they are partially pinpointed in the blots:

Flexibility: An inhibited, rigid person is spotted by the small number of his total responses. Many of the things he does see have form only and no color.

Intellectual functioning: Found mainly in the quality and number of human responses.

Sensitivity and understanding of people: What he sees in the gray spaces.

Not excessively defensive: The person who is too defensive and doesn't communicate sees a great many small details.

Rorschachians like to present their inkblots as specific and scoreable, but some more objective practitioners warn that strict adherence to scoring can lead a tester astray. The skill, they say, lies in the depth of the tester, not the instrument. W. Mons, an English psychiatrist, in his primer on Rorschach repeats the warning: "I was to discover that neither standards nor conception had any uniformity of character, that unless every response was fully understood for its significance for the *particular person* being tested, a reliable and clear personality picture could not be hoped for."

The job seeker is obviously caught in the middle of a battle over whether the Rorschach is really a test, or merely a tout sheet for psychological hunch betters. In any case, there are certain ground rules that have been developed over years of inkblotting. The following is a reasonable glossary of what people are "seeing" in blots these days:

1. Unreal responses—humans with two heads, monsters, animated trees, scenes from Mars—are schizoid responses that may indicate the subject is living in two worlds.

2. Psychotics tend to react to color emotionally, seeing the color itself and ignoring the form of the blot. "Normal" people tend to blend color and form, as in "a yellow lion."

3. Seeing the cards as a whole is typical of adolescents. In an adult, it can be a sign of mental simplicity. If the man is known to be intelligent, it can mean a predilection for abstract ideas.

4. Picking out large details in the blots is a sign of common sense. The more details, the more sense.

5. Choosing very small or minute details is less favorable, and may indicate a taste for the unorthodox or too great an interest in petty matters. It may also be an escape from reality, including an attempt to hide true personality from the psychologist.

6. Seeing things not only in the blots, but in the white spaces between them, can be a sign of a rebellious or overly stubborn personality.

7. Seeing inanimate objects in motion represents deeply buried unconscious forces. Detached feet that seem to be kicking, or fingers that are pointing, are pathological signs.

8. Animals in motion are generally typical childhood responses. In adults this may indicate feelings of inferiority, or mental defectiveness. In intelligent adults, it is a clue to neuroticism. (Some testers believe *large* animals are positive responses.)

9. Seeing human figures in motion, however, is generally the expression of a mature adult. It shows his ability to absorb experience and learn from it.

10. Reacting to the chiaroscuro, or gray areas, without making out a definite form—such as seeing "gray clouds" or "dark waters"—is symptomatic of a person with strong inner anxiety.

11. One of the most favorable Rorschach responses is to combine the gray tones and a form into a realistic three-dimensional image. The response "looking down a tree-lined street," for example, shows a person has a good insight into himself and an understanding of others. It demonstrates finer intellectual faculties, and literary taste and/or ability.

12. People who see textures in the blots, such as "grained wood" or "marble" (touch-feeling response) are exhibiting a strong pleasure drive, and possibly a dangerous sensuality. When combined with form, it can mean an awareness of other people's moods and good business "tact."

13. Unstable people react strongly to color, while overly controlled people tend to ignore it. When there is an excitable response to red—without any form—it indicates passion, temper, and a disposition for uncon-

trolled emotional outbursts. It may also mean the power to love strongly, and to possess deep passionate feelings. When the color dictates a form that is not there, such as a part of a body, it indicates the person is more apt to follow his heart instead of his head.

14. Seeing anatomical charts in the blots—lungs, hearts, bones—is normal in doctors, artists, athletes, or anyone with a "justifiable" occupational interest in the human body. For others, it is a clue to hypochondriasis.

15. Seeing "blood" or "flesh" is associated with highly neurotic and perhaps violent tendencies.

16. "Fire" responses are also neurotic.

17. Rejecting an inkblot without giving an answer is considered the sign of a dullard who can't make anything out. Or it may be the response of a man who is afraid of what he has just seen.

As many critics believe, there is of course the strong possibility that imaginative brain watchers see more in the blots than is actually there. The thought has been confirmed by a few firms and psychologists interested in checking out the Rorschach's employee-picking power. One validity trial, which used insurance sales executives as guinea pigs, turned out to be a devastating denouement of the inkblots. The experiment was done by Dr. Albert E. Kurtz of Pennsylvania State University and the Life Insurance Agency Management Association of Hartford, Connecticut.

As the first half of the test, 22 Rorschach "experts" examined a group of both successful (42 men) and unsuccessful (38 men) life insurance sales managers from eight different companies and used their answers to construct a Rorschach scoring key. The new inkblot scale was supposedly a portrait of the "inner man" of a successful insurance sales executive. Using their new success scale, these same experts inkblotted an unidentified group of 41 other life insurance sales managers—20 poor and 21 good—then tried to predict which of them were actually successful and which were washouts. (The definition of success was the company's confidential records on the man's dollar-and-cents performance.) The testers failed utterly, predicting not much better than poker-playing chance. They even labeled almost a third of the crackerjack sales managers as being psychologically confident of failure. In fact, if they had judged the men on age alone, it would have been *sixteen* times as accurate as the Rorschach.

The heavily advertised image of the Rorschach as a "progressive" and "Freudian" personnel tool almost disturbed the emotional stability of the world itself. The United Nations, at the suggestion of a medical consultant, at one time considered using the blots to choose "cooperative" UN staffers whose personalities would not clash with members of diverse cultures and races.

Fortunately Dr. Eugene W. C. Shen, a Nationalist Chinese who was then the United Nations' director of examinations, refused to accept the Rorschach on face value in such a potentially world-shaking assignment. He put the inkblots through one of the most extensive projective personnel validity tests ever conducted. The sample included 58 members of the UN Secretariat, representing virtually all the continents of the globe. Each person took the Rorschach and two supplementary tests, the Machover Figure Drawing, and graphology, or handwriting analysis.

The results were much like previous trials. The inkblots and their projective helpmates generally failed to choose the better from the unsatisfactory members of the UN Secretariat. "When we compared the tester's opinions with our supervisors' rating of the staff members' work, the results were generally negative," says Dr. Shen, who studied at Leland Stanford University. "The reliability of the Rorschach trial was too low for us to consider using it as a selection tool. Quite a few of the members doing good work were graded by the tester as being psychologically unsuited for the United Nations, and vice versa."

Of the 58 Secretariat members, the consulting "expert" found that only 38 were acceptable. Fourteen staff members doing good work were *rejected* by the tester, while five who were not acceptable to the United Nations on proven experience would have been retained. In answer to the question: "Does the staff member get along well with equals, superiors, and inferiors?" the tester came up with a *negative* correlation—lower than chance—a pretty difficult accomplishment outside a gaming casino. Of the 22 Secretariat employees whom he identified as misfits, *21* had been rated by supervisors as getting along well with others.

The UN then cagily made it a little difficult for the tester, asking him to evaluate a staff member's punctuality from the blots. Again, he failed, incorrectly identifying 18 workers as being lateniks. On the key question: "Would you continue to employ him or her?" the tester's recommendation—if projected against the entire Secretariat—would have required firing almost one-third the entire United Nations staff!

The unsuccessful shakedown trials of projectives in industry have given some sensitive brain watchers pause, but they have not braked the dollar-making boom. Like brassiere salesmen, projective testers are versatile and adaptable. They are heartened by the ample supply of old tests and the sheaves of new unproven projectives introduced each year for clinical work with the disturbed, most of which can be adapted for commercial ends sooner than detractors can debunk them.

One old projective standby, handwriting analysis—finding a man in the waves and idiosyncrasies of his script—has long been popular as a selection tool in Europe, where a fine hand is carefully cultivated and admired. Occasionally, it finds its way across the ocean to our penmanship-poor culture, where the results appear to be disastrous. (The Manhattan classified phonebook lists ten "handwriting analysts," three of whom specifically mention "personnel" selection.)

One young man, then a recent college graduate, applied for a sales promotion job with a $30,000,000-a-year aluminum fabrication firm that makes metal sheets and tubing. He conscientiously filled out the application blank in his normally crude, almost juvenile hand, a shortcoming shared by many of his countrymen. He was turned down for the job with a verdict that his handwriting showed that he was "untrustworthy," and that he possessed "no growth potential." The story, however, has a happy conclusion. He now holds a similar job, as a trusted, well-paid associate member of a Manhattan firm that specializes in management and sales consultation for industry. The handwriting tester, however, has left him one legacy: to this day, he has strong feelings of inferiority about his penmanship.

Current psychological bulletins are brimming with new projective ammunition for tomorrow's testers. The KTSA, the Kahn Test of Symbol Arrangements, is a new Rorschach-like test that, instead of inkblots, substitutes a set of sixteen miniature objects—Scotty dogs, hearts of various sizes, a ship's anchor—which the subject arranges in order of preference, then explains what each one means to him. The hardened person who places the heart last, says the tester as an example, is showing his negative attitude toward love. The enthusiastic author, an Air Force psychologist, feels the

KTSA is superior to the Rorschach in some ways. His little charms, he believes, obviously mean more to people than do lifeless blobs of India ink.

Several testing firms have even turned the once-innocent application blank into a surreptitious projective test that probes more for psychological *style* than for the prosaic information it pretends to seek. The McMurry Company of New York and Chicago, one of these practitioners, reveals some of its application-blank trade secrets in an article in *Personnel,* "The Application Form Revisited."

An applicant's lack of energy, for example, may be spotted simply by scanning his list of "favorite high school subjects" on the application blank. The tip-off: "the mention of one subject only." Clues to a man's "aggressiveness" are also telegraphed, in this case by the cavalier fashion in which he handles the blank. The aggressive form-filler belies himself by compulsively "writing into words printed on the form" and "crossing out words or letters printed on the form." There are other application blank giveaways to hostility: listing a former superior by his "last name only" and distorting or misspelling, with malice or otherwise, the corporate name of previous employers. Slang references, such as "Monkey Ward" for Montgomery Ward, are among the most revealing.

Nothing is wasted. Significant projective indications can be found anywhere on the "revisited" form, the McMurry people indicate. The oral skills supposedly associated with effective salesmen are even hidden there, easily extractable from the application-blank information on "fathers and brothers." Say the testers: "An applicant is more likely to possess oral skills if his father is a lawyer and his brother is a salesman, than if his father is a geologist and his brother is in civil service."

The sin of narcissism, what the *Shorter Oxford English Dictionary* calls "a morbid self-love or self-admiration," is tipped to the tester mainly by the way an applicant fills out his name, says the *Personnel* article. If the name is "spelled out in full when this is not called for on the form, as 'John Jonathan Jones,' especially if 'Jr.' or 'IV' is added," says the tester, you are exhibiting narcissism—even if you happen to have been born a "Jr." (A competitor, Worthington Associates, looks at names and narcissism somewhat differently. Placing an initial at the front of your name, as in "J. Jonathan Jones," is a clear sign of narcissism, says

Worthington, while the use of a middle initial, "Jonathan J. Jones," is only "mildly compulsive.")

The clinical testing world encompasses a sizable slice of the profession, but, fortunately, some psychologists are able to laugh at their colleagues' excesses. One academic psychologist, writing in a professional journal, smilingly proposed a "Gesundheit" projective test that would be graded on how a man reacted to his own sneezes. The test "kit" would include a snuff box, a face mask, a large jar of powdered snuffs, and a facial tissue dispenser. The testee is to sneeze three times, followed by the tester's "Gesundheit." As a guide to scoring, the test author suggests: "How much snuff does he take? (aggressive or reticent behavior?); Does he sneeze directly at the examiner? (possible sadistic personality component or hostile attitude toward parental figure?); How does he apply it? (a foppish manner by male or a vigorous approach by female may be indicative of possible psychosexual conflict or outright homosexuality)."

One tale, possibly apocryphal, is aimed at the blind clinical man who insists on working without flesh-and-blood subjects. The story—told and retold in testing circles—involves a woman psychologist who made involved interpretations of a finger painting "projective," only to discover to her horror that the subject was a young chimpanzee.

Despite the rebuffs, the projective tester's miracle claim to "cheat-proof" methods has accomplished near wonders, especially during the past half-decade. For management, it has approximately doubled expenditures for testing, and has provided a feeling of being involved in "real" psychology. For the working stiff ($50 a week to $50,000 a year) it has been the largest nail in the coffin of his privacy and of the right not to be an involuntary guinea pig in an unlicensed pseudomedical experiment. To the brain watcher it has meant fatter take-home pay. But at the same time, it has produced a growing anxiety that this excursion into the clinician's field may have put him in too deep—into psychological waters that may yet submerge him entirely.

4
TESTING MEN ON THE JOB: YOUR PERSONALITY IN LIVING COLOR

When air travel and bustling auto vacationists disturbed the sales graph of the Greyhound Bus Lines downward not long ago, it drove the company's president into the always-receptive arms of the tester. The assignment was to prune costs by mass firings, on a psychological basis. When the brain watchers had completed their testing of the entire management with a battery of tests which included a "neurotic" personality inventory and, appropriately enough, a sense-of-humor test, several hundred employees, including two vice presidents, were reportedly fired.

The day the testers descended on Greyhound is well remembered by its employees, some of whom still appear to carry the emotional scars of their narrow escape. The spokesman for the Cleveland office recalls the debacle. "A tester who previously had been at Westinghonse did some of the original work, and the company also called in a Chicago consulting outfit," he explained. "Of the three hundred men we had here then, about one hundred were fired and a handful were promoted. The company tried to use testing as their guide instead of experience, but I don't believe it worked out too well. We have a new president now and the whole thing has been cut out."

The social damage done in *l'affaire* Greyhound was vast, and although an extreme case, it points up one of the gravest threats to our traditional concept of "working your way to the top"—the mass, indiscriminate testing of men already on the payroll, either when up for promotion or suddenly lashed out at by the brain watcher when contemplating nothing heavier than last month's expense account. It is possibly the tester's most traumatizing, and lucrative, activity.

Unlike selection work, testing of men "on the job" involves not just the turndown of an applicant for a tempting opening. It can be the major determinant of who shall be lofted into executive suites to manage our industries, who shall be arbitrarily frozen in uncarpeted, frosted-glass cubicles, and who shall be discarded, often at early middle-age, when the Corporation's judgment of a man shapes the remainder of his life.

Figures on how many firms test men who are already employed, and were once thought immune to a tester's hasty evaluation, are not fully reliable. Some organizations, like the U. S. Civil Service, do not personality test applicants, but do often put men eligible for promotion through brain-watching paces. (A spokesman at the Brooklyn Navy Yard states frankly that its use in government agencies for upgrading is "common.") Over-all, few personnel men doubt that brain watching on the job—what is euphemistically called "human inventory" and "manpower audit"—has been accelerating at a frightening rate.

One set of flesh-and-blood statistics in a recent report in *American Business* Magazine showed that the management consulting firm of Booz, Allen & Hamilton, for example, used a battery of tests to determine the promotability of 1,427 executives in twenty-five companies, giants varying in size from $10,000,000-a-year sales to over $1,000,000,-000. The tests "found" that 35 percent of the men were promotable, 54 percent were satisfactory in their present jobs, and the remaining 11 percent were considered unsatisfactory, with no undecideds, no imponderables, and no tester self-doubts.

The tester's entrance into the field of on-the-job testing is understandable when we realize that there are some 4,000,-000 managers in industry today, each of whom represents a potentially sizable price tag for the tester. One testing firm, Herrold Associates, reportedly received $100,000 for a recent psychological inventory of a single management team.

The "how" of testing employees for movement upwards, sideways, or down is, like all brain watching, an unpredictable operation. In fact, occasionally a man's rung in the corporate's hierarchy may depend upon his sudden measurement with a single personality test or even a single trait scale. A psychologist in suburban Great Neck, Long Island, recently described such a chilling situation. "A large mail-order advertising firm used to have their main headquarters here before they moved into New York City a few years ago," he recalls with amusement. "While they were here I gave all their executives the Allport A-S Reaction Study, which measures ascendancy and submission, the tendency to dominate others or be dominated by them. I turned the results over to the company, and I have since heard that they have been using these same scores for the promotion of all their executives." Undoubtedly the mail-order executives never dreamed that the Allport's simple inquiries into how they would react on a bus or at a school meeting could be so very final. A similar situation turned up at Westinghouse's plant in East Pittsburgh, Pennsylvania, not long ago when the "Cattell Sixteen Personality Factor" personality test was used to screen technical men hoping to be promoted.

Although just as potentially dangerous, the typical management audit is considerably more involved and psychologically taxing than these one-shot psychometrics. Richardson, Bellows, Henry & Company, for example, which charges $250 per executive for its on-the-job assessments, executes an involved operation that includes an hour-and-a-half depth interview, an I.Q. test, a battery of ten paper-and-pencil tests, including the Kuder Preference, the Allport-Vernon "Study of Values," and a sentence completion followed by a Rorschach inkblot. "Three different psychologists give the Rorschach, the paper-and-pencil tests, and the depth interview so that we can get three opinions on each man," says an RBH spokesman. Another consultant, John R. Martin Associates, located on New York's Park Avenue, relies almost entirely on a lengthy "depth" interview.

The end product of much of this frenetic activity in assaying a corporation in one mind-swoop is an organizational map unlike any ever dissected in a business seminar. The chart appears to be an innocent table of organization with the president of the firm, or the vice president of a division, at the apex of a pyramid with lines of responsibility going downwards. The names of underlings—regional managers, salesmen, production foremen—are ensconced in small rectangles and suspended hopefully below. The difference in the tester's map is that each man's rectangle is shaded in with a different color of the rainbow, showing management at a glance every employee's future—in living color.

Testers have naturally developed their own favorite color schemes to decorate their "manpower audit" maps. In a promotional booklet to clients, one testing outfit explains its rainbow key: "Each man is represented by a rectangular block such as you will find on any organization chart, coded in one of the following four colors: green—to indicate potentials for upgrading; blue—to indicate continuation of current status; yellow—to indicate need for study and investigation of personal problems; red—to indicate downgrading."

The John R. Martin consulting organization, which also specializes in these awesome charts, has a color scheme which clashes somewhat with its competitor's. Its blue represents "very superior." Green is for run-of-the-plant "superior," and gray is for average men. Yellow and red, the traditional stop signals in on-the-job assessment, are also Martin's failure shades reserved for psychological rejects. Yellow means "other placement suggested" while red is blatantly "unsatisfactory." The yellow man is likely to be shifted or reduced in rank, while the red man is likely to be pushed out into the street to look for a new job.

These color charts, drawn at sizable expense to the corporation, are no mere exercises. As one tester points out: "Our recommendations are followed at least 90 percent of the time." The earnestness with which management regards these half-day brain watchings of twenty-year employees was illustrated in a recent volume, "Executive Selection: How Psychologists Can Help," prepared by graduate students at Harvard Business School in collaboration with psychologists and management, including representatives of Raytheon, Textron Corporation, and various important testers. "Almost inevitably an audit will give top management a better feeling of the human resources of the company and may bring about a 'facing up' to deadwood and incompetence," says the report.

It unemotionally describes such a case of chopped-out "deadwood" taken from the files of one of its participants. "One large consumer products company hired a psychological testing firm to conduct an extensive search. In one eighteen-month period they appraised over 1,000 people. The company wanted to do a major job of restaffing and was looking for unsuspected specific managerial talents. Such talent was found. One important side effect was that a number of people lacking in management ability were discovered. They will eventually be transferred and replaced by newly discovered talent." Like most testing reports this one fails to follow up with a study on whether the new faces produced as well as, or worse than, the deadwood.

The serious game of corporate chairs can be quite emotionally disturbing even to an innocent onlooker. During the research for this volume, the author solemnly watched in testers' offices on at least two occasions as the color personnel maps of two sizable corporations, the entire marketing department of a giant machine-maker and a division of a company which manufactures everything from tubes to atomic reactors, were dramatically unrolled. The sight of the colored-in future of more than 100 striving executives—a judgment seldom fully revealed even to them—was virtually blinding. The author felt compelled to glance aside rather than to risk the possibility of remembering the names of the "yellows" and "reds"—whose careers were doomed—generously dotted across the chart.

The typical manpower audit has another outstanding facet, the depth interview, the couchless equivalent of the psychiatric session. To some testers this face-to-face joust between psychologists and employees is one of the few viable tools in the business. (Others, of course, are just as adamant that it is totally worthless.)

One proud proponent of the depth interview and a strong critic of conventional personality tests is John R. Martin, Ph.D., proprietor of John R. Martin Associates, fellow and diplomate of the American Psychological Association. "I don't see how anyone would stick his neck out and evaluate a person without seeing him," says Martin. "To me the depth interview is the most important part of the evaluation. I do use a short personality questionnaire as a guide to the interview, but I think tests such as the Bernreuter are worthless. In fact my whole attitude toward psychometrics in general compares to that of an atomic scientist toward high school physics."

The depth interview, which can run anywhere from half an hour to half a day, is the tester's technique of softening, then opening up an employee and having him voluntarily expose his psychological innards for the corporation. Unfortunately it is not too difficult a job. The employee has already been conditioned by our culture to regard excessive personal privacy as somewhat Victorian. Confessional articles in books; market motivational research which probes into his eating, buying, sex, and fantasy habits; public opinion polls; school guidance counselors; and credit checks have made the employee almost aggressively voluble about himself without too much prodding from the tester.

Most testers verify this national foot-in-the-mouth disease. "People like to talk about themselves," says Dr. Theodore A. Jackson, chief psychologist of Stevenson, Jordan & Harrison, management engineers. "After two minutes they open up." Another tester who finds his subjects magnificently talkative adds: "It's amazing what they tell you. We set up a sort of doctor-patient relationship to put them at their ease. Then we try to find out about his home, his attitude toward his boss, his likes and dislikes, how his family feels about his job. It's very difficult for him to cover negative attitudes in an extensive interview."

A testing psychologist at management consultants George Fry & Associates, who states that he has evaluated 5,000 people, describes some of the finesse of the depth interview. "During the interview I make the man feel as comfortable and as much at home as possible. I never apply stress. I may ask him about his work, not because I care about it, but as a camouflage. It's easy for people to talk about their jobs. I wait until I have him almost supine. I can tell by the change in his muscle tone or by his verbalizing to the effect that he will take his hair down or will get on the couch. Before that everything is superficial. After that he reveals himself quickly and I learn a great deal about the man."

The clever depth-interview technique is a threatening experience for the man who weakens his guard even for an instant. Many interviewers have a standard patter: What are your father's best traits? What are your mother's best traits? What do you think of them? In what way are you like them? What is your effect on other people? Were you in the service? Did it help you? Did it change you and how? Even these preliminary questions (similar ones were once used as a mail-order depth interview by *Medical Economics* Magazine in New Jersey) will trigger the confessions of the typical loquacious employee, who is either flattered by the serious attention to his blabbings or confused by the role of the psychologist-tester.

As the session progresses the interviewer begins to sound more and more like the "doctor-counselor" who is seriously interested in the employee's problems. Actually he is listening with anticipation for some small psychological confession that he can develop into a possible syndrome. "I wait until a man makes a comment that is clinically significant," says one tester. "Then I chase that rabbit for a while." As many management men have sorrowfully learned, this near-sighted view of the psychologist as a "friendly counselor" can be an expensive error.

The typical depth interview is perfectly stage-managed to trigger such confessions, and most testers do not hesitate to use the precious information against their man. One sales-man for a vending machine company was going through a mass evaluation of the marketing department of his company. He was given a typical depth interview and during the session he yielded to the tester's art and relaxed sufficiently to confide in the interviewer. Just a few days before, he told the tester, he had learned that his child was anemic and he was very troubled about it. In fact, he was forgetting small details on the job. His candidness in airing this temporary personal problem was rewarded with a new, and even greater one. "We had to grade him yellow for caution," the tester explained dispassionately.

Some test interviewers boast that holding back on the corporation, or trying to lie, is a futile protest against their advanced art. "A person can almost never keep up his guard for any lengthy period of time," says the George Fry psychol-ogist. "When they are going to lie they always first signal ahead. They give a whole host of clues. Usually there is a dilating of the pupils, change in the complexion due to the capillaries in the cheekbones, a shifting of their body. Some are better liars than others, but few are really good."

Each tester has his own technique for spotting cagey inter-viewees. "The smart guy who tries to fool us is the easiest one to catch," says the John Martin spokesman. "When he be-comes defensive, the things he is talking around are the things that he is giving away to us."

Because the depth interview is as much bread-and-butter to the brain watcher as it is to the applicant, the tester often goes into this modern combat much like the guerrilla fighter, unhampered by any rules of gentlemanly procedure. One tester, for example, explains his ingenious technique for opening up men who have been too guarded during the guts of the discussion. "I make a motion of finality—perhaps move the papers to one side of the desk as if the whole thing is over," he explains. "Then I say: 'Do you have any ques-tions about the interview?' After that I learn a hell of a lot."

The day a man meets his psychologist may well be the most important one of his life and no one can afford to harbor hostility or insecurity for that vital hour or hour-and-a-half. As frank testers admit, the depth interview freezes a man in his attitudes in a moment of time (and an eight-page report) rather than the ten, twenty, or thirty years he may have worked in the firm. At that moment of corporate truth any slip by the employee or error by the psychologist is potentially dangerous. However, the danger is increased at least to the square when the employee comes up against an interviewer more intent on improving the "art" with absurd psychological experimentation than trying to fairly assess the man staring at him from the other side of the desk.

During the past few years, for example, hundreds of executives have been stopped in the middle of a depth interview given by one prominent New York psychological firm, and asked the simple question: "Please think of your very best friend. Now would you please describe him for me."

"I use the best-friend technique as a verbal projective," says the tester, whose office walls are covered with nine giant file cabinets containing evaluations of over 1,000 executives in one mammoth metal firm. "They start talking about their best friend at first, but soon without realizing it they have projected themselves into it. After that the person they are talking about is not their best friend but actually themselves. Remember, birds of a feather flock together. I can learn more about a man by asking about his best friend than by putting direct questions to him about himself.

The shocking "best friend" gambit has, of course, no proven validity nor is it even rooted in common nonpsychological horse sense. As an experiment, the author sat patiently through one of these best-friend tell-alls and vividly described a pal of long standing, with an equally large but quite different assortment of neuroses. At the conclusion of the session, when asked what he had learned, the tester threw back a digested but quite competent description—not of the author—but of his best friend. Fortunately the friend is a well-employed executive who has no intention of job-hunting. Judging from this experience, we will never know how many "blue" or "green" management men on the escalator up, and how many discarded "reds" buffeted from one executive recruiter to another, owe their fate to the maturity, the bad-luck marriage—or the reverse—of their very best friends.

Some on-the-job testers have a pragmatic concern with a man's work record, not only as a concession to traditional techniques but as a hedge against monumental errors. Many other brain watchers, however, will not check a man's work record beforehand. They prefer not to have their manpower audits tainted by a man's record of accomplishment, what they call psychological "contamination." This approach can naturally result in an embarrassing chasm between the corporation's longtime opinion of an employee and the tester's half-day report. The difference of opinion can even ruin a promising career, especially if the self-confident tester rationalizes to back up his "expert" point of view.

One such tester evaluated the sales department of a large candy company recently. The sales manager of the division, who covered several southern states, was graded as "awful." The management, who had always considered him one of their crackerjack men and best producers, were dismayed. "We were a little concerned with our report at first," admits the tester. "But after we checked it out we found that we were right. He really wasn't as good as they thought. The sales manager's area included many poor sections. It turned out that he was doing well only because the candy was one of the main items in their daily food diet."

The depth interviewer, often reinforced by projectives and paper-and-pencil tests, presents a formidable professional front and is often considered the leader in his art. But his reports, like most others in the brain-watching establishment, can be disappointing exercises in generalities enlivened only by a layer or two more of professional jargon than usual. Browsing through some of them it seems incredible that management can appreciate, or even understand, what they are buying at upwards of thousands of dollars a day.

Here are two authentic samples voluntarily provided from one Park Avenue tester's file. The first, an accountant being evaluated, was graded "superior" both in his job and in his possibility for advancement. The report read:

> His repressions of his feelings and his philosophical acceptance of unresolved adjustment situations have resulted in the accumulation of backdrop of feeling tone within him. This makes him cautious and leads him to take the view of an observer who sometimes senses a futility in much that goes on and who can move among people and yet feel somewhat alone.

Obviously, this repressed introvert is what the doctor ordered in the accounting department.

The second, an ambitious, impatient executive, was not recommended for higher things:

His impulsiveness, his strong need for rapid personal advancement with accompanying power and material benefits, his general loss of enthusiasm in intensity of personal application when the solutions to problems require slow-moving routine follow-through are the major reasons why he is not recommended.

If the Corporation believes that this one-shot management audit is worth paying for, testers have asked themselves: Why not a continual psychological watch on a man? How much more fruitful and lucrative if we could stay with the same man five, ten, fifteen years or even ad infinitum.

The answer, now called "management development," invites the psychologist into the corporation for frequent visits to look, listen, question, and tell. It is probably best espoused in the field by the firm of Rohrer, Hibler & Replogle, which, although not quite the originator of the technique, is the prime proponent of this type of big-brother psychology.

"Rohrer," as it is known in the trade, was started by Perry Rohrer, former Cook County court psychologist, who in the late 1930's convinced the management consulting firm of Stevenson, Jordan & Harrison to set up a psychological division with him at its head. By the end of World War II, with the impetus of the testing of servicemen (see Chapter X: Once Upon a Mind), the division had swollen to anywhere from twenty to thirty-five psychologists, depending on who relates the story. In 1946, Rohrer and some twenty of his colleagues left SJ&H to form the nation's first full-time firm of psychologists for the Corporation—a move that is affectionately known in the business as "The Revolution." Since then RH&R have spawned dozens of similar operations throughout the country.

RH&R is a testing network of seventy-five Ph.D.'s who have made escape and careful feigning a virtual impossibility by a tenacious around-the-calendar brain watch. Working out of ten central headquarters in New York City, Chicago, Dallas, Cleveland, Minneapolis, San Francisco, Los Angeles, Detroit, Milwaukee, and Atlanta, the intrepid RH&R men are "attached" to the top management of some two hundred corporations. A psychologist is assigned to one or more executives in the firm and stalks his quarry at lunch, at his home for dinner, and even on the golf links —for weeks, months, even years at a time.

This unusual private-eye psychology was frankly discussed by an RH&R partner, the head of one of its offices. "We are not a clinic, a psychological department store, or management engineers," he says. "We are 'Psychologists to Management' and we concentrate most of our work at the top level. One of our clients is a billion-dollar corporation with over five hundred thousand employees, and we have been working with only the top twelve to fifteen executives in the company for a number of years.

"After initial evaluation our work is all informal," he continued. "Originally, our psychologist sees a man about twice a month but after that it varies—anything from once a month to even two or three regular visits a week. Our psychologist actually lives in the environment of the firm and learns a great deal about his man. The psychologist on the job will lunch with one or five executives at a time, will know all the wives, and have dinner with all the families frequently in their homes. At first, as when any professional man visits the home, the situation may be a little formal. Then the psychologist-client relationship comes off. Naturally every man wants to know if he is a bust as an executive."

If the psychologist's divining rod spots such a failure, he feels obligated to have the man face it squarely. "If a man is bumping his head against a ceiling I try to get him to see himself realistically," says a John R. Martin psychologist who is active in management development work. "This type of person gets heartbreak every time someone is promoted over him."

The work of the big-brother psychologist has set up an unusual balance in many corporations. It places RH&R and similar firms in the enviable spot of having accumulated more intelligence on the company's executives, from their niblicks to their marital problems, than the corporation itself possesses.

The value of these swollen dossiers has not been lost on management. In fact, many of them have granted the consultant a supracorporate power, including the virtual handpicking of a company's new president. Many of the top personnel announcements heralded in the business-news pages of *Fortune, Time,* and *Newsweek* were born not in executive suites, but more likely in the psychologist's fertile mind over an after-dinner demitasse or on the nineteenth hole during a chitchat with a personable candidate who has learned to appreciate, and perhaps cultivate, this new seat of power.

In this depersonalized atmosphere of the public company, the psychologist sometimes knows the heir apparent long— even years—before anyone else. "I would never tip my hand to the man with the mantle on him," says an RH&R psychologist. "I would just tell him that he can go as far as he wants to in the corporation."

This awesome power of the consultant was hinted at by another tester, whose operation also includes long-term testing and development. In fact, the story he recounted shows that executives with bad evaluations sometimes find that the black psychological mark is virtually impossible to erase. "A man we had turned down for vice president came back to us and asked why he had not been recommended," the tester explained. "We told him. Then a few years later he was appointed president of the very same company and he called us in to work with him. After a few years he ceased to be president. It was for the very same reason he had originally been turned down for the V.P. slot—his attitude toward his wife, his son, and himself."

The continuing management development arrangement between the tester and the corporation is generally a $200-per-day look-see and therefore the most highly priced business in the field. The John R. Martin psychologist describes what companies get for their money, the ritual of what brain watchers like to consider the "therapy" that follows up their original "diagnosis." "I have been working with one firm for a period of sixteen years," he says. "I see them once a week and generally start by dropping in to talk to the president for a half-hour or an hour. I ask, 'How's things?' and he usually answers that 'everything's fine.' But when we talk a little while longer, he finally tells me what's really on his mind. I might then go to see the V.P. for sales, and after a while gravitate toward the point of strain in his department. I talk to the man in question and help him to get his feelings out in the open. If he thinks somebody he works with or under is an S.O.B., I might end up by taking them both out for drinks. Soon they are both going steady."

On-the-job testers with an audit or development program try to create the image that their probings will hurt no one and that their therapeutic balm will, in fact, evoke harmony. When trying to get their foot past the corporate doorjamb, for example, they seldom talk about the psychological "dead-wood" and "red downgrading," or the definite possibility that if the cocktail therapy on a man doesn't take, the guy who thinks his boss is an S.O.B. may well be cursing him on the unemployment line.

Their sales pitch invariably has an up-beat approach that starts by courting the No. 1 man. Some unsubtle testers find that by the simple act of chalking in blue or green—the exceptional colors—in the president's box and working down the color scale from there, he becomes automatically convinced of the validity of their program. Other psychologists work on the national infatuation with "self-improvement," being cautious not to get too deeply involved for fear of alienating their potential patron.

"When I examine the president I leave my white coat at home," says one on-the-job expert. "I give him a depth interview patterned after the typical personnel one. Then I feed it back to him. I tell him some of his problems and what he can do about them. We might have four or five follow-up sessions and he gets so intrigued that he wants me to extend it to the entire firm. He is also interested in the program because the top guy is a lonely fellow and he needs somebody like me to talk to."

Bringing along the firm's chary executives—with a hell of a lot more on the line than the president—is part of the tester's art. One company evaluated a key executive by disguising the psychologist as an employee from "another city" and had the two men share a company hotel suite for a few days. The two chatted during the evenings, and with this—plus a close-up view of such personabilia as the executive's snoring and toilet habits—the psychologist made his secret evaluation.

Another tester, to prevent the rallying of resistance against a mass brain-watch operation, admits to carrying two sets of business cards, only one of which describes him as a psychologist. On the other he is described as a less ominous "human relations specialist." If employee resistance gets its back up, he simply conjures up the human relations card and poses as a company Dale Carnegie.

The more typical technique is a "positive" letter sent by the president to all employees, a masterful sell-job that attempts to assuage their all-too-real fears, yet impress them with the management's firm interest in the psychologist's findings. One such letter was quoted by a George Fry psychologist. It read:

This is one of the tools of modern management in

order that each one will be able to function at the greatest personal satisfaction and hope of success. This obviously redounds to the benefit of the company.

This procedure will include paper-and-pencil inventories of your attitudes and interests, and will be followed by an interview with a consulting psychologist.

Each one will have an opportunity to discuss their personal problems and their strength and shortcomings in order to best utilize the assets and minimize the shortcomings.

Another letter, an appendix in the Harvard volume *Executive Selection*, shows the Lorelei appeal to advancement and promotion. Yet despite the stage-fronting, the simple description of the brain watcher's operation has a stiffening effect:

To: General
Executive Memo: 7–56
From: [The Company's President]
Subject: Management Development Program

We must get better acquainted with our own people. There are areas in which an individual's greatest potential lies, as well as areas in which he is less likely to develop. He can do a better job and management can help him to prepare for advancement if dependable methods are used to become aware of his potentials.

In the scheduling of groups for appraisal, dates had already been set up for two groups: the week of October 15 is reserved for those who may be included from the Accounting Department, and the week of November 12 for those who may be included from the Receiving and Operations. Arrangements will be made later for scheduling of other groups.

The tests and questions consume less than a full day and the interview will use less than one-half of another day. A written report of the appraisal, including the interview, as a matter of central control, will be mailed to my office and will be forwarded unopened to the general manager of the appropriate operations or to the manager of an independent department for his use. The reports, with respect to their subordinates, may also be used by division managers reporting to operations general managers but should not be available to anyone else within the operations. After their usage the reports will be returned to my office for storage in a locked file and will be available for reference in future staffing.

The ethics of whether or not a "doctor," to whom the Ph.D. test psychologist likes to compare himself, should subject his "patients" to compulsory psychological examinations undoubtedly tortures some brain watchers. To help alleviate their guilt, they, and many of their clients, go to lengths to create the impression that the whole process is really quite voluntary. The comparison to World War II Army volunteers—"you, you, you, and you"—is irresistible, and the Harvard volume *Executive Selection,* in a guarded understatement, points up the transparency of the volunteer idea. Says the Harvard document: "Again it seems fair to generalize, considering the normal aspirations of such a group of executives, that most of them will volunteer. . . . Also a man's unwillingness to take a test, if it is known that no promotions will be made at any level without tests, would not help but work against him."

Rohrer, Hibler states that the refusal to go along is rare, and points out the "extreme case" of a "stubborn" production executive who sat it out for three years before capitulating to "group pressures." In most cases the nonvolunteer, if not dismissed, becomes a corporate celebrity, an unenviable spot unlikely to lead anywhere except down.

Very occasionally an enlightened company, or a tester, will shy away from using the corporate whip. They will try to set up a testing program that grants employees the prerogative of volunteering or not and upholds the confidential nature of the report. But one current experiment indicates there is something in the very nature of corporate psychology that works against it: a brain-watching Parkinsonian law that states that employees must always take tests that management offers, and that a hot testing report on an executive must inevitably find its way up to the surface and into the boss's hands.

The Worthington Corporation, which sells $185,000,000 worth of pumps, compressors, and air-conditioners a year—in collaboration with Kenneth F. Herrold & Associates, a team of Columbia University educational psychologists who have gone into testing—ostensibly worked out such a commendable libertarian, voluntary, and confidential operation.

A *Business Week* article headlined the innovation: "Testing Managers Without Heat: Worthington Corporation says it puts no pressure on its men to take personality tests or to do anything about the results." The article glowingly describes the admirable attitude of Worthington's president. However, it stops briefly in the midst of its description to hedge it with what skeptics expected all along. "Theoretically," says the *Business Week* writer, "no one is required to take the tests if he doesn't want to, *but a request from the boss is often almost an order."* (Italics mine.)

On the absolutely "confidential" nature of the tester's report, *Business Week* adds: "A potential leak in the secrecy of personal records is the occasional request of a superior for a subordinate's personality test analysis. This is given only if the subject of the test gives his permission. But there could be times when it would be hard to withhold his permission. *There are also company personnel men who are beginning to wonder if it wouldn't be helpful to have all those test results in the files."* (Italics all mine.)

As part of the pseudohumanistic "doctor" pose, most on-the-job testers insist on some kind of follow-up or counseling session afterwards. "To leave a man unaided after he has bared his problems," Rohrer has been quoted as saying, "is to invite frustrations and confusion." In actuality, however, the typical counseling session in the business—especially in the case of a bad report—is carefully designed not to tell the man the full truth, or even enough to stimulate a holy crusade to disprove the tester and clear himself, or to be the seed of a corporate rebellion against the power of the psychologist. Many a "yellow" and "red" man has been kept ignorant of the most damaging accusations against him, and thus condemned without defense.

Miller Associates, for example, is one of the few which will give the subject a written copy of his report. In cases of "emotional difficulty," however, Miller will make a *separate* confidential report directly to management. RH&R interprets its reports to the man orally, but states that it might withhold negative information if it is concerned that the individual will "worry," especially if he is the "introspective" type. With this cunning playback that controls how much employees ever know about their evaluations, the tester has covered his flanks. He is commended by the men whose reports are glowing and he has carefully prevented the dissemination of harmful evidence and the crystallization of hatred against him by those whose careers he may have already destroyed.

(The playback session has become so popular that some

firms, including one electronics giant, have decided to train their supervisors to do the $200-a-day psychologist's follow-up work. This is being done despite professional warnings against turning supervisors into "amateur psychotherapists" and the common-sense fear that for every cocky and expansive psychologist there are at least a dozen psychologically untrained, unknowing supervisors.)

The on-the-job tester is hopelessly involved in a moral and ethical tussle. Enlightened testers are seeking answers to the dilemmas of compulsory evaluations, confidences, and the entire question of whose welfare they are really concerned with—that of the men they examine or that of the company? Is there a doctor-patient relationship, as the brain watcher so ardently swears, or is he committed to protecting the corporation who both calls and pays for the tune?

In practice almost all consultants offer fealty to the corporation. "Our patient is the total organization as the whole," says Dr. John R. Martin. "We try to get the employees to relate their satisfactions to the policy and purposes of the company. If not, we feel they don't belong there, and must tell the company president." Dr. Martin feels that ethics require him to share "specifics" with the corporation, but not "confidences"—a twilight zone that is not easy for the layman to interpret.

Other testers, of course, consider confidences not only something to be shared with the company, but the shiniest wampum of the business. One tester tells of being helped greatly by employees who sidle up to him and say: "I know all about Joe. I'd like to tell you." Martin complains about this and points out that some clients expect their testers to act as "Gestapos" for them. He cites the case of one former client, a large corporation which he dropped for this very reason. "They wanted me to feed them confidential information on their executives and I was not willing."

This dilemma of the psychologist's dual role, the serious question of whether he can ethically have a corporation rather than a person as a client, has been raised—not by disgruntled employees—but by sage professionals. Dr. J. L. Otis of Western Reserve University, former president of the Division of Consulting Psychology of the American Psychological Association, labels much of what has been going on as "psychological espionage."

"Psychological espionage is not a nice phrase; yet it does characterize some of the work we are doing and describes the attitude of some of our examinees and clients toward us.

. . . But does he [the psychologist] identify with the company or the examinee?" he asks. "It is very difficult to do both. . . . There is no doubt in my mind that psychological services to industry are often purchased in the espionage situation since espionage is not only the art of spying; it is also the employment of spies. It is the use a purchaser may make of psychological services that is the real problem and this is the area of responsibility the psychologist must face. The professional person may never act in a hostile manner toward an examinee, but that does not mean that the employer will not use the reports and results to serve his own ends.

"Perhaps we can resolve this dual role by refusing to accept it. Would industry continue to purchase our services if we stated that it is the welfare of the examinee that comes first and last, and that we can best serve our clients by insisting that the human beings we see must benefit from our recommendations?"

It is highly doubtful. The day the tester accepts Dr. Otis' advice at face validity, and rolls up his color charts and cagey depth interviews, corporate brain watching on location will have joined the ranks of medieval bloodletting.

5 SICK, SICK, SICK: HYPOCHONDRIACS, HOMOSEXUALS, AND HEAVY DRINKERS

I have diarrhea once a month or more.

I believe I am being plotted against.

The top of my head sometimes feels tender.

In walking, I am very careful to step over sidewalk cracks.

I dream frequently about things that are best kept to myself.

I am a special agent of God.

These brash questions and their answers (all emphatically "No") have brought the brain watcher into a field he has publicly denied: abnormal psychology. To block off a whole area of opposition to his controversial work, he has always carefully advertised himself as the "normal man's tester," not really interested in exploring the dark recesses of his subjects' minds. He is devoted, he says, only to the shadings of personality of functioning men and women who are working, or, at the very least, looking for a job.

Actually, however, the tester sees himself as a self-appointed bastion of normality. He is convinced that there is a legion of untouchables—psychotics, hypochondriacs, near-psychotics, alcoholics, homosexuals, and other misfits—battering at the doors of the Corporation, while others are already surreptitiously populating it, protectively garbed in gray worsted. He believes that psychotics are more numerous out of institutions than in, and is too impatient (and for his boss, the fee-paying employer, too cost-conscious) to wait to see if a man will crack or bear up under the pressures of the business world.

The Bernreuter-type tests, the Edwards, and other instruments could only hint at maladjustments. The Rorschach is too expensive and difficult to administer on a mass basis. What the tester really wanted was a cheap and scalpel-like tool to rip away the clean white shirt and polite smile, cut through the work record and references painstakingly built up over the years, and reveal the tortured soul underneath, ready to explode. By thus playing psychiatrist, he hoped to duplicate the mass screening job done by thousands of physicians in World War II (a valiant effort, incidentally, which recent studies indicate was substantially less than successful. See Chapter X: Once Upon a Mind; and Chapter XI: Brain Watching: Science or Cult?).

The answer to his wishes is the Minnesota Multiphasic Personality Inventory, which is sampled in the above handful of impertinent questions. A giant 566-question test, it asks queries once considered too embarrassing to pose in the corporate environment. The test was created in 1940 by two University of Minnesota researchers and since World War II has received accelerated attention and controversy. The *Fifth Mental Measurements Yearbook* lists hundreds of technical articles on the instrument, most either ferociously pro or con. In the testing world, which embraces, then rejects tests cyclically, the MMPI—as it is always called—is "this year's" test. In fact, a panel of hundreds of corporate personnel men organized by the Bureau of National Affairs recently stated that of some eighty psychological tests used by their companies, the MMPI was the single most popular personality instrument.

The MMPI is a deep-water test that does not trifle with gauging a man's sociability or self-confidence. It has nine awesome scales: Schizophrenia, Psychopathic Deviate, Hypochondriasis, Hysteria, Depression, Paranoia, Psychasthenia (phobias), Hypomania (mild insanity), and Masculinity-Femininity. The test was constructed by comparing the responses of 800 psychiatric patients at the University Hospital connected with the University of Minnesota with those of 700 visitors to the hospital. The questions that *seemed* to distinguish between the two groups were made part of the inventory. The norm of all scales is set at 50. Scores of 70 or more are generally considered evidence of bad adjustment or possible psychopathology—placing the applicant considerably closer to an institution than a stock option.

The MMPI dwarfs all other inventories in its size, scope, and pretensions. It contains 19 "general neurological" items, 5 about your "cardiorespiratory system," 26 on "family and marital" problems, 16 on "sexual attitudes," 46 on "political attitudes," and others on delusions, phobias, religious and social points of view. It also reserves 15 questions for the inevitable "lie" scale.

The MMPI tester, for example, is fascinated with our religious opinions in the hope that he can spot the hypothetical link between first normal devotion, then fanaticism, and finally psychopathology. Fair employment practices laws and antidiscrimination statutes in many states have forced most testers to curb their curiosity about religious attitudes. Others avoid it for fear it would stimulate rebuffs from powerful quarters both in the public and the clergy with whom the brain watcher is still too insecure to tangle.

The brazen MMPI, however, bristles with spiritual overtones. In fact the test makers have empirically decided what is "healthy" in religious beliefs and how much devotion is likely to become clinically significant. It is normal, says the MMPI, to believe in God and a life hereafter, and to pray *several times a week*. However, it is not clinically sound to carry faith to such extremes as being *very* religious, reading the Bible several times a week, or, as some groups sincerely do, believing there is only one true religion. A person who denies the second coming of Christ, surprisingly enough, is penalized on the *depressive* scale, with no forgiveness for those who have not yet accepted the first coming. In one generous gesture, the MMPI has made it equally acceptable to agree that Christ did change "water into wine," or believe that such miracles are simply "tricks."

The MMPI has probably the most highly developed set of scales to trap artful dodgers not anxious to be labeled psychopaths, including not only a typical "lie" scale but a subtler "K" (for "correction") scale for those who try to fudge rather than prevaricate. The lie scale has the usual goody-good items which *must* be answered "True" in the confessional way. For example: "I would rather win than lose in a game." The K scale is a set of thirty statements, "once in a while" admissions of minor flaws which the applicant should also admit to, such as: "I certainly feel useless at times." (True.) For tweaking the tester by not admitting one of these small sins, your profile is not only penalized a K point, but by some inexplicable statistical gyration, the penalties are added in full to your schizophrenic scale!

Does a high schizophrenic score mean that you are a schizophrenic, or even have tendencies in that direction? Incredibly enough, it doesn't. In her text *Psychological Testing*, Ann Anastasi poses the same question. "Does a high score on the SC scale indicate schizophrenia? Do schizophrenics usually obtain a higher score on the SC scale than is found in the case of other psychiatric groups?" she asks. "The answer to each of these questions is 'no.' The majority of investigations concerned with the validity of individual scales have yielded negative results."

Even the test authors warn against taking their scales, or even a set of highly psychotic scores, very seriously. The MMPI manual makes this astounding statement: ". . . it should be continually kept in mind that the great majority of persons having deviant profiles are not, in the usual sense of the word, mentally ill, nor are *they in need of psychological treatment*. [Italics mine.] Having no more information about a person than that he has a deviant profile, one should always start with the assumption that the subject is operating within the normal range."

The test authors' caution is supported by experiments. At Northwestern University, where 39 percent of a group of randomly selected students scored a sick 70 on one of the scales, and 14 percent on two of them, the faculty man who did the study felt compelled to defend the undergraduates. "There is no other supporting evidence to indicate anything approaching that high degree of abnormality among Northwestern students," he says. There is also considerable doubt that the tester's norm of 50 is meaningful. The same study at Northwestern came up with norms of 60.4 on the PT (phobia) scale, and at the University of Minnesota students produced very high norms: 59.8 on Hypomania and 58.3 on Psychopathic Deviate. These new statistics indicate that possibly thousands of employees have been falsely and irretrievably identified as mentally disturbed in corporations all over the nation.

If the scales are not accurate, the norm scores are open to debate, and if the scales do not mean what they say, why the test? Why its extensive use in the selection of personnel? Cognizant of the weakness of the individual scales and, like most brain watchers, petulant about giving up a test until fashion has called it in, MMPI enthusiasts have fallen back on an old gambit: "If a test is weak, build a battery; if a scale is weak, build a profile." To evaluate a man with the MMPI today, a tester must spend hours poring over almost a thousand sample case profiles in the MMPI "Atlas" to find a zigzag graph that fits his unlucky subject.

At best, the MMPI is a rough instrument in which, as a rule, psychotics do score higher than normal people. But of course there is no experimentation that indicates that its 566 questions do any better than asking the subject just one: "Do you believe that you are mentally ill?" The danger is in the bushelful of false positives—perfectly normal souls suddenly labeled otherwise—that it scoops up along with true psychotics in its giant psychological maw. In one experiment of borderline cases who scored 65 to 80 on the test, the MMPI not only failed to identify 34 percent of the abnormal women, but incorrectly identified 41 percent of the normal women as being distinctly otherwise.

Despite its prime status in the testing fraternity, some outspoken psychologists have been willing to take on the quiz monster. William A. Wheeler, psychologist at the Veterans Administration Neuropsychiatric Hospital in Los Angeles, writes in the *Journal of Consulting Psychology* that the claims that the MMPI measures "clinical syndromes" are "questionable." Dr. Albert Ellis, a prominent New York consulting psychologist—the type of professional for whom the test was originally designed—says, in the same publication, that any psychologist "worth his salt" can do better than the test.

The potential damage packaged in MMPI and its fancy psychological labels is clear to anyone willing to rummage through the extensive literature. In fact, some of the MMPI work, like one "research" job recently done on big-league and minor-league ballplayers, and reported in *Research Quarterly,* is more bizarre than its intended victims.

This amazing ballplayer study, based on MMPI forms filled out by 64 players in the major leagues and by 49 of their colleagues in the minor leagues, hoped to ferret out the supposed personality defects that kept minor-leaguers swatting in Buffalo and Phoenix instead of the Yankee Stadium. When the MMPI's were scored, the averages varied only a few insignificant points. The big-leaguers got 47 in Schizophrenia to 53 for the minors, and 53 to 57 in the Psychopathic Deviate scale.

Even though the differences were less than those in measurements of MMPI norms, the article's author gleefully (and naïvely) concluded that the big-leaguers had made it because they were nonpsychopaths, while the minor-league boys were doomed—not because of their youth, inexperience, or low batting averages—but simply because they were irresponsible locker-room roués. Their MMPI scores, says the author without tongue in cheek, "seriously suggest that the minor-league players are more apt to digress from the socially accepted mores. *Their deviations would tend to occur in the form of lying, stealing, alcohol or drug addiction, and sexual immorality.*" (Italics mine.)

Despite the poll showing its popularity in industry, corporations who psycho-hunt with the MMPI are very reluctant to discuss their work. Law enforcement groups, however, are more candid about their understandable desire to screen out sadists and near-psychopaths from putting on protective police blue, and many of them have warmed up to MMPI in the hope that it will do the difficult job. New York's former police commissioner Stephen Kennedy, whose force "experimented" with the test at the Police Academy, stated his fear that some police candidates are what he reportedly called "rejects from private industry."

The Personnel and Testing unit of New York's Police Academy has given the MMPI (plus the Strong and Kuder) to certain candidates over the past five years on an "experimental" basis. The tests have been administered and handgraded by regular policemen despite serious warnings that only qualified psychological personnel should handle them. "If a man does badly on the MMPI," says a Police Academy spokesman, "we refer him to the medical bureau, where he gets more professional treatment. After that he has to be okayed by the Medical Bureau and recertified by the Personnel Department."

Detroit Police, who have a local psychologist administer the MMPI at $25 per man to all candidates who have passed their mental and physical tests, use it because they think "it is difficult to cheat on." "We have tried the Bell and Thurstone but the results were discouraging," a spokesman says. "I know it is not foolproof, but it is a check. If a man scores high on the MMPI 'lie' scale, for example, we give that information to the investigator handling his case. Perhaps then we will take with a grain of salt other statements that he has made in regard to his character." Los Angeles also gives the MMPI to all police candidates, and according to one report, 11 percent of 12,000 would-be policemen were rejected for "psychiatric" reasons, one of which was a bad MMPI score.

Despite their own flirtation with the MMPI, New York's "finest" disagree. Three personnel men involved in selection work for the New York force, in a recent issue of the *Public Personnel Review,* strongly chastised their Los Angeles colleagues for their blanket use of the controversial test in psychotic screening.

No brain watcher can conscientiously congratulate himself on keeping the corporation sterile unless he has cleansed it not only of psychos, but the suspected "homos" as well. Homosexuality has never been a sufficient problem to prompt a personnel managers' conference on the subject. Apparently strongly effeminate men whether homosexual or not generally ignore the corporation, and prefer to seek jobs where they are more easily accepted, in such fields as window display, theatre, and fashion. Those who attempt to join the corporation are usually politely turned away by the personnel man, unjustly or otherwise, and just as politely return to more approving environments.

The suspicious brain watcher, however, is convinced that *secret* homosexuals bearing the bodies, manner, and garb of virile men, but the souls of women, are infiltrating corporate ranks plotting toward eventual control by the emasculated. To flush them out, he uses the MMPI, the Strong, the Terman-Miles, and others with built-in masculinity-femininity scales. The tests are generally disguised as "interest" tests on the debatable assumption that a man's virility can be deduced from his hairy-chested attitudes and hobbies.

In a recent case, a twenty-five-year-old surveyor, married, with two children, lost a chance to accumulate a sizable bankroll on a construction job near the Arctic because of suspected homosexuality. His test forms had been sent to an assembly-line quiz man. After his Strong Vocational Interest Blank was graded, he was rejected as "unsuited" because of his low score on its masculinity-femininity scale. "The clients would have been worried about him. After all, he would have to live for months with a rugged crew of construction workers at an isolated camp site," says the tester.

What evidence of potential homosexuality did the tester find? What touch of reversed ardor, of Freudian imbalance, had the subject let slip through his test answers? Actually, the Strong had gauged his "masculinity" simply by counting the number of *virile* items he had checked that he "liked" as opposed to the *feminine* items that he did not "dislike." A study of the Strong test items shows plainly that, like all such scales, *the man's man* is equated with the stone-age personality. The suspected homosexual may just be the cultured, mechanically-deficient man who would rather be the "author of a novel" than a "machinist" or "secret service man." Or, like the poor surveyor, he may only be a domesticated suburbanite, better conditioned to family "picnics" than "stag parties."

Your virility is sampled on these typical Strong items. The he-man choices are marked "L" (like) and the female, "D" (dislike). The Strong asks whether you like, dislike or are indifferent to the following:

Climbing along the edge of
   a precipice (L)
Bridge (D)
Snakes (L)
Detective stories (L)

Social problem movies (D)
Art galleries (D)
Pursuing bandits in a sheriff's posse (L)
Poetry (D)

If you now feel that you are in an exposed position in sexual neverland, relax. Protecting your virility on the Strong is simple. Just conjure up the image of a do-it-yourself neighbor with few cultural interests and answer with his libido. Or, if necessary, merely withdraw mentally twenty years or more back into your life and relive the time when climbing along precipices, chasing bandits, and playing with garter snakes did not seem as ludicrous as it does now on the tester's page.

Sophisticated testers chuckle at masculinity scales as measuring only a man's cultural level, but the tests nonetheless have a great deal of currency in the field. "We sometimes tolerate lower scores for creative jobs," says one New York tester, "but we would expect higher scores for engineers, pilots, truck drivers. Very low scores are usually a tip-off to homosexuality. We find that some of these men score even lower in masculine interests than the average woman."

The proliferation of M-F scales today started with the extensive Terman-Miles test based on male and female interests in the culture of the 1930's, when men were perhaps more manly. Despite the striking change in our culture and the increasing similarity in interests of the sexes in the 1960's, the questions on the Terman-Miles are admittedly the source material for most of the homosexuality scales in use today. The MMPI 55-question M-F (masculinity-femininity) scale, for example, is admittedly "inspired" by the outdated Terman-Miles. (The masculine responses are indicated. The femininity scale for women, to spot repressed Lesbians, is exactly the reverse.):

I enjoy a game better when I bet on it. (T)

I would like to be a journalist. (F)

If I were a reporter I would very much like to report sporting news. (T)

I like to be in a crowd that plays jokes on each other. (T)

I like *Alice in Wonderland* by Lewis Carroll. (F)

I would like to be a soldier. (T)

In addition to craving military action, the man with the proper hormone balance, according to the MMPI, does not like expensive clothes, horseback riding, and socials, except dirty and loud ones. For some reason, the *compleat* male is supposed to prefer George Washington to Abe Lincoln.

Since the test is touted as a clinical instrument, the MMPI adds a handful of Freudian table-droppings to the masculinity scale. For example, it is unwise to admit that the person whom you most admired as a child was a woman—mother, sister, or aunt. For quick spot-scoring, it even asks the direct homosexual question (No. 69 on the form): "I am very strongly attracted by members of my own sex." (False.)

Using tests like the MMPI to predict which individuals are sexual deviates is a serious business. Premature claims that they can do the job are published, but are inevitably followed up by thorough debunkings. Three enthusiastic researchers at UCLA, for example, claimed that they had developed an MMPI scale for "sexual deviations" that had proven correct 88 percent of the time on the UCLA campus, at the expense of 11 percent "false positives" among the student body. Even though that many young lives put under a shadow made such a scale impractical, the impressive claims of validity prompted a researcher in the Texas prison system to retest the scale. He gave it to 60 sexual offenders and 60 nonoffenders among his inmates and reported the results in the *Journal of Consulting Psychology:* entirely negative.

The fallacy of homosexual-hunting with interest scales is

pointed up by Dr. George W. Henry, New York psychiatrist and former Cornell Medical College professor, who has devoted thirty years to the diagnosis and treatment of homosexuality and has written extensively on the subject (*Sex Variants* and *All the Sexes*). According to Henry, the technique is fruitless because many homosexuals are quite masculine, in both physique and interests.

"There is no specific trait that you can depend upon with any certainty in the identification of homosexuals," he says. "Test results of this type are not reliable. Some men who have feminine traits compensate for it by engaging in virile activities. Would you pick a prizefighter, a truck driver, or a military man as being feminine? Well, I have had many of them as homosexual patients. Many individuals are quite masculine in their physique and interests but passive or feminine in their love relationships. That is more important."

Just as the Corporation subscribes to a healthy mind in *corpore corporato,* it is equally insistent that its members not only have healthy bodies, but be convinced that they do. The peripatetic executive, governing a vast domain with the help of a desk-top drugstore, is an outdated stereotype. The new high-pressure management man handles his problems without suffering either psychosomatic illness or even the dread of it, or at least the brain watcher would like to think so.

To spot such a man in advance, many companies use standard personality instruments with at least a handful of health questions. Others, like the Standard Oil Company of New Jersey, have developed their own hypochondriac-hunters. A man's attitude toward his health is an important factor in success at Standard Oil, a testing spokesman for the oil mammoth points out. "If a man feels that a whole raft of things is wrong with him, he is a dubious risk," says the SONJ representative.

Health questions have been included in personality tests since their inception, generally as part of their "emotional stability" scales. Of the 140 questions on the Bell Inventory, for example, 34 are concerned with health, including many that read more like a physician's medical history than a personality quiz. For example:

Do you have many headaches?

Have you ever had a surgical operation?

Have you had considerable illness during the last 10 years?

Do you wear eyeglasses?

Do you have teeth that you know need dental attention?

Have you ever had a skin disease or skin eruption, such as athlete's foot, carbuncles, or boils?

No medical admission, even recent surgery or an abscessed tooth, can be anything but harmful. The brain watcher has none of the caution of theorists in the field of psychosomatic medicine. As the straightforward medical questions on the Bell indicate, he has developed a simple unsubstantiated theory that sickness and emotional stability are in essence one and the same. Neurotics get sick and believe they are sick. The adjusted either do not become ill or do not admit it, even to themselves.

On this shaky premise the tester has built an intricate Gothic structure which he calls a "hypochondriasis" scale, the most elaborate of which is naturally in the MMPI. The scale is not only the study of general health but of neurological, cranial nerve, motility, sensibility, vasomotor, cardio-respiratory, and gastrointestinal symptoms—all in 33 questions. Typical of the "depth" of the MMPI, its hypochondriasis questions, such as one query on whether you have ever vomited or coughed up blood, include many of the symptoms of severe illnesses, including cancer, tuberculosis, ulcers, cardiac disease, and other "imaginary" ailments. The average test taker can afford only five health confessions regardless of the true condition of his health. Otherwise you will have convinced the tester that you worry more than you should (the norm) about your body.

Do these scales really measure hypochondriasis or have they merely isolated the less healthy for double punishment? The *Shorter Oxford English Dictionary* defines "hypochondriasis" as being "chiefly characterized by the patient's *unfounded* belief that he is suffering from serious bodily diseases." The MMPI manual's definition of its scale is substantially the same. But is an executive suffering from sinusitis harboring an *unfounded* belief when he says that his nose is full? Is a person suddenly losing weight because of any one of a dozen serious ailments *imagining* his bathroom scale readings? Is vomiting blood the red stain of a hypochondriac? The suspicion that the person who scores high on the

MMPI Hs scale may well be either a little too frank or a bit less healthy (no known detriment to business success) than other testees was confirmed in a recent Detroit study on the MMPI. Two hundred and thirty-eight workers and supervisors who had had a recent illness took the MMPI. They scored quite high in the health queries, checking—in 66 percent of the cases—those items that specifically applied to their illnesses, making the MMPI, as many have suspected, of more value as a medical history than a spotter of compulsive pill-takers.

When fighting spurious enemies like the hypochondriac who is not really there, the brain watcher can be very zealous. Other times, however, when he is faced with a real psychological opponent, he just as quickly abdicates his responsibility. The serious national problem of alcoholism on the job, for example, has cut billions in lost energy out of our gross national product and has produced more than its share of tipsy after-lunch conferences, bad executive decisions, and broken lives and careers. The National Council of Alcoholism recently estimated that some 3 percent of the work force was "alcoholic" and that the incidence was especially high among executive groups who have ample opportunity to drink both on and off the job. The Du Pont Corporation, for one, has reported that it had at least 950 alcoholics in its work force.

Dr. Frances I. Colonna, acting director of the Alcoholism Clinic at the New York University–Bellevue Medical Center, points out that early detection on the job and subsequent treatment is vital. Instead of "predicting" who is alcoholic with spurious tests, some companies use the common-sense approach of simply looking for heavy drinkers. The Consolidated Edison Company of New York, for example, has begun a responsible training program for supervisors in the early recognition of incipient alcoholism, including the sneaked drink on the job and unexplained disappearances.

What has the brain watcher contributed to the solution of this serious problem? It would be hopeful to say that the extent of alcoholism has had a sobering effect on his methods. Actually, however, the hire-for-fee tester looks at alcoholism much as he does at ascendancy, neuroticism, or any other trait. If that's what you want to find, he promises to replace serious individual detection of the illness with a twenty-minute quiz. For a modest fee, he can smell out any alcoholic—potential, latent, active, or otherwise—among the corporate pack of moderate drinkers and teetotalers, give or take a few score thousand mistakes.

A representative of The Personnel Laboratory, a blind projective house, says that it can pick an alcoholic from his clinical test blanks most of the time, with only a few unfortunate errors. A more prevalent method is the use of alcoholic questionnaires, the most popular of which are two by the same author, Morse P. Manson, Ph.D., who has developed the Manson Evaluation and the Alcadd Test, both designed to spot heavy drinkers. "Several large firms have bought our tests for use in personnel selection," says Manson.

The Manson is a disguised instrument that asks no swigging questions. Much like other simple personality tests, it operates on the theory that the maladjusted person can be equated with the alcoholic. By simply testing a subject's adjustment with his quiz, Manson claims, he can pick out male alcoholics 79 times out of 100 and females 80 out of 100. If his claims are accurate, which most researchers doubt, there are still no apologies for the one out of five misbranded teetotalers.

The Alcadd Test, unlike the Manson, is a surprisingly candid census of a man's drinking habits, based on the debatable assumption that everyone who drinks too much is either naïve or anxious to slobber out the alcoholic truth. As follows:

I need a drink or two in the morning. (False)

My father is (or was) a heavy drinker. (False)

I often go to a cheaper neighborhood to do my drinking. (False)

I often have a black-out when I drink. (False)

People who never drink are dull company. (False)

The brain watcher's alcoholic problem is once again his steadfast allegiance to a jerry-built idea—that a conglomeration of traits can describe any personality deficiency. Manson lists the supposed alcoholic traits measured by his tests: anxiety, depressive fluctuations, emotional sensitivity, resentfulness, aloneness, etc. Other researchers have used the MMPI to come up with an "alcoholic profile." In the *Journal of Abnormal and Social Psychology*, one researcher theorizes an entire-family history in which the alcoholic is a product of a domineering but idolized mother and a stern and autocratic father, whom the patient feared. He had a strict, obedient family life, has strong feelings of guilt and need for religious security, has lack of self-consciousness but marked ability to get along with people—especially members of the opposite sex—with whom he has possibly had extramarital relations.

The best contemporary research, however, indicates that all attempts to catalog the alcoholic personality, or spot it in personality tests have been frustrating. Dr. John D. Armstrong, medical director of the Alcoholic Research Foundation in Ottawa, Canada, in the *Annals of the American Academy of Political and Social Science,* sums up the current responsible attitude. "The limited experience of many investigators leaves the impression that there are certain features unique to the personality of alcoholics," says Armstrong. "However, scientific reports to date do not permit us to define such an alcoholic personality, or even to come to any substantial agreement as to what it may be like."

Armstrong hits the use of psychological tests for alcoholism, pointing out that the results depend mainly on which alcoholics are being tested. "The current tests," he says, "are based on individuals selected by some *bias* from the total alcoholic population (arrested, committed, rich enough for one clinic, poor enough for another). Such methods might be compared to evaluating a nation's dental health by examining only the residents of an old people's home."

The brain watcher has valiantly tried to construct a specific personality for the alcoholic, a psychological 100-proof that he could sample at will. However, one by one, his hastily constructed concepts have been knocked down by independent researchers. Fordham University studies, for example, have shown no significant correlation between alcoholism and emotional stability. Dr. Solomon Machover, chief psychologist at Kings County Hospital in Brooklyn and an authority in the field, explored another favorite pet hypothesis—that alcoholics are latent homosexuals—which he found equally negative. Machover chose 39 male alcoholic patients at Kings County at random and gave them the MMPI Masculinity-Femininity Scale, on which they scored 51.24, a very "normal" masculine quotient. Like Armstrong, Machover is convinced that the alcoholic has many different syndromes. "The commercial screening of employees and applicants for potential alcoholism with current personality tests is premature," he says. "I wouldn't like the responsibility."

But the brain watcher would. At stake is not just the income from probing alcoholics, homosexuals, and other untouchables. Just as important is the tester's fierce reluctance to admit that any group of individuals in our society is so complex that its members cannot be measured easily and cheaply with his ubiquitous tests.

PART TWO

The Brain Watcher and Your Career

6 *TESTING THE OPINION MAKERS: FRONT PAGE TO MADISON AVENUE*

"What kind of personality do we look for in an advertising copywriter? A good agency man should have both creativity and control. Most important, though, he should conceive of himself basically as a salesman, in words, and recognize that he is not writing the great American novel. We don't want a frustrated novelist with guilt about his copywriting that will keep him from doing a wholehearted job. When a man is making as much as forty thousand dollars a year, the effort better be all the way."

This comment on the debilitating effects of Freudian guilt in the advertising agency world, uttered recently by a prominent Park Avenue tester, is symptomatic of a new agonizing trend: the brain watching of "creative" employees in the key communications field—the opinion makers in the advertising, newspaper, magazine, public relations, and radio and television industries.

Men in these privileged, responsible fields had little or no contact with the tester until a decade ago or less. Originally this exceptional animal—whether hired for his non-testable ability to write Pulitzer-winning editorials, burnish shinier public relations images or compose mouth-salivating

TV beer jingles—was considered immune to the tester's
onerous overtures.

However, when the brain watcher became frustrated by
his failure to develop special tests of creative talent, he
simply decided to apply his regular tools, from the Rorschach
to the Bernreuter, to the selection of "communicators."
Today, the brain watcher is increasingly prevalent in these
glamour fields and has convinced many managements that
their workers—whether an editor for the Los Angeles *Times*,
a public relations executive at Ruder & Finn, or a copywriter with Kenyon & Eckhardt—are little different from us
all and equally measurable.

The tester is successfully making a strange anomaly stick:
men weaned on the credo of the unharnessed individual and
hired for their talent to self-think are being personality tested
for their ability to same-think, and even same-feel, or go
packing elsewhere for a job. Unfortunately, the tester's typically platitudinous search for the overadjusted American has
even graver potential for harm here than in most cases. He
has intruded into the arena where much of our culture's
mass opinions and actions first take firm hold, and whenever
he can get away with it, he is shouldering more than his
share of the great crusade to nudge our opinion makers into
a tighter, more controllable mold.

The advertising agency, with its affluence and wifely link
to industry, offered the tester his first chance for just such a
toehold. One of the largest mass testings in any industry was
initiated by the advertising profession after World War II
by the 4A, the ad agency association, which saw the tester
as a predictive genius who would solve all its problems about
who should be permitted to join the golden fraternity. Dub-
bing it a vocational guidance service, the 4A invited young
hopefuls to be personality tested at $25 per head (the 4A
made up the $15 difference). During the next ten years
(1946–56), some 7,000 young men paid to be assayed with
blind projectives given at a Park Avenue testing firm, where,
among other things, they drew sketches of the female form.
The results, a written description of the unseen candidate's
personality plus a prognosticative rating on how he would fit
into the advertising field, were given to the 4A with a copy to
the man himself.

What did the tester search for? What exacting criteria
separated the good advertising man from those of us in the
general population who might one day have to look at his

creations? The 4A confesses that it left this entirely to the tester.

To protect the identity of the 7,000 hopefuls, each man was given a code number and reports, identified only by number, were sent out to all 4A agencies. The men with promising reports (about one out of every three tested) ostensibly got the most responses, and for interested agencies, the flesh-and-blood candidate was produced. The man who received a bad report yet still had the gumption to disregard the tester's opinion and make the rounds of agencies was a little conspicuous by the absence of a test report, which if he had any brains, he discarded. Says the 4A spokesman, "If the results were bad, I wouldn't think a guy would carry them around in his pocket."

The testees, indifferent or otherwise, were all followed up one, three, and then five years later, in the hope of validating the tester's predictions. In 1956, the entire program was dropped, partly, as a 4A spokesman states, as a result of what was learned. The expensive arbitrary program had accomplished little, if anything, and had barefacedly failed to separate the winners from the losers. "Sizable numbers of men rated both good and bad ended up in the advertising business, anyway," says the 4A man. "And from what we could learn, they were apparently doing well."

Not only had the tests failed to separate those with advertising potential from others, but the "unfit" who eventually proved their competence had to work against greater odds to break into the field—possibly one of the greater negative correlations in modern brain watchery. Says a BBDO spokesman who served on the 4A Personnel Committee: "It was a highly questionable program."

The extent of personality testing in the selection of advertising men today is difficult to gauge exactly, although one 4A executive offers this guess: "Of the twenty leading agencies, almost all are using or have used tests. Of the next one hundred largest, I would say fifty test, while fewer of the smaller agencies do." Although this estimate is high (several large agencies refuse to use tests), the influence of the tester in the advertising world is reasonably potent. His activities are not confined to any one advertising specialty but most stress is naturally laid on the two vital components of the business: the copywriter who composes the ads, and the account executive who oversees the operation and tranquilizes the client's anxieties.

Personality testing among advertising agencies takes many

forms. Some, like Chirurg-Cairns, train two or more of their staff to function as blue-ribboned "AVA Analysts," and operate a layman's couchless operation. Others use testing consultants or, like Kenyon & Eckhardt, a 4A agency in New York which bills more than $100,000,000 a year, have staff psychologists who conduct a full-scale testing operation. K & E's chief personnel officer is a certified psychologist (New York State), and although restrained about testing in the abstract, he has used it in virtually every phase of his hiring operation, from junior accountants to the selection of copywriters.

The K & E testing program is basically in personality quiz form. Their battery includes a group intelligence test, the Kuder Preference Record, and two specific personality instruments—the Edwards Personal Preference and the Adams-Lepley Personal Audit. ("We were using the Study of Values, but it didn't seem to add enough," says the K & E man. "Ninety-nine percent of the applicants got the expected results—high on political and economic drives.")

The K & E tester has nightmares similar to those of the Park Avenue oracle who fears the "frustrated novelist" looking for a $40,000-a-year handout, and he describes how this misplaced Hemingway is spotted in the tests at K & E. "We look for a high literary interest on the Kuder plus a high score on the persuasive scale. This indicates that he wants to sell through words. But too high a social service interest would be negative—it could mean that he's a guilt-ridden 'pure artist.' I have dealt with people of this type. The guy starts getting superego problems that he is prostituting himself producing copy instead of writing the great American novel."

In addition to a guiltless soul the good copywriter should also be decisive about his work, even though it is not deathless prose, says the K & E man. "If a guy doesn't have enough confidence in his ideas [confidence is measured on both the Adams-Lepley and the Edwards] he'll submit ten ideas for an ad instead of one or two, and throw the decision in someone else's lap."

The tester's contention that an ad creator must be a copywriter-writer who wants to sell, rather than a writer-writer who wants to create even though it must be ads, may explain why so many contemporary advertisements appear to be written in gibberish, in a strange inbred advertising trade language no longer emotionally meaningful to (or even translatable by) anyone except fellow "sales-oriented" copywriters. The testers' comments on "guilt" and "frustrated novelists" appear bizarre even to the lowliest of us who write. In the writing community it is assumed that all writers worth a jug of sharpened pencils are hungrily envious of Shakespeare, Molière, and company and, in their frustrated daydreams, contemplate Broadway hits and Nobel prizes, not two-page, four-color bleed toothpaste spreads in monthly magazines.

One reader of national magazines and newspapers who has learned the expeditious habit of not even seeing most advertisements was pleasantly surprised by a quite readable full-page ad in the New York *Times* for Rover cars. It was written in English—not by a superadjusted copywriter-writer but by an envious, healthily frustrated magazine and book writer-writer named Ken Purdy, who knew how to interest readership, not impress the brain watcher.

There is considerable friction among agency testers as to whether a copywriter's "creativity" can be isolated and judged by personality tests. One psychologist at George Fry & Associates, Inc., whose testing division has worked with five large undisclosed advertising agencies, claims that elusive creativity is instantly visible to the knowing tester. He has tested several copywriters and states that he finds the creativity in the subject's inkblots and sketches—specifically in the "movement and elaboration" a potential copywriter sees in the Rorschach, and in the "aliveness" of his human-drawing test. (There is little validation that the art work of writers is distinguished by its "aliveness" or even its recognizability.) The same tester states that a slightly shaky psyche is not inconsistent in creative people. "I would be afraid to turn down a copywriter for emotional instability, unless, of course, it were something serious, like an unresolved Oedipus complex," he points out.

The K & E tester, who apprenticed with the George Fry firm, may agree about the danger of a close mother-son relationship, but he has become disenchanted with the hope of pinpointing talent among his agency's creative staff. "We tried to test for creativity," says the K & E personnel man, "but we had practically zero results. We tried projectives, including the Rorschach, on our art people, but couldn't see that they told us anything about their creativity. We also used a test of 'Critical Thinking' by Glaser on executives and copywriters, but the results were not consistent."

The copywriter's immunity to brain watching varies, but his colleague, the advertising account executive (sometimes derisively referred to on the Avenue as a man with only a "shoeshine and a smile"), is heavily subject to the tester's nod in many agencies. Two mammoth agencies, McCann-Erickson and Benton & Bowles, who seldom test copywriters, insist on putting account men and other executives up to the senior officer level through the personality hoop. However, testing is usually confined to selection and not used in upgrading. "It would be bad for morale," says a B & B spokesman. "Too much of a shock for our organization."

One of the most vulnerable targets of the tester at both agencies is the fledgling advertising man just graduating from one of the nation's graduate schools of business and about to be funneled through an "executive training program." B & B (whose founders, Chester Bowles and William Benton, have gone on to untested public responsibility) scour the campuses of the "better" business schools—Columbia, Ohio State, Harvard, Northwestern—in search of "outstanding men" for their "A" Management Training Program. The likeliest young men are given a four-part test battery that includes an intelligence test, a test of verbal skills, and two personality measures, the popular "Study of Values" and a Guilford-Martin Temperament test. Those who conquer the hurdle then spend a year in the field, doing test marketing, after which they return to the home office for assignment in media, research, traffic control, or contact work, the training ground for future account executives.

The McCann-Erickson organization, headed by exuberant ad man Marion Harper, is another enthusiastic Madison Avenue proponent of testing. It, too, recruits future account executives (and ostensibly board chairmen) from the business college campuses, where each year it culls some fifteen candidates. After an initial screening at college, the men are brought into New York for a grueling regimen, including a full day of interviews followed by a four- to six-hour visit to the consulting and testing firm of Dale, Elliott & Company. McCann's tester (who also does the screening for B & B) publishes a deceptively soft-sell booklet, "Why We Are Asking Dale, Elliott & Company to Take a Look at You," and the pamphlet is distributed to McCann and other clients to give to their apprehensive testees whose visions of five-acre Wilton and New Canaan estates may have begun to fuzz away. Under the heading "Regarding the Psychological Tests," the reassuring booklet states:

Those who have not taken tests before may have a natural reservation, and possibly some apprehension regarding their value and fairness. The Dale, Elliott firm is well aware that psychological tests have been mis-used and poorly interpreted in many instances, and that tests can, when mis-used, do more harm than good. With their many years of experience in the testing field, the Dale, Elliott principals are fully aware of the need for skillful professional interpretation.

This clever advance flanking of test criticism is probably effective, especially since the tester implies that his firm's "professional" interpretation is more skillful than that of other practitioners and therefore less to be feared. This is especially interesting, considering that Dale, Elliott openly states that it does not employ a single psychologist, and that all interpretations are conducted by laymen. To avoid total confusion, the Dale, Elliott firm refers to itself as "management consultants" rather than testers.

What do these nonpsychologist testers probe for in the psychological make-up of a McCann-Erickson advertising novitiate? Basically, they say, they are seeking a somewhat more creative, sales-oriented executive than the typical businessman—and hope to identify him through a personal interview (two and a half hours over coffee); a series of vocabulary tests; the George Washington Social Intelligence Test common in sales selection (see Chapter IX: So You Want To Be a Salesman?); a color vision test; Dale, Elliott's own "Buying Motives" test, which ostensibly measures ability to concoct sales ideas quickly; and the Guilford-Zimmerman Temperament Survey, a ten-scale personality test.

Madison Avenue self-flattery that its narrow streets incubate a special breed of male is a delusion not shared by its testers. On the Guilford-Zimmerman, for example, the ad man is undistinguished by any deviations from the non-existent wholesome male conjured up by all testers. A Dale, Elliott spokesman details the personality requirements for an agency man: "The good ad man should score high on Activity. On the Ascendance-Submissiveness scale, he should come out in the middle or higher—although if his score is too high there is a chance he will be overriding and arrogant. On Thoughtfulness-Reflectiveness, he should be a bit toward unreflective, and on the Seriousness-Impulsiveness scale, he should score as reasonably serious, otherwise he will go off half-cocked."

The Guilford-Zimmerman test includes ten traits, and the McCann man is plotted on all of them: he is more sociable than shy; more objective than subjective ("otherwise his feelings will be hurt easily"); more cooperative than critical ("otherwise he might be fault-finding"); stable rather than unstable; more friendly than hostile; and reasonably masculine.

Such involved, and highly theoretical, calculations are by no means accepted by the entire Avenue in toto, or even in part. Rod Funston, personnel director at Batten, Barton, Durstine and Osborn, is a convinced test skeptic with considerable experience in test-oriented firms, including Lever and Benton & Bowles. In fact, a perfunctory Kuder test given previously at BBDO is no longer given to appplicants. Funston, an M.A. in psychology, is unconvinced that testing offers any help in the selection of ad personnel and BBDO gives no tests, not even an IQ, to prospective or current employees. The BBDO applicant, says Funston, is instead "very thoroughly screened" in traditional interviews with both superiors and peers.

The equally sizable Young & Rubicam also shies away from testing. "I would not use tests," states a copy chief at Y & R. "We test a man by putting him up against practical problems and seeing if he can solve them. I believe the best way to select a good copywriter is to have other good copywriters on your staff interview him. We make it a point to see everyone with a professional background. We speak with him, study his samples, and make our judgment. We keep meticulous records on the people we have seen and actually hire ninety percent of our copywriters directly from these records."

If the advertising world has any agreement about its personnel practices, it is that creativity is a highly prized if ephemeral asset. "Anyone who can find a test for creativity will make a fortune in this business," a former personnel man for Cunningham & Walsh stated recently. The thought has not been lost on testers, and the latest entrant into this debatable high-cash sweepstakes is the agency-active Dale, Elliott firm—which is now attempting to "validate" a battery of "creative tests" with the help of various agencies including McCann, B & B, and Carl Byoir & Associates, a leading public relations firm.

The basis of the DE battery is a group of tests published

in Los Angeles, plus DE's own "Buying Motives" and a common intelligence test. The test battery was administered recently at Byoir to twenty public relations men who had been divided into two groups of ten. One was supposedly a "creative" group, and the other ostensibly not. The result: four tests failed to distinguish between the two groups, but a Dale, Elliott spokesman says four others—the IQ test, Buying Motives, and two of the Los Angeles scales, "Originality" (the ability to produce remotely associated, clever, or uncommon responses) and "Fluency" (ability to evoke a large number of ideas) produced "significant group differences." By discarding the first four tests and "weighing" the other four, the DE nonpsychologists supposedly have arrived at a critical score that, in nine out of ten cases, isolates the creative PR or advertising man from his dullard colleagues.

Awesome? Hardly. Although in borrowed psychometric jargon DE states that the Byoir sample was "pure" (most creative men vs. least creative men), the facts are considerably different. The Byoir vice president who collaborated in the experiment frankly states that although the ten "creative" men were PR executives of proven ability, the other ten were not "least creative." Rather, they were ten "mostly new" men who were not yet in a position in which they could exercise creativity. In actuality, many of these "least creative" may well eventually prove to be the most imaginative in Byoir's shop. DE is heartfully continuing its experiment at McCann, Erickson, ignorant that the initial sample was more contaminated than pure.

BBDOer Funston is on the hot-prospect list of the "creative" testers, but he maintains a firm skepticism. "I don't know of any good tests of creativity. Furthermore, if we get to the point where we believe we are actually assaying creativity, we ought to head for the hills. All we'll succeed in doing is destroying creativity altogether."

Two of the giant communications fields—radio and television—are considerably freer of the tester's ranklings, possibly because they are considered an outgrowth of the theatre, where enforced brain watchery could be a violent affront and management is more than hesitant about flapping back the sensitive psychic skin of its creative staff. In addition, neither field has yet been made a prime target of the tester's near-demonic salesmanship, as have industry and portions of the advertising world.

There are, however, important exceptions: several inde-

pendent out-of-town radio and TV stations use local and
New York testers to evaluate key personnel, and the tester
has directly long-armed himself into television through ad
agency personnel connected with major TV productions.
The George Fry organization, for example, has screened
more than one television producer, a job whose personality
requirements are esoteric, if nothing else. A good TV producer, says the tester, should be "compulsive, somewhat impatient, and have the ability to win respect. He must be
able to pick on people and have them like it."

One television executive at a major ad agency tells of a
painful, but successful, party of an attempt to extend personality testing into his department. "We wanted a man
for film traffic manager, and fortunately we found a twenty-
five-year-old fellow with CBS experience who was just at the
right stage of his career for this job," the TV executive recalls. "We interviewed him and decided that he was just
the man. We sent him to personnel for the necessary routine
and were surprised when they had him take a battery of
personality tests. Personnel reported back that he had
scored much poorer than another guy—who hadn't impressed us—and recommended against hiring our choice.
We had to fight them to hire him, but we finally won out.
Incidentally, he has worked out beautifully on the job."

Of all the communicators, the professional man with the
wispiest image, yet collectively one of the firmest molders
of national opinion, is the public relations executive, a three-
button variety less than a generation removed from the flack
publicity man. "Do you want to sell a product, win a proxy
fight, fumigate an odious reputation, project a new 'corporate personality,' sway a Congressional vote, publicize a
worthy cause or just get your picture in the paper?" asks
author Irwin Ross in his book *The Image Merchants*. He
answers his own query: "If you have any of these desires, you
are obviously in the market for public relations. Public relations is without doubt one of the most volatile and fastest-
growing service trades in the United States today."

Anyone with experience in the public relations field—and
this includes former newspaper reporters, editors, magazine
writers, eager corporate and agency PR men who trained in
the persuasive art in college, and unclassified drifters who
have found an occupational haven in publicity—knows that
speaking generically of the PR man, ideal or otherwise, is
an impossible task. The good public relations man may be
a barker news-salesman huckster without journalistic skill;

a discreet corporate type indistinguishable from the client he peddles for a fee; a voluble individual with a flexible expense account, an ethical code to match, and a barrelful of contacts; and occasionally even a professional so adept at editorial skills that he need not ballet-walk, press release humbly extended, before his superiors of the fourth estate.

The impossible job of test-assessing a man's value as a public relations executive is related to the simple fact that there is no one type. Each successful man in the trade tackles his sometimes semiridiculous tasks with a different frame of reference, and an individual personality-approach. The Public Relations Society of America, in a report of its Vocational Guidance Subcommittee, underscores the difficulty in finding superior men for this complex work. Says one executive: "There is a dire shortage of people who can think problems out, sell to management, and perform the work." Another outlines the problem this way: "Avoiding the person who just likes people and finding someone with the professional approach."

The brain watcher, however, as usual, sees the complex job of assessing men for this still-undefined craft in his own simplistic terms: create a personality profile of the PR man, and match it up against an applicant, sizing it carefully for any ragged psychic edges that show.

Some desperate firms which employ public relations men have bitten at the attractive bait. According to a survey conducted by the Public Relations Society, one in four PR employers uses tests to "show aptitudes and personality make-up." Among business firms which employ their own PR men, the percentage was higher, between 33 and 41 percent, while among straight public relations firms and advertising agencies with PR departments, it was between 15 and 18 percent. As in other industries, the type of testing varies, including clinical and quiz tests, the use of outside consultants, and testing done by the personnel department.

Newspapermen anxious to replace $150 a week and potential glory with a steady $10,000 to $15,000 berth are prime sources for public relations executives. However, as much as they admire their editorial skills, many testers are fearful that a Hildy Johnson *Front Page* character will disrupt the equanimity of the corporate PR department, where demeanor is often more highly prized than sheaves of news-clippings, one of the reasons why so many corporations with sizable PR departments must still go outside to a hell-bent-for-results public relations agency when they want a job properly done. (Union Carbide Corporation, with a sizable PR staff of its own, recently hired an agency one-fifth the size to promote its new glass-and-black-steel Park Avenue skyscraper.)

An example of the tester's innate fear of talent, and how it can keep corporate PR departments sterile, was illustrated by a recent case, recounted (as a testing coup) by the vice president of advertising and public relations of a large national milk foods corporation in New York which uses a blind clinical projective testing company on Park Avenue to evaluate its people.

"I interviewed a young newspaperman looking for a job in our public relations department. He seemed extremely bright. He had worked for a sizable newspaper in town and I checked him out with his editor," he recounted. "He got a good report: that he was a fine chap, aggressive, enterprising, likable, and according to his editor 'writes like a house on fire.' I sent him up to the tester and I was surprised when they recommended against hiring him. They said plainly that this fellow was obviously talented but that he was 'trouble.' They felt that he couldn't work well with people and would feel that his colleagues were stupid. He's a good reporter, but in a big company like this he would be frustrated at every turn with problems of clearance. The tester saved me a lot of anxiety. This fellow could have turned this place upside down."

Incredibly, the testing company's evaluation of a candidate they had never seen was respected by a reasonably intelligent vice president despite its conflict with his own and the editor's description and estimate of the man as both talented and likable. In actuality, the tester, with his distate of the exceptional male, played it safe by predicting chaos in a situation where this bright thirty-year-old, having decided to leave the newspaper field for greener grounds, might just as well have tolerated his "stupid" associates for his own advancement—and the possible improvement of the company's public relations force.

Although a corporate PR man is more likely to be test screened, the agency publicist, the survey indicates, is also suspectible. One of the broadest testing programs in the entire field, in fact, was conducted by a medium-to-large PR agency, Ruder & Finn, a 120-man operation with gross billings of approximately $2,000,000 per year. R & F first called in a consulting psychologist in 1958 to set up an evaluation program for the hiring of executive applicants. Writing about the firm's experience in an article in the *Public Relations Journal,* partner David Finn described how some five years prior one applicant had casually been sent to a tester for a $150 evaluation. "The report we received was a detailed description of the man's psychological make-up and personal history, much of which was embarrassing to us and completely irrelevant to the job situation," Finn writes.

Instead, Ruder & Finn invited a consulting psychologist into the organization for an extended stay to get its feel. Falling into the brain-watching type-trap, R & F asked him to make "a comprehensive effort . . . to determine what caused our successful members to tick," as if Ruder & Finn men had been cross-bred from identical chromosomes. The tester was happy to oblige and for approximately a year he exposed their team of public relations writers and executives to a testing battery which included the Rorschach and other clinical tests.

The personality profile of the model PR man obtained from the inkblots, etc., was subsequently published in the *Quarterly Review of Public Relations.* Says the R & F psychologist exultantly about his results: "From all this material I have been able to evolve a 'public relations profile' which now serves effectively in the selection of new executive personnel. Having determined the patterning of executives of proven ability, I am now able to evaluate the potentialities of new candidates." During the next two years, according to publicist Dave Finn, the tester tried precisely that with fifty PR job applicants, and his recommendations were scrupulously obeyed in all but two cases.

What special qualities—stealth, strength, sagacity—enable the ideal public relations man to secure prestige magazine and newspaper coverage for a paying client? Surprisingly, the PR personality pattern turns out to be the usual conglomeration of executivese, plus a touch of nobility that few people in the business had suspected they possessed. The image merchant, says the R & F tester, is responsive to tension, has freedom for action, persistence, drive, energy, objective thinking, flexibility in attitude, friendliness and likability, lack of self-consciousness, the ability to do well in many tasks without special aptitudes, and the kicker: he is endowed with "a service concept of the self."

In effect the tester sees the public relations man as a dedicated social servant with facile mimeograph, as a literary Martin Arrowsmith with typewriter and shoulder-rest telephone—a personality glorification that PR men will find humorous or, at the least, unrecognizable.

"Among successful public relations executives there exists a spontaneous effort to help other people . . ." says the Ruder & Finn tester. "To the cynic this consistent tendency to help others often appears to be a casting of bread upon the waters. This cynicism is, however, unwarranted. There is little deliberate planning or 'favor trading' present in the public relations executive's tendency to enjoy being of service to others. It is rather a general way of adjusting to the world, which is learned in early family relationships . . . At any rate an individual with this kind of social identification reacts to the successes and failures of others as if he himself shared in the other's happiness or disappointment."

This observation is ridiculous to the professional PR man and does an injustice to the realistic publicist who is trying to earn a reasonably interesting living within the business framework without having sophomoric comments about his service or lack of service to mankind thrown in his face by reverse innuendo. Furthermore, nothing rankles the "helpful" PR executive more than seeing a colleague's boardful of tearsheets when his own campaigns are falling on deaf editorial ears.

As a writer, the initial rumors that newspaper editorial personnel—reporters and editors—were being personality tested on several major dailies hit this author with disbelief. The personal enterprise of the American reporter, no matter how diminished his zeal might occasionally seem, was too ingrained a folk virtue, it seemed, to be tampered with by the brain watcher. After a few interviews and leads followed from one tester to another, however, the list of important American newspapers that insist that bylines be preceded by personality tests grew—the Los Angeles *Times,* the St. Petersburg *Times,* the Wilmington *News-Journal,* the Atlanta *Journal and Constitution,* the Miami *News,* the Columbus *Ledger-Inquirer,* the South Bend *Tribune.*

The editorial man, in the words of one tester, has been the last "holdout," a tower of opposition that now appears to be tottering. Aside from newspapers, several trade publications regularly test editorial people, and even the publishing giant of McGraw-Hill, as we shall see, has submitted some of its beginning editorial people to the personality test. One national woman's magazine, for a brief period a few years ago, even converted its personnel men to blue-ribboned "AVA Analysts."

In no part of the editorial world, however, has the tester been able to intrude so successfully as in the daily newspaper, where he crashed the city room only after seeing the linotype and pressroom operations capitulate. The two most active testers of newspaper personnel are Harless and Kirkpatrick Associates in Tampa, Florida, whose clients include a large group of southeastern newspapers, and the New York firm of Robert N. McMurry, which among other things has helped select the last three managing editors and full editorial staff of the South Bend *Tribune*. The Personnel Laboratory, a blind projective house in New York, has also tested a number of varied editorial people.

To produce a reporter on the Wilmington *News-Journal*, for example, the McMurry people send a staff psychologist to Delaware to first interview, then administer a battery of projective instruments, including their own seven-card version of the Thematic Apperception Test, to the bewildered journalism graduate. On seven blank sheets of paper, the reporter writes seven stories that are stimulated by the drawings in the TAT cards. The stories will never carry his by-line in print but will have an indelible effect on his writing career.

The Harless group, although it does give projective tests such as the Draw-A-Person and Sentence Completion, tests its reporters and editors (it started with the St. Petersburg *Times* and has worked up as far north as Columbus, Ohio) with scoreable quiz tests including the Study of Values, the Kuder Preference, and the popular Guilford-Zimmerman Temperament Schedule. The evaluation of a city editor or other management editorial personnel is worth a $200 fee, while a police-beat reporter can come as low as $100.

Comments on the decline of the American newspaper can hardly be blamed on the tester, for his is a relatively recent intrusion. However, the criteria most testers have adopted to scale down flesh-and-blood newspapermen illustrate that they are aware of the decline of the individualistic journalist, and intend to perpetuate the unfortunate new image of the reporter-editor who has become much like us all—a bit more docile, balanced, and conquerable than the preceding generation. "If H. L. Mencken applied for a job on this paper today," says the personnel director of one large daily, "he wouldn't get past the personnel office."

What are the psychological guideposts for today's underpaid journalist? How must he alter himself for this $150-a-week guild journeyman pay, give or take a few dollars? The tester's immediate response to this appears to be triggered by a violent distaste (or fear) of the personal journalist of the 1920's and '30's who had such an impact on the thinking of his and succeeding generations. One tester talks about journalists as if he were selecting a docile governess for his children instead of a unique professional for whom a special amendment was written into our Constitution. "The most important things we look for in editorial personnel," he says, "are their ability to take criticism and the absence of possible alcoholism."

The Harless-Kirkpatrick testing group in Tampa is quick to point out that emotional stability is vital for a newspaper reporter, although there is little evidence that adjustment to our cultural norm, which is one of the bases of stability measurements, is any stimulus for a vibrant journalism. This same tester is wary of the "opportunist" reporter, the young journalist more interested in his own career (and properly so) than in being loyal to the newspaper and its management. Although "high aspirations" is an asset for a reporter, testers are wary of someone with "too many job changes."

The St. Petersburg *Times,* which uses the Harless-Kirkpatrick organization, has published a booklet, "Editorial Testing Program," outlining the findings of personality tests on thirty of its editors and thirty reporters. It divulges the distinctive personality characteristics of "successful" newsmen, traits that ostensibly are avidly sought in new applicants and beat-wary reporters being considered for editors' slots. The findings on this minute regional sample of newspaperdom present a strange profile of a journalist, who appears to live not in fact or fiction, but only in St. Petersburg, Florida. Here's the modern journalist as this tester sees, and hires, him.

1. Editors are more sociable than reporters.
2. Editors are serious, reflective, and cautious.
3. Reporters are impulsive.
4. Reporters are more hostile than editors.
5. Reporters have both belligerence and diplomacy ("This is a difficult combination to find, but necessary in a topnotch reporter," says the tester).
6. Both reporters and editors are quite stable, but editors more so.
7. Editors are more objective than reporters.

Behind much of this is a tester bias that a reporter should

be little more than a baggy-suited junior executive with a writing flair. As for editors, the tester is convinced that like all "managers," they too must be business-oriented. "If a man is being considered for city editor or managing editor," says a spokesman of the Tampa firm, "we would expect that on the Study of Values, he would score high on the Economic scale," the same admonishment, incidentally, that Sears, Roebuck makes to its executives.

The drive to nudge the newspaperman into a controllable norm is most obvious at the Los Angeles *Times,* which for the past fifteen years has given the controversial Humm-Wadsworth Temperament Scale to all applicants for reporting and editing jobs. The H-W is a 300-plus item questionnaire that uses Yes or No responses to questions ("Does it make you nervous to be on the water?") to construct a personality profile cached in seven impressive clinical terms: Normal, Hysteroid (self-preservation, selfishness, crime), Manic (elation, excitement), Depressive (sadness, caution), Autistic (daydreams, sensitiveness), Paranoid (fixed ideas, conceit), and Epileptoid (ecstasy, inspiration).

A personnel spokesman for the *Times* frankly explained that the complex test is simple to apply to editorial job selection. As he states, the newspaper "plays the percentages" and prefers reporters to score as close to the newspaper's test norm as possible.

As adjuncts of the business economy, it was natural that the industrial habit of testing employees would also infect the nation's trade newspapers and magazines, an area of communications that employs a vast amount of editorial talent, much of it of high professional caliber. Many of the editors of leading trade magazines—*Modern Packaging, Modern Plastics, Chain Store Age*—have been pretested, as have some forty editorial people at McGraw-Hill Publishing, men now serving as editors on its diversified magazine list, from *Business Week* to *Electrical Merchandising Week.*

This McGraw-Hill testing program is six years old and involves members of its editorial training program who are selected out of college or journalism school for apprenticeship in a McGraw-Hill career. ("They have done better than average in the company," says the former assistant to the editorial director, now a managing editor, who was the company's first editorial trainee.) Another of the forty trainees, who has been a successful McGraw-Hill editor, recalls that shortly after he graduated college, McGraw-Hill sent him to The Psychological Corporation for a day and a half of tests, including one that listed 100 traits and asked that he pick the ten that "most described" him and list them in order. Another of the tests was the behemoth 500-plus question MMPI, which, he thankfully recalls, he was familiar with from college.

Since only certain editorial employees have been tested, the existence of a personality screen is not general knowledge at McGraw-Hill; nor is the fact that the giant publishing firm has embarked on an "experimental" testing program for editorial people that may soon affect considerably more of its editors at its Eighth Avenue headquarters building.

Of all the professionals who have been thrown into ego combat with the brain watcher, the proud journalist and his prostration before the tester have created the most disheartening spectacle. However, one writer who recently faced his tester down, and vanquished him, may provide the courage and example for other communicators.

A prominent magazine writer, a frequent contributor to the *Reader's Digest* and other major magazines, applied for a special project writing job with a leading record company and was interviewed by a company "executive" whom, by his "jargon," the writer quickly identified as a psychologist. "He kept probing into my personal life, and as he asked me questions about everything including my sex and toilet habits, I felt my blood pressure rising. It was a ridiculous, humiliating experience and I told him I would not cooperate. I would be a loyal employee, but, I said, my private thoughts were my own business and my subconscious was not for sale. I left the interview shortly after.

"That night, Friday, I told my wife about the sickening experience. Monday morning I received a call from the record company. 'When can you start work?' I was shocked but I managed to answer, 'Hold on. Haven't you spoken to your head shrinker? Didn't he tell you I wouldn't cooperate?' He answered: 'Sure. That's why we want you. He said your reaction was great. It showed that you were a stubborn, dedicated, introverted man, the kind that would make a great writer.' "

The experience was uplifting, for a sophisticated tester had recognized the virtue of psychological integrity or had been shocked back to reality by it. However, other defiant communicators should not expect similar encouragement for their rebellious notions, for the brain watcher has gotten heady over his successes and the fact that he does not have to extend any special psychological bill of rights to the creative opinion makers. Increasingly, the modern communicator must shape up, within the strict image set for him, or go peddle his papers elsewhere.

7 BRAIN WATCHING IN OUR SCHOOLS: THE THREE R'S THROUGH GRADUATE SCHOOL

For two fateful days in March and April of 1960, half a million students in junior and senior high school throughout the nation resolutely completed a battery of achievement and aptitude tests that have become expected, if not beloved, aspects of American secondary education. Immediately after, however, they were asked several hundred prying questions on their personality, personal life, and family background, not unlike those father has come to expect in the adult job-seeking world.

These students were involved as compulsory subjects in Western culture's most massive testathon, "Project Talent," financed mainly by the U. S. Office of Education of the Department of Health, Education and Welfare at a cost approximately $1.00 per twelve- to eighteen-year-old. The awesome endeavor is centered at the University of Pittsburgh, where high-speed IBM 7070 computers have by this time electronically deposited almost a billion bits of information about our children, first on IBM punch cards, then on magnetic tape for permanent recording and instantaneous recall.

The youngsters were scored not only on "aptitudes" such as their literary and mathematical skills but, much more important from the brain watcher's point of view, on how well they measured up on "personality," specifically on Talent's scales for "self-confidence," "conventionality," and "calmness," and a store more traits.

Although psychologically gargantuan, Talent is far from the brain watcher's first excursion into the lucrative school system. The enriched tax coffers of school districts have provided not only increased salaries for teachers and long-needed classrooms, but a willingness by many school districts to invest sizable sums of the taxpayer's money for the investigation of not only how smart Johnny is, but what makes him tick.

Some of the probes have had reasonable motivation: guidance on a counselor-to-child basis or individual diagnosis of obviously disturbed children. During the past half-decade, however, much school testing has followed the errant path of personality testing in industry. Millions of our youngsters have been subjected to mass psychological screenings with doubtful paper-and-pencil personality tests and have had their ever-changing ten- to sixteen-year-old personalities translated into recognizable percentiles that are indelibly entered on their school records along with grades and IQ scores for easy misinterpretation by teachers and school authorities.

They have had the profiles of their "interests" (literary, clerical, etc.) plotted on awesome Kuder Preference Record graphs and proudly brought them home to Mama from the eighth grade as misleading vocational guidance "evidence" that they should be future scientists or salesmen. Unknown to parents, and often to the whole community, entire classes of children as early as second grade are gathered in group confessionals where they fill out "problem checklists." Scores on a child's worries and fears, on sex, dates, Mom and Dad, fights over the car, family finances, and even teen-age menstruation—once considered the exclusive province of parents—not only become part of the child's school record, but are inevitably bandied about in certain school authorities' knowledge.

School testers have inaugurated an even more disturbing phenomenon: crude "mental health" analyses that, in an imitation of the psychiatric screening techniques that failed in World Wars I and II (see Chapter X: Once Upon a Mind; and Chapter XI: Brain Watching: Science or Cult?), have put Johnny to the extreme test. Instead of waiting to judge his behavior and performance, many impatient school brain watchers are using psychological test scores to label him "maladjusted" or "potentially maladjusted," and even to predict which of a given underprivileged group of six-year-olds will trouble the community as delinquents a decade later.

Increasingly, personality tests are being used in public school systems to select those youngsters who have no evident behavior problems—but do have poor psychological test scores—as patients for their burgeoning staffs of school psychologists. The California Department of Education, for one, has begun operating a master scheme of personality test evaluation—basically conducted by the schoolteacher—that will identify *your* "emotionally handicapped" child early and possibly even isolate him from *my* Johnny or Jane before he can cause the state pain or extra tax expenditure.

As awesome as the cataloguings appear, they hardly reflect the full extent of the brain watcher's activities in our public and private school systems. The tester has also been working furiously to find a statistical correlation between personality and school, especially college, grades. If he can convince school authorities that his measurement of a seventeen-year-old's "sociability," for example, has more meaning than just the titillation of an undertrained guidance counselor, he will have opened a vast new commercial market. (One researcher recently announced, for example, that the less "heterosexual" college boy—possibly undistracted by girls and orgiastic dreams—is *statistically* the better student.)

Far from an Orwellian concept, the College Entrance Examination Board—whose quest for the scholarly elite now stupefies parents of high schoolers for two years beginning with the junior year—recently awarded research grants to psychologists to find the personality types or traits slated for college academic success. If "perfected," the grand scheme is to use these tests to predict which high school seniors have the personality makings and which are to be eliminated because they have failed their *"Personality Boards."* If these ill-conceived plans reach maturation, parents of the later 1960's, and beyond, will not only have to search their dedication and genetic heritage to understand why Johnny (or Jane) did not score a resounding 600 or 700 on the College Boards. They will have to plummet their psyches to comprehend why their children were turned away from the nation's better campuses as psychological and emotional misfits. (Even the National Merit Scholarship Corporation has recently begun a search for the superior student "personality.")

In fact, as we shall see, on several college campuses, in many medical schools, and *most* theological seminaries, the brain watcher is *already* operational, screening out thousands of hopeful ministers, engineers, and doctors on the basis of their "personalities."

Johnny may have been personality tested earlier in his school career, but he will probably first meet his brain watcher on entering junior high school, when one of his first introductions to secondary education may be a personality test thrust under his nose. Despite his subject's youth and the chilling fact that this parentally unauthorized probing is tax-supported, the school brain watcher is no less curious than his colleagues in industry. In fact, the common personality "counseling tests" given to our children—the SRA Jr. Inventory, the Minnesota Counseling Inventory, the California Test of Personality: Intermediate—are just as, if not more, pugnacious than similar adult tests.

The California Test of Personality, which comes in various versions from elementary to college level, is one of the most common. The CTP is a short Bernreuter-type "Yes" or "No" test that envisions the youngster as a dodecagon, a twelve-sided psyche that can be measured simply by asking the student fifteen questions about each of these traits. He is graded for "nervous symptoms," "feeling of belonging," "anti-social tendencies," "family relations," etc., and his percentile scores on each trait are marked on a graph on the face of his test. The connected dots take form as the student's "personality profile," with which the teacher or guidance counselor can—and does—compare him at a glance with his classmates.

The test is like many Dad has taken, but Johnny, unlike his father, tends to be honest, and freely creates a juicy, if somewhat distorted, twelve-year-old's view of his life. The questions are often intimate, and cover such a latitude that parental attempts to impress Johnny's teacher that he is from a good family, by teaching him to scrub behind the ears or not to spread the family's secrets about school, are laughable. On its "Family Relations" scale for example, the CTP asks naïve youngsters these far-from-bashful questions about their home life:

Do you prefer to keep your friends away from home because it is not attractive?

Are the people in your home too quarrelsome?

Another common student test poses a set of "family" questions to be answered "True" or "False." No amount of PTA polish can reshine the tarnished family image if Johnny's answers are wrong. How would (or *has*) your child handled the following?

I become nervous at home.

One (or both) of my parents is very nervous.

There is very little love and companionship in my home
    as compared to other homes.

I get less understanding at home than elsewhere.

The actions of one or the other of my parents have
    aroused great fear in me.

School personality tests also have the inevitable emotional
stability and neurotic scales, which are often softened for
the youngster's consumption to "calmness" or "nervous symptoms, freedom from." The CTP, for one, evaluates Johnny's
stability on a heavily health-and-hypochondriasis scale. For
example, should an eighth grader—whether or not he has
hay fever or weak eye muscles—answer "Yes" to many
questions of the following type, the label "nervous" is
likely to follow him closely through school:

Do your eyes hurt often?

Do you frequently have sneezing spells?

Industry has been castigated for its devotion to testing,
but for all its excesses, it has sometimes hired trained psychologists to do its personality analyses. Many school systems,
however, have blithely handed over the responsibility to
barely trained personnel, few of whom have adequate backgrounds in testing procedures. Great Neck, the educational
pearl of Long Island's North Shore, for example, had "experimented" with the CTP, then discarded it because, as one
school authority states: "By and large, the teachers and
guidance counselors tend to place more confidence in the
test scores than they deserve."

Johnny's brain watcher is most often this naïve guidance
counselor. Almost always a nonpsychologist, the school counselor is either a regular classroom teacher with "empathy"
who doubles in the job in lieu of a few hours off from
teaching or, as is increasingly common in our "better"
(wealthier, suburban) districts, a full-time "professional" who
after a few months' additional training is given the responsibility of guiding the school careers of several classes, an
entire grade, or even a small school.

In most cases, guidance people are woefully untrained to
handle the proper interpretation of personality tests, a job—

as we have seen—that is nearly, if not actually, impossible for the Ph.D. psychologist. In progressive New York State, guidance counselors need only as much graduate work as secondary teachers—credits toward a master's degree. In fact, New York school *psychologists* who actually diagnose students (Rorschach, etc.) are not even required to have a master's. In other areas of the country, guidance people need even less training and, by and large, counselors are naïve about the pitfalls of personality testing.

Despite admonitions to keep these volatile tests out of the hands of laymen, most school districts (even those with staff psychologists) allow guidance counselors to give, score, and interpret the tests. In a typical operation, the guidance counselor will give the test to an entire class on a routine basis, supposedly so that the student can "learn more about himself." In actuality, however, the test is the counselor's psychological lever, or as one counselor states it: "a clue to what to discuss with the student and his parents during conferences."

The counselor, in effect, uses the test as a child-spotting tool to eliminate the necessity of waiting for problem youngsters to show their pimply faces. In fact, in some schools the personality test is casually introduced to unwary kids as a seemingly innocent part of a modern educational project. In Port Washington, Long Island, for example, all members of the incoming seventh-grade junior high school class are given the Mooney Problem Checklist to fill out as part of a ten-week course in "Human Relations." "It's a wonderful timesaver," exuberantly says the seventh-grade guidance counselor. "Through the Mooney we can often find children who need help that we might not have found otherwise."

Whether these children should have been "found" and subjected to intensive guidance and even possible referral to the school psychologist for diagnosis and psychotherapy is a moot question. Is a possibly introspective, or candid, youngster, who is admittedly not maladjusted enough to come to the firsthand attention of the counselor, disciplinary authorities, or the school psychologist, being helped by being "found" by personality checklists? Probably not. Do our schools have the right to risk grave psychological harm to youngsters by using their insignificant test scores and probably transient problems as a make-work project for under-trained, but enthusiastic, guidance counselors?

Of all the school personnel who have worn the brain watcher's mantle, the least qualified is the classroom teacher.

Yet many of these tests are advertised for his use and scoring. The Mooney Problem Checklist, a form of personality quiz which asks students to "pick out problems" which are "troubling" them, is openly sold to teachers under the advancing contemporary theory that not even growing youngsters are to be permitted privacy of the soul.

School brain watchers have had valuable assistance in indoctrinating our youngsters to accept their prying as a normal aspect of the modern schoolhouse culture. *Scholastic* Magazine, for example, has published a special supplement, "Meeting The Test," meant to gracefully introduce naïve preteen and teen-age students into the blessings of testing. Obviously composed with the help of testers, the supplement strains to make the student's upcoming brain watch sound like an inoffensive "positive" experience. "If you and Johnny took a personality inventory at school many of the differences between you would show up. Your counselor—and perhaps *your teachers* [italics mine]—would also get a better picture of what each of you was like. They might also get a better understanding of the different problems you were facing," it says.

One large test distributor, in promoting the sale of the Mooney to school systems, lists its "wide variety of applications" including its use by teachers for a "livelier, easier-to-teach class" in "adjustment," a public seminar which often revolves around the confessions which have just been forced out of the trusting youngsters. "In modern schools, a number of problems of adjustment of young people are met through special courses or units within courses," says the test distributor's bulletin in educational jargon. "Varied though they are, they have in common the teacher's aim to work through the group some of the needs felt by members of the class. Often a good starting point for such a class is the administration of the Mooney Problem Checklist."

The Mooney comes in several stages: Junior High, High School, College, and even Adult. The Junior High form, for example, has 210 frank "problems" that the testers feel encompass the world of the twelve- to fifteen-year-old. The youngster checks off those statements, in seven different areas, that are problems for him: Health (Afraid I may need an operation), School, Home and Family, Miscellaneous, Boy and Girl Relationships (Thinking too much about the other sex), Relations to People in General and Self-Centered Concerns (Sometimes wishing I'd never been born). After the student marks those items that gnaw at him—at least for that day, or hour—his score in each category is registered, then totaled, and recorded as a semipermanent profile of the tortured twelve-year-old.

(The high school version of the Mooney is similar, but longer—330 problems in ten categories—and brasher. It lists such problems as: "ashamed of the house we live in," and even "worried about sex diseases." On the college level, problem checklists are often given at freshman orientation time, when a women's college freshman class is liable to be kept after dinner to check off such possibilities as "thoughts of suicide.")

In a strong sense, the youngster is promised anonymity when he fills out these blanks, but he soon learns that if he scores reasonably higher than the national "norm" provided to the teacher and counselor, he is fair game. He is often selected for further counseling, or possibly even a visit to the school psychologist for further "diagnosis" with the Rorschach, the Thematic Apperception, and even the Blacky Pictures, a photo dog story that supposedly gives the tester insights into a preadolescent's sexuality, among other things.

Most school systems that personality test not only fail to respect the carefully nurtured impression that tests scores will be held confidential and not passed on to other school authorities (students are never informed that they become part of their school personnel folder), but they try desperately to create the impression that no compulsion is involved. This is another tester-educator false front. At the end of the Mooney, for example, the child is asked whether he would like "to talk to someone" about his problems.

The child who is secure enough to refuse this offer of help soon learns that the system is, in fact, not voluntary. As one counselor on Long Island, a nonpsychologist, put it: "Even if a child does answer that he wants no help, we might call him or her in anyway if we felt the child was troubled enough." The child with self-pride, or acting under parental instructions, who leaves his paper blankly trouble-free, is—says the school brain watcher—fooling no one. "The fact that a kid doesn't check off any of the statements might be a counseling problem in itself," he says. "It could be indicative of a greater underlying problem."

One of the great dangers of school brain watching is that the teacher, or counselor, will become self-deluded that his use of personality tests has transformed him into an active "psychologist," with carte blanche to exaggerate minor clues into impressive syndromes. The danger is especially grave when school testers inflict the clinically derived personality tests on their helpless student bodies.

One of these, especially designed for high school students, is the 355-question Minnesota Counseling Inventory, an obvious derivative of the famed psychosis hunter, the MMPI (see Chapter V: Sick, Sick, Sick). The MCI, like its grandma MMPI, has the same raw Freudian approach, and, in fact, uses many questions similar to those originally obtained from testing psychotics. The MCI starts casually with such true-or-false statements as "I seem to make friends about as quickly as others do." It then warms up rapidly, becoming increasingly psychotic-searching as the test progresses. For example, your child may have already been confronted with such queries as these:

The things that some of my family have done have embarrassed me.

I hear strange things when I am alone.

Scholastic, in its testing supplement, explains how the counselor uses the MCI to translate a fifteen-year-old's scores into a verbal description of Johnny. "To be more specific, let's see what the test would tell a counselor about students who score 'high' and 'low' on the 'Conformity' scale," says *Scholastic.* According to the magazine, high school students who are high conformers on the MCI are "usually reliable and responsible, conforming to rules and behavior codes even when they may not agree with them. Instead of rebelling against regulations, these students attempt to have them changed through orderly procedures. They ordinarily show respect for persons in authority. Although not necessarily docile or oversubmissive, they understand the need for social organization. Such students cause little disturbance in school . . ." At the other end of the scale, the nonconformist student is described as "irresponsible, impulsive, and rebellious." Adds the indictment: "They may appear to learn little from experience, committing the same offense repeatedly even though verbally acknowledging it may be wrong. These students are individualistic and self-centered."

In a grand generalization, the MCI's author—and his appendage, the conforming school counselor—have decided that the conforming child is the preferable school student, and therefore, the preferable adult. Not only has individualistic nature been equated with the delinquent personality, but the tester insists that this type of youth "learns little from experience." With little sophistication, many counselors and teachers are taken in by this gibberish, with a resulting myopic look at our true educational needs, especially the shortage of secondary school graduates who are sufficiently individualistic to make vocal contributions to our culture.

Personality tests in school counseling situations have also been criticized on scientific grounds, as tools of the naïve. The authors of *Measurement for Guidance*—John M. Rothney of the University of Wisconsin, Paul J. Danielson of the University of Arizona, and Robert A. Heimann of Arizona State College—are quite cynical about their use in the schoolroom:

"There is a great deal of evidence that personality questionnaires, controlled interviews, and interest inventories are widely used in counseling," say the authors. "Just why this is so in view of the demonstrated inadequacies of these devices is difficult to understand. It seems that it must be a combination of amazing psychometric innocence on the part of the users, naïveté in considering the counseling job as a 'quickie' affair rather than a complex longitudinal problem, mistaken faith in the statistics on the part of the inventory producers and consumers, expediency, and a desire to keep up with the other fellow who uses them for any of the above reasons. . . . The popularity of the instruments may be due in part, then, to the psychological support that counselors, working in a relatively new area, and without adequate evidence of their effectiveness, may feel that they need; and the round-the-clock hucksterism in the sales of the instruments must account in a large measure for the widespread use. Certainly it cannot be justified on the basis of logical reasoning or experimental evidence."

Another critic, L. F. Shaffer, in the *Third Mental Measurements Yearbook*, points out that the use of personality tests in school guidance tends to overlook the fact that the student is a person, not a set of doubtful statistics. Says he: ". . . Those who have real professional training will not need a system. Those who lack psychological knowledge will help pupils more effectively by using simple human warmth and interest than by thumbing a handbook of over-simplified recipes."

One of the tragedies of school brain watching is the amenability of our youngsters. Today, in many classrooms under the umbrella of guidance, the student's trust in teacher is being used as a facile brain-watching tool. Little Johnny generally will not tell only all about himself and family on

command, but is being conditioned as a psychological ac-
cessory to divulge all he knows about his classmates as well.

Through a little game, "Guess Who," based on the theory
that "peers know each other better than the teacher," the
seven- to fourteen-year-old student plays neophyte brain
watcher as he rates his classmates for teacher or counselor.
The student is given several general descriptions, including
the following: "Here is someone who always seems rather
sad, worried, or unhappy, and who hardly ever laughs or
smiles." He is then asked to "Guess Who" and fill in the
name of the youngster alongside the description.

Another device used by classroom teachers is the "Sociogram." By asking each child to name himself, and his three
best friends in the class, the teacher constructs a chart of the
class's "social structure." When scored, each child becomes
a keyed circle, large if popular, small if insular, and arranged
either at the center or edge of the group depending upon the
child's importance in the class structure. A sharp arrow
drawn from one child to another indicates that he has chosen
the "target" as a friend. If the child is rejected by someone
whom he has chosen, the arrow is blunted.

With definitive graphite strokes the impressionable classroom teacher has "charted" the child's social caste and assigned to "rejected" youngsters the onus of social ineffec-
tiveness or even emotional instability. In actuality, all of us
who have attended grammar school—surely including most
teachers and guidance counselors—must recall that social
position in grade school often varies from year to year depending on the other children in the class and indeed on the
teacher herself. There is, to state it kindly, no significant
research that the "sociogram" is either a valid predictor or
describer of a child's personality.

These classroom parlor games can prove annoying to children who are not born mixers, and a bright seventeen-year-
old's progress may be impeded by an inexpert guidance counselor enamored of personality tests. A child "spotted" in
personality quizzes by his poor scores and casually labeled
as "troubled" may even find his hopeful future cut off
sharply. However, no school testing program has the proportions, and potential danger, of a project now underway
in California. If continued and expanded as planned, tens
of thousands of children in that state, and perhaps considerably more on a national level, may be falsely identified as
emotionally disturbed.

The project, a technique supposedly for the "early identification of emotionally handicapped children" in school, is being conducted by the California State Department of Education under a research grant (California Senate Bill 62, 1957 Legislature) of $108,000. After three years of research, the educators and psychologists involved in the problem have developed a technique that has been used to test 70,000 school children in 50 school districts and to label thousands of these California youngsters as other than normal. In fact, in some parts of the state—Redwood City, Alhambra (elementary grades), Palo Alto, Sequoia (high school grades), and San Jose (junior high)—educators have, at the suggestion of the project directors, taken these supposedly "emotionally handicapped" children from their regular classrooms and grouped them in special "adjustment classes" in virtual isolation.

The California work is plainly a brain watcher's dream. The existence of an uncategorized society is at the core of his neurosis, and for some time he has warned us that we must give up some of our freedom of action to enable him to test, then separate us, according to our adjustment. The unverbalized threat has come true in California, where the project directors point out that they must detect and isolate in childhood what they call a "vulnerability that may lead to psychosis, neurosis, suicide, repetitive automobile accidents, alcoholism, narcotic addiction or criminal behavior." (Responsible researchers of each of these groups have failed to produce any agreement as to the personality defects, if any, involved. See Chapter V: Sick, Sick, Sick.)

The secret of how to identify these disturbed youngsters who will one day drain the state's welfare treasury and be unproductive citizens is remarkably simple, say the Californians in effect. In a report issued in the spring of 1961, they reveal that the key has been hidden all this time under a handful of paper-and-pencil personality tests and the superpsychological eye of the fourth- and fifth-grade elementary school teacher. The child is given a question-and-answer test, "Thinking About Yourself" ("This girl has bad dreams. Are you like her? Do you want to be like her?"), and then a surreptitious quiz presented as a "Class Play." The student is assigned the role of "director," and then asked to select classmates for various "parts," such as "Someone who could play the part of a bully." The scores on these two tests are meshed with the teacher's personal evaluation, and the unfortunate child who does badly on two out of three is screened out as a candidate for the tag "emotionally handicapped."

The painful indictment is obviously not husbanded in California. In the initial Department of Education study, *14 percent* of the 2,198 children tested in grades three to five in three school districts were given what may one day be the scarlet "E" for their efforts.

What check has been made on the researchers? What carefully controlled validity trials insured that Johnny isn't being disturbed by the testers rather than his emotions? The Department of Education's so-called "validity" experiments are far from convincing. In fact, if the report is studied carefully, it indicates that large numbers of normal, adjusted California youngsters are being falsely identified by the program. While the tests "uncovered" more than 300 disturbed youngsters out of 2,198, the principals and school psychologists at these same schools, from their intimate experience with these same 2,198 children, nominated only 150 as being emotionally disturbed. In fact, of the 300-plus children, the testers and the school authorities agreed on only 90!

The California Department of Education has asked for a state law to enlarge its testing activities, and to grant a special incentive subsidy to those school districts using their plan to test, identify, then possibly separate the children. If passed, we can expect the California Education Department to "identify" *almost half a million* emotionally disturbed children in the state—70 percent of whom will probably be considered quite normal by school authorities.

To side-step this obvious statistical trap, the California testers show their agility in a display of turnabout logic that makes *the test the criterion for its own validity experiment.* Says the testers' preliminary report unsmilingly: "It appears that seven out of ten children who are most probably emotionally disturbed are not noted or observed by the principal or school psychologist."

As another supposed validity trial, the California testers had clinical psychologists evaluate the children screened out by them. Of 30 "disturbed" youngsters chosen by the test procedure, the clinicians agreed on 24. The testers present this as corroboration, but had they reread their college texts, they would have been reminded that checking one evaluation procedure with another is no sign of true validity.

The California project is especially awesome for it brings the power of a sovereign state to compulsory pseudoscientific evaluation. Equally serious, it asks for specific community-state action toward the child based on this evaluation. In a fantastic letter to the state legislature, on December 23, 1959, the researchers try to hard-sell the idea that this is the natural role of the benevolent government.

"The research program presented herein represents the first known major attempt by any branch of government to identify early these children who will need some educational assistance because of emotional problems and to discover ways of helping them within the school program," says the letter. As justification of their work, they state that *"many of these children* [italics mine] will one day be part of our society who will seek revenge, retribution or withdrawal from life. They will become part of the vast population in prisons, mental hospitals, alcoholic wards. They will be found among the accident-prone, the narcotic addicts, the suicidal, and the melancholy. They will be seen in the divorce courts, lonely rooms, mental hygiene clinics, city streets and farms."

This is abject nonsense. Of course they will be part of this population and will also be seen on *city streets and farms*. There is, however, no proof that the pressures of an unknown culture ten, twenty, thirty years from today will place any more, or less, strain on these "screened" youngsters than anyone else. In their final report of March 31, 1961, the testers state unequivocally: "There seems to be little doubt that as they get older they become delinquent, drop out of school after age sixteen, make poor grades, are frequently referred for disciplinary action by school authorities, or need the attention of a child guidance clinic."

How does this check with the testers' own follow-up, conducted in 1960 on youngsters judged "disturbed" in 1955? Had they all become drop-outs as predicted? Hardly. According to their counselors, more than half—57 percent—would, in fact, graduate from high school. What about their inevitable clash with the law? Actually less than one-fourth the group had delinquency problems, and 76 percent of the predicted law-breakers had confounded their doomsday testers. In fact, of the "control" group of "average and *above average*" children, half as many (12 percent) had an unexpected delinquency rate. Hardly a successful prognostication of blighted lives.

The pitfall in these crude measurements (which could probably be done just as inaccurately by comparing the bottom portion of a class with its leaders), is that no responsible investigator of emotional disturbance can be any less scrupulous than a jurist is with criminal liability. There is no allowable statistical error, let alone this wild flaying about of unsubstantiated predictions of twisted lives.

No critique of this California test blight could be more revealing than a peek at the testers' salesmanship of their operation. The closing page of their report to the state legislature dramatizes two newsclippings—an Associated Press story of the trial of seven boys for murder in New York and a local California clipping announcing this test study by the Department of Education. Asks the broadside: "Which costs more? Juvenile trial may cost $250,000. EDC (Emotionally Disturbed Children) Budget For 3 Years $190,000." The answer, that exaggerated claims by testers are always more expensive in the long run, is not given.

What about parental annoyance at these threats to their child's sanctity? Where are the outraged cries of mothers and fathers whose hovering care can turn a split knee into a trauma, while a badly open psyche appears to leave them unmoved?

The fault does not lie with most parents. Personality testing in our schools is a near-furtive affair conducted by classroom teachers, counselors, and psychologists without, in most cases, the knowledge or permission of the parent or sometimes even school board members themselves. While Johnny's parents must usually sign a legal release before school authorities feel confident enough to have a licensed doctor jab him with a hypodermic, no one feels obligated to ask or inform the parents that pseudomedical experiments are being conducted on his mind.

A spokesman for the California emotionally-disturbed program, for example, admits that although parents of screened children are often invited for group counseling, they are not "directly" informed of the tester's diagnosis. In New York, a full-time school counselor on Long Island—after claiming that there is little parental opposition to his junior high's testing program—confessed that the parents are not told of its existence: "Information on our testing program is not part of the general information given to members of the community."

The ominous spread of school personality testing does not indicate any approval by the nation's parents. For all their submission to corporate testing to get and hold a job, adults who yield to the Goliath who pays them are on quite another footing in their homes as school-district taxpayers. The power of parents and their anger at school brain watching is substantiated by action in several communities where there has been a breach in the school's veil of secrecy.

In Island Trees, Long Island, a suburban neighbor of Levittown, the wrath of parents recently forced the school district to drop the use of a personality test for one group and to re-evaluate it for another. Island Trees had been testing beginning junior and senior high students (seventh and tenth grades) on a mass basis with a popular test, the SRA Youth Inventory. When parents of junior high school youngsters learned from their children that they had been asked about their parents, home, religion, and sex, they complained vociferously.

School authorities took a second look at their procedure and retreated rapidly on the testing of seventh-graders with an instrument that was curious about their dating habits. The test will no longer be given to seventh-graders, but whether Island Trees tenth-graders will continue to undergo the brain watch is still undecided. And, as a spokesman of one school district involved in a similar hassel points out with quiet satisfaction, they have not retreated on any principle of personality testing and still have other testing armament in reserve that parents have not objected to, or even know about. Despite such skirmishes in several communities, the battle between the tester and the parents for our children's minds has yet to be really joined.

In East Meadow, New York, one parent has cast the gauntlet before school testers in an emotionally charged protest that may clarify the controversy. Edward J. Van Allen, the father of a junior high school youngster, angrily initiated court action against local school officials to allow him to see his son's school records. He won in a decision of the New York State Supreme Court which reaffirmed the common-law concept that a parent has the right to know what is happening to his child.

While examining the records provided by the school under court duress, Van Allen saw a notation that projective personality tests—including the Rorschach and TAT—had been given to his twelve-year-old son, but that the full details of the psychologist's report were absent. The school board finally "requested" the district's guidance director to show the testing notes to the father. Although satisfied with their compliance, he is now disturbed at the immense power of school testers. "I don't think they had any right to give him the tests in the first place without written permission from me," he told *Newsday*, the Long Island daily. Added the newspaper report: "Van Allen said he might take the matter of giving tests without permission to the Legislature for possible corrective action."

The question of whether a child can be given a personality examination, by either a school psychologist, a guidance counselor, or a teacher, without parental permission is at the core of the argument. It is in the courts and the state legislatures that this fight will take place, and the expansive power of the school brain watcher will either be curtailed or the natural rights of parents will be atrophied.

Parental ignorance of the implications of school testing was demonstrated in the spring of 1960, when 440,000 high school youngsters in 1,353 schools were each given a card and a number that would be their *nom de psyche* in a sweeping longitudinal brain watch that will not be completed for twenty years or more. These two days of intensive testing, which were part of Project Talent, financed by the U. S. Office of Education, may well be the most significant in these youngsters' lives. The motivations of the study may be quite honorable. In fact some of the electronic heaps of statistics on their mental prowess spewed out by an IBM programing of the 5,000,000 punched results should prove of great educational value.

But despite the opinion of Talent's chief psychologist John Flanagan (head of the U. S. Army Air Corps testing program in World War II) that personality inventories are of little value, the youngsters were also subjected to a staggering brain watch. After completing their academic chores (English Punctuation, Arithmetic Reasoning, etc.), each student was put before three personality hurdles: an 800-item Student Information Blank; a 400-question Student Activity Inventory; and a Student Interest Inventory.

The personality test results are already filtering back to the schools, where they are being touted as of great value to guidance counselors. In fact, Project Talent people are already speaking in jargonese of the "predictive value" of the results —which children shall and shall not someday succeed in a particular profession as gauged by their interest and personality test scores.

Project Talent's battery is a typical conglomeration of personality instruments not unlike those faced by any prospective salesmen in industry. The Student Information Blank is a depth prober on everything from a boy's dating habits to his father's education, occupation, and financial status. The questionnaire is actually a biographical inventory, part of the tester's shadowy plan to find a statistical correlation between an *individual* child's success and his family history—to perpetuate the myth that a *specific* child is better suited for higher things depending on his father's income and the number of books in his house.

Project Talent tries to camouflage this nosy socioeconomic probe as a way "to provide data essential to an analysis of college plans, need for financial assistance, etc." Behind it is actually the tester's gnawing desire to predict which of our children have the better *statistical* chance of success, and thus be in a position to influence their destiny. A preliminary report on the first 440,000 children tested substantiates the suspicion: the testers have already correlated students' intelligence with their fathers' occupations, with these results: (1) Students whose parents are workmen or laborers scored 105 on the general information test; (2) Children of skilled workers or foremen scored 123; (3) Children of business executives and professionals scored 140.

Talent has come up with an obvious fact, that on the *average,* children from underprivileged areas with lower cultural backgrounds and inferior schooling provided by communities and states which pour tax funds into newer, higher-income areas become students with less general information. The disservice of such reports is that the bright numbers are a chance for brain watchers to predict that a young Pablo from East Harlem, or the son of a cab driver, has a smaller "predictive" chance of entering college and enjoying later success—thereby perhaps nudging the prediction toward becoming an unfortunate reality.

Project Talent will be conducting regular follow-ups of its half a million student guinea pigs and, judging from early results, will regularly be inundating school guidance people with easily distortable information. One recent Project Talent report provided this exotic morsel to already confused guidance staffs: "Much of this information may have a bearing on achievement. For example, *it has been found that the number of brothers and sisters is related to whether a student will enter college, and perhaps whether he will complete college."*

The Student Activities Inventory is Talent's conventional personality quiz with a fistful of seventeen traits including vigor, sociability, and even "talkativeness." The test asks the student how well a statement ("I am usually the leader of my group") describes him, varying from "very accurately" to "not at all." The results, state the testers, will be compared to later behavior and success. In fact, personality profiles of four groups—1,250 senior high school girls, 1,153 senior high school boys, 990 ninth-grade girls, and 1,152 ninth-grade boys—have already been released.

There have been no surprises. While achievement in mathematics and music showed a reasonably high correlation, and vocabulary and social studies a very high correlation (.731), the personality scores hovered around chance in relation to academic achievement—a very fortunate fact for tomorrow's school children. However, of all the traits, only "conventionality" showed a consistent *negative* relationship with achievement, which should shake up rigid school guidance counselors used to interpreting students' high conformity scores as a positive sign, and vice versa.

During the next decade, we can expect a steady flow of personality correlations emanating from Talent's IBM machines in Pittsburgh and Washington, statistics of which we should be very cautious. "With respect to the scores for Sociability the nurses [actually, girls hoping to become nurses] were highest, and the elementary school teachers the lowest," says a Talent report. Having uttered this, Talent's administrators—and parents of daughters—can now only hope that gullible guidance counselors will not shuffle a generation of brilliant but *sociable* girls out of elementary education into the hospitals where they supposedly "belong."

The third personality technique in Project Talent is the Student Interest Inventory, one of the interest tests which operate on the assumption that by having a youngster check off activities that he "likes," you have uncovered vocational guidance information that will lead him to a fruitful, lucrative career. The brain watcher learned some time ago that parents have an insatiable desire to type-cast their eight-, ten-, and twelve-year-olds in an occupational slot (well-paying professional) and he has willingly tapped this sizable commercial market through the school system. No brain watch is more familiar to Johnny, who has taken them all—the Kuder Preference Record, the Strong, the California Occupational Interest Inventory, and others.

Early each fall, scores of thousands of junior high youngsters bring their plotted Kuder graphs home to Mommy so that she can study and misinterpret the scores. The popularity of these tests, especially the Kuder, is illustrated by a survey of 30 New York school districts which shows that 17 administer interest tests. As we have seen in industry, the Kuder is a simple test that "measures" scientific interest by asking Johnny if he would like to "visit a museum of science," while assuming that looking forward to a trip to an "advertising agency" is a sign of "persuasive" interest.

Each of the interest testers sees the youngster as composed of differing parts. Project Talent's "Student Interest Inventory" believes that the youngsters' likes and dislikes are divided into fourteen areas, while the Kuder zeroes Johnny in with a bare ten: outdoor, mechanical, computational, scientific, persuasive, artistic, literary, musical, social service, and clerical.

The art of converting a high Kuder score (seventy-fifth percentile or more) into a suitable vocation for Johnny is explained in the "Examiner's Manual," a bible for many naïve guidance people. Under "Artistic," for example, the Kuder manual lists the gamut of jobs suitable for the art-interested child: from curator of an art gallery to furrier. The student with high musical interest could be a composer or a chorus girl, among other things. What of a high social service interest? It obviously portends a career as a physician, or perhaps a county agricultural agent.

The Kuder coding system is more complex when a child claims interest in more than one area. The Kuder defies befuddlement, however, and simply combines the interests into a vocational blend. The child with outdoor and clerical interests—rather than becoming a CPA who welcomes an occasional mountain fishing trip—should, says the Kuder, be encouraged for a career as a "grain buyer" or "purser, ship." What chance for Johnny if he likes both music and numbers? There is only one logical possibility, says the Kuder manual: a business agent for musicians.

In most school districts, Mother and Father are uninformed about the meaning of their child's Kuder scores, and in the enthusiasm of seeing a high "musical" interest, for example, many assume that the school tester has verified their suspicion that young Gertie is a prodigy after all. The interest tests make no pretense of being "aptitude" measurers, but this is seldom understood—not only by parents, but by teachers as well.

Dr. Fred Brown, testing supervisor of the Great Neck, Long Island school system, makes the point strongly. "Too many people—teachers, parents, and students—consider interest tests as measures of ability and aptitude, which is, of course, far from the truth. A person may like to play golf but still be a duffer, and be absolutely unsuited for a golfing career. In our field it is generally conceded that interest tests have been 'oversold' to school systems, and that there is a great deal of misinterpretation of the results of the Kuder Preference Record."

To offset the danger of misinterpretation of psychological testing in schools, Dr. Brown has compiled a teacher's manual which other school districts might do well to copy. (The manual does not include personality testing, for Great Neck has tried and dropped it.) Says the Great Neck manual about the Kuder, straining not to appear patronizing to the state-licensed teacher: "It is suggested that the teacher first read the description of what the scores mean printed on the back of the profile sheet."

Dr. Benjamin Shimberg of the Educational Testing Service —whose organization has developed a non-personality-testing guidance program—concurs in this viewpoint, but points out that ignorance of student interest tests can go high in the educational hierarchy. He tells the story of attending a school system meeting to speak on guidance. During the discussion, the principal of the school, which tested its youngsters with the Kuder, avidly described the test's ability to measure "aptitude."

The threat to a child's career happiness from such an unsophisticated approach was illustrated at a meeting of the Guidance Institute by Dr. Henry Dyer of Educational Testing Service. Dr. Dyer was in the midst of exhorting his audience "On the Reduction of Ignorance About Tests in Guidance" when he recounted a chilling school brain-watching tale. "A sixth misconception," he began, "is that interest inventories measure some kind of basic orientation of a student irrespective of the kinds of experience to which he has or will be exposed. Do I need to spend much time on this one? Let me cite just one example of where it can lead. A presumably well-trained guidance counselor in a high-grade high school where a large majority of students go on to college was confronted by a girl with top-notch scholastic standing in all of the college preparatory subjects. Her parents were college-trained people; they had always expected that she would go to a liberal arts college; the daughter had always entertained the same expectations. The counselor, however, was apparently bewitched by one of the girl's scores on an interest inventory which indicated that her major interest was in clerical work. Disregarding all other evidence in the situation, the counselor insisted that the girl was unfitted for the work of a liberal arts college and would be happy only in a secretarial school. Tears on the part of the child, anger on the part of the parents, and hell-to-pay all around."

In *The Personnel and Guidance Journal*, John M. Rothney retells another school interest test anecdote that is near-legendary in the field. A semiliterate country boy received the school's highest score in literary interest, ranking at the 85 percentile. When the surprised counselor asked if he read a lot, he answered: "Naw, I don't read nawthin' much—except onct in a while a detectif magazine." The would-be Faulkner had a high "literary interest" only because he thought it would be nice to be an author, someone who he believed had "nothin' to do but write books."

This common disparity between a student's talent and his interests, among other liabilities, has convinced some critics that interest tests should not be given on a wide-spread basis in our schools. These same authors, Rothney and Schmidt, state in fact that the tests are "not only wastful but potentially very harmful." Says their critique: "An author [of interest tests] frequently chooses to name a test, a group of items or a single item, say, a measure of mechanical interest because he thinks it is. . . . Then, of course, after he has christened it he chooses a system attaching numbers to it, and it seems to become a scientific test."

Asking youngsters to mark off "interests" as a clue to a satisfactory life's work makes little sense, say the authors, especially when the children are unfamiliar with the alternatives. One popular interest test, for example, asks junior high school youngsters to choose among the following:

1. Sort and catalogue a valuable stamp collection.

2. Write a popular article on how a diesel engine works.

3. Determine the cost of manufacturing a new soap.

Obviously, Rothney points out, thirteen-year-olds would be intimate with only the first item, and have no experience of any kind with the other two. A guessing game of what Johnny "might like" if he knew about it could hardly be construed as valuable vocational guidance information.

In *The Personnel and Guidance Journal*, Joan R. Hess of the University of Wisconsin details a study in which Kuder scores of high school students were checked against occupations they eventually went into. The results: young people rarely enter occupations indicated by inventories taken while in school. Miss Hess does not, however, denigrate the "entertainment" value of such tests, and quotes one school-teacher: "The two periods in which the two pupils take the

Preference Record, score it, and plot their profiles are the two periods in the course that they like best." She adds her own postscript: "Interest inventories don't offer much more than that."

The obvious fact is that children's interests change (otherwise why isn't everybody a fireman?). One reason, that as parental influence decreases in later adolescence, true vocational interest—rather than parental pressure—begins to evolve, was pointed out in the *Guidance Journal* by William C. Cottle, professor of education at the University of Kansas. He tells the story of a boy of a prominent business family who scored high in "business" interest on entering college. After two years of schooling, however, his score on "social welfare" interest rose meteorically, passing his "business" interest. Says Cottle: "Now his pattern is really beginning to represent his own interests rather than those to which he was exposed in the restricted family environment."

For the past half-decade, we have heard the plaintive story of our nation's overcrowded colleges. However, as has finally been admitted, the college crush is a selective one: Johnny mostly has trouble finding a berth in the college of his choice, invariably either Harvard, Yale, Princeton, Columbia, Cal Tech, or other prestige institutions. In the name of this excessive supply of youngsters, we have seen the creation of the "College Boards," an academic joust which supposedly gives college admissions officers a better insight into an applicant's chances of successfully completing his B.A.

The College Entrance Examination Board test (the Scholastic Aptitude Test, or SAT), the Ohio State University Psychological Examination, and others, are taken by a majority of our high school seniors every year. How successful have they been? How well do they predict college success? Although not a brain watch in the strict sense, these tests—as we shall see—are heading toward testing areas which our youngsters, and behavioral science, are far from ready to handle.

In the *Review of Educational Research,* several authors have summed up the findings of "College Admissions-Selection Studies" over the past years and found a startling fact: despite the plethora of testing, high school grades are still the best single predictor of Johnny's success in college! In 263 studies, high school grades correlated roughly .50 with comprehensive freshman-year intellective criteria. The SAT (College Boards), the ACE (American Council on Education Psychological Examination), and the Ohio State averaged somewhat less: .47. Several achievement tests in widespread use, such as the Iowa, did about the same or worse—averaging .43 in eighteen studies of college freshmen. To try to give meaning to these coefficients, bear in mind that IQ scores and school grades generally relate about .50, as do the heights of fathers and sons—a less than satisfactory measure which makes it statistically possible to predict a "C" performance from a student and have him come up *magna cum laude* without ruffling the numbers.

Combining the high school grades and the SAT, for example, supposedly makes the prediction more accurate. But, according to twenty-one studies on the subject, using this dual peek increases the accuracy by only .07. Whether the scramble and strain is worth this minute improvement (in group statistics) over and above the youngster's high school record, we will leave to obviously enthusiastic member-subscribers of the test, and obliging high school educators who have made obeisance to college admissions people and College Boards their very way of life.

As a group, students appear to be surviving whatever obstacles the College Boards have conjured up. However, there is less chance that the youngsters (and our culture) will survive the next onslaught of college entrance testing, a new revolution being prepared by the brain watchers. Unfortunately, it is being encouraged by the desperate college admissions people, who have become obsessive in their desire to know beforehand how well Johnny will do.

Dr. Henry Dyer of the Educational Testing Service points out that college admissions people feel they know something about Johnny's academic ability, but now desperately want to know how hard he will *try*, once he gets to college, and hope that some personality test formula will lay bare this secret motivation. Dr. Dyer, who is skeptical about the creation of such a tool, states: "Because they feel the need is so great, they are convinced it must exist."

Dr. S. A. Kendrick, vice president of the College Entrance Examination Board, shares this skepticism, yet his organization has already spent "hundreds of thousands of dollars," and is in the midst of a search for just such a test. "Our membership wants personality testing, for they keep looking at cases of a bright boy with good SAT scores who should be a Phi Beta, but folds up instead," says Kendrick. "There are no devices at present sufficiently keen to measure these things accurately. If there were something that could measure persistence and motivation, we would like to have it. Now we can only infer this from a student's aptitude scores and grades. There is no research I know of now that could be carried to the point of the admissions office. Most of it has been self-report personality tests, but in spite of lie scales, they can be handled by bright students. Projectives are not terribly well worked out. Take the Group Rorschach—occasionally it can give you a fairly reliable estimate of psychosis. But if it tells us that a sixteen-year-old is dependent, so what? Do we want dependent sixteen-year-olds? Who knows?"

Dr. Kendrick's refreshing candor seems to place the personality tester light-years away from menacing high school seniors and their collegiate futures. Yet the encouragement actively being given to personality testers by Mr. Kendrick's own organization may make it a reality within a matter of years. The fact is that six years ago this very same College Entrance Examination Board, hearing the bray of its member college admissions men, placed announcements in almost every psychological journal asking psychologists to submit detailed proposals to test the "noncognitive" aspects, or personality, of college applicants. "We received approximately 120 proposals," says a College Board spokesman. "A lot of it was junk—but some of them appeared promising." Of the "promising" ones, the College Boards have supported some half-dozen with research grants, one of which may one day be the personality obstacle that will cast your Johnny (mine will be sufficiently informed) onto the education refuse pile as emotionally ill equipped to enjoy higher learning.

What kind of "promising" personality tests may students have to face? A recent College Board publication, "A Biographical Inventory" ($2.00), describes one, a Fordham University research project based on the assumption that answers to a scored student biographical form can distinguish "positive" from "negative" students and thus choose future alumni. The Fordham researchers first picked out three groups: 50 positive, 50 average, and 50 negative students, graded by a faculty jury of three and based on such items as their faculty advisor reports, student government records, Office of Psychological Service records, academic records, and even their ROTC military rating.

The Fordham personality test operates on the thesis that there is a successful "Fordham type" and that he can be described in detail, then found in others by comparing life histories, background, and likes and dislikes. All the test groups filled out the biographical inventory which pressed the undergraduates for such items as the number of siblings, rank in high school graduating class, magazines and books read, hobbies, part-time work, favorite plays and movies, reading and TV habits, and a checklist of problems. Using the tests for comparison, they found that 80 items *appeared* to discriminate between the groups (using any items that had the insignificant significance of .20 correlation, or more), then winnowed it down to a test of only 27 questions.

Who is the successful Fordhamite, by tester standards? He is typically good-man-on-campus with the appropriate number of high grades, extracurricular activities, aim for graduate work, plus a few surprises: he enjoys the *Saturday Evening Post,* Latin was his favorite high school subject and social studies was least liked. The College Board Magazine, *The Review,* in its Spring 1960 issue discusses the Fordham experiment and touts what it calls "its successful use of a biographical inventory in predicting adjustment and achievement of college students." The facts, as revealed by the research report itself, are considerably less. Had the Biographical Inventory been operational as an admissions screen at Fordham, it would not only have failed to distinguish the "negative" from the "average" control group, but would have refused admission to a *majority* (52 percent) of Fordham's best students!

The college testers fall back on the statistical rationalization that such a biographical screen would (in their opinion) keep out more "negatives" than "positives." Even if true, which is unproven, it is little reason to adopt an arbitrary personality admissions policy that turns away brilliant New Yorkers—more interested in the social sciences than Latin —from the city's only Jesuit institution.

A somewhat different approach, to mesh the personality of students with the "personality" of the college, is being researched at Syracuse University under a grant from the same College Board. The testers believe that, like students, stone-and-ivy have a psyche. They have already personality-tested 100 colleges with their College Characteristics Index, a 300-question inventory filled out by students who rate their *schools* on such traits as "Sexuality-Prudence." How do you rate a school's eroticism? Simple, says the brain watcher: with True-False statements. Try these on your college's psyche:

Bermuda shorts, pin-up pictures, etc., are common on this campus.

Some of the more popular students have a knack for making witty, subtle remarks with a slight sexy tinge.

Having established the personality profile of the college on such traits as "rebellion, objectivity, dominance, change, order," the tester sets these up as environmental "presses" while the student's own personality is described as a "need." Knowing the emotional ills of the alma mater, all they need to know is how students, tested on a 300-item "Activities Index" with the same traits, will score. By checking his "needs" against the school's "presses," the tester can easily spot an ill-fitting outlander. For example, the student who does not enjoy "seeing love stories in the movies" or avoids "flirting" may not be permitted to don the school tie of an institution where Sexuality is high and Prudence is low.

The ridiculous idea of mating student and college personality (if it really exists or could be measured), of inbreeding the faults as well as strengths of the school, and excluding diverse types of students, would not deserve a critique no matter how negative, if the work were not being done with the financial backing of the College Board. Reason will undoubtedly intervene before such an idea is adopted. If not, not only may youngsters have to go into intellectual training for schools noted for an academic personality, but they may have to start all-night carousing in their early teens to prepare for some of our more socially oriented institutions.

Whether to use personality testing, with all its implications, is a ponderous decision for the college admissions man, who is usually not a psychologist. Although not guiltless (his shrill cries for more measuring tools are what encourage the obliging brain watcher), he is confused. He can hardly wade through, let alone evaluate, the hundreds of research reports in professional magazines—*Personnel and Guidance Journal, Journal of Educational Psychology,* and others—on the supposed relationship between a student's grades and his personality test scores.

Many of the studies are sober, carefully constructed experiments and others pure exercises in statistical fancy that hopefully will not be seen by admissions officers. But one factor is always present: complete and chaotic disagreement. D. C. McLelland, using Thematic Apperception cards, for example, claims a .51 correlation between his projective evaluations and college grades. In the *Journal of Psychology,* E. L. Lowell found the same test to be an abject flop (.05) in predicting the scholarship of testees.

In *Educational and Psychological Measurement,* two faculty members of state teachers' colleges found that the Guilford-Zimmerman Temperament Schedule—when given to students and checked against their grades—showed no correlation for most traits including emotional stability, objectivity, and friendliness, and only very low (.13 to .16) correlations for "purposiveness, cooperativeness, and masculinity." At the same time, in *The Personnel and Guidance Journal*—while stating that the standard MMPI appeared to be of no use in predicting scholarship—an author claims to have created his own personality scale (Z) from the MMPI which supposedly correlates .61 with grades.

Dr. Harrison Gough of the University of California's Institute of Personality Assessment and Research came to the conclusion after studying 6,000 high school students that the venerated traits of industry, patience, honesty, conscientiousness, and warmth were present in scholars, while the villainous characteristics of "autocratic, blustery, conceited, and stubborn" were signs of the dullard. Dr. John French of the Educational Testing Service, however, exploded this gentlemanly hypothesis when he found that a set of equally admirable traits was not at all related to college academic accomplishment. In probably the broadest validation study ever attempted in this field, French tested 4,833 collegians from eight colleges in 1953 with a battery of achievement, aptitude, interest, and personality tests, then followed them up in 1957 with a thorough check of their four-year grades.

Were the scholars, as the California researchers said, the resolute, the tolerant, persistent, stable collegians? Likely enough, the scholars and nonscholars proved out like everybody else, including a proportional number of neurotic, intolerant, daydreaming louts. Dr. French's research report states that his work "reveals no consistent or particularly meaningful relationships between any of the criteria and any of the personality scales."

A candid article by a University of Minnesota researcher in the January, 1960 *Personnel and Guidance Journal* (after failing to construct a workable "Scholastic Interest Scale" from the Strong) summed up the responsible opinion in this very complex, and very emotional, field—an opinion that hopefully will be studied carefully by every college official before embarking on any exotic adventures in brain watchery. "Although considerable research effort has been expended," says the author, "college grades are not predicted more accurately today than was the case ten or fifteen years ago."

The inability to find the measurable link between intellect and personality distresses the tester, who writhes at the sight of dangling unstructured threads in the loom of life. His pain would be eased considerably if he could learn to look at the search for intellectual achievement as being related to an individual's *own* personality, and the test as one that measures whether he properly exploits what he has.

Although it occurs to few psychometrists, some bright introverted students use their ease in isolation for thought and worthwhile introspection, or at the very least, for extra study time. The extroverted student of equal capacity can generally find enough time away from people he enjoys to do his study chores; meanwhile his affair with life brings, for him, a flood of stimulation. The bright persistent student hammers away at a problem until he thoroughly conquers it; the bright impulsive student spurts ahead of his instructor and the curriculum to new avenues of intellectual excitement; the conforming student absorbs all that is thrown at him within the structure of accepted ideas; the rebellious student questions and offers some of his own ideas. All use their own personalities to explore different dimensions of intellect. Despite sophomoric statements by some testers, no one personality, or trait—as studies indicate—has any monopoly on good college grades, accomplishment, or intellectual achievement.

Although some colleges, like Colgate University, are reportedly using personality tests "experimentally" to screen applicants, the tester has not yet cracked the undergraduate college on any sizable basis. He has, however, heavily infiltrated the professional schools in the past decade, and today thousands of would-be ministers and doctors must produce personality credentials in order to join the fraternity of Hippocrates or that of Jehovah. In fact, if a recent personality project at law schools had not fortuitously failed, the legal profession would be in the same uninviting situation.

The theological schools are deepest in psychological testing, in the business of shaping our future ministry with dull psychological tools. A survey of 53 Protestant seminaries by the National Council of Churches shows that 37, or 70 percent of them, use personality tests in selecting applicants for the ministry. The most common tests are the Minnesota Multiphasic (21 schools), the Bernreuter (12), the Strong

Vocational Interest Blank (21), and the Rorschach inkblots (8). Two large denominations, the Presbyterian and the United Lutheran, have worked out a basic personality battery for almost all their applicants: the MMPI and the Strong. Last year, the United Lutheran, the largest of the Lutheran groups (2,500,000 membership), gave this ready-mix "Ministry" battery to 2,000 ministry candidates applying to their ten seminaries. The same tests are used in the eight seminaries of the United Presbyterian Church, with local variations, such as the addition of the Guilford-Zimmerman Temperament Schedule at the Princeton Theological Seminary in Princeton, New Jersey.

Why these tests? What makes a good Protestant minister and how do you test for such an elusive commodity as a divine "call"? One testing officer in the United Lutheran Church is frank about his group's psychological screening: they really do not know what makes a good Protestant minister. They are hopeful only that the MMPI will help them screen out the "psychotics," and that the Strong Blank, when used with a theological twist, will help pinpoint seminarians who are oriented in the direction of the new socially-conscious ministry rather than the fundamentalist hell-and-brimstone religion, which modern church leaders consider antediluvian. Both the Lutheran and Presbyterian testers confess that the Strong scale for "minister" is outdated. (It compares the attitudes and prejudices of the average minister of a generation ago with those of the applicants.) In fact, a good score on the "minister" key is not important to many denominations; they prefer to see an applicant score well on Group V of the test—as a YMCA secretary, social worker, or social science teacher.

How a devout young man is evaluated for a ministry career was described in detail by the New York central office of an important Protestant denomination. The student had been interviewed by a local church committee, which, once satisfied with him personally, had him take the Strong and MMPI tests. His test blanks were then sent on to the church's main office in New York, which dispatched them to Testscor, a midwestern electronic scoring organization. Once scored, the raw tabulations were returned to the church office, where a psychologist-minister—who had never seen his devout subject—made an impressive verbal interpretation that was to quash the candidate's hope of ever ministering to a congregation.

"He showed a high interest in Group V on the Strong,

which is favorable. It indicates that he likes to work with people," the minister-tester stated. "But we have to ask ourselves 'Why?' He scored high in the minister scale too, which, because of the old standardization sample, favors a more narrow and prejudiced type of person. He also came out high on the 'policeman' and 'YMCA physical director' scale, which I do not consider favorable. The most important indication that he is not minister material for our church is his profile on the MMPI. High scores on the Ps, Sc, Pa scales indicate that he is an autocratic individual, blustery, undiplomatic, with a negativism that he uses to protect himself. He is compulsive, rebellious, and disidentified with people. He is the sort of person that has to be in control of the situation, and although he prefers to work with people he does it in a dogmatic way."

This casual use of the MMPI and the Strong is highly uncalled for in the serious job of choosing Protestant ministers. In fact, despite warnings that untrained personnel should not attempt to interpret the MMPI, the United Lutheran Church has faculty members at its ten seminaries— often not psychologists—give and interpret the test to 2,000 prospective ministry students every year.

Judging from conversations with several church psychologists and those responsible for selecting ministerial candidates, it appears that personality testing has replaced a thoughtful analysis of what a minister should be in the current American culture. The clergyman-psychologist who conducted the blind MMPI analysis laments the fact that many men now entering the ministry are "passive" types unable to make a profound moral, social, or religious impact on their communities, an impact that is needed if Protestantism is to stem the tide of mounting indifference. Yet despite the crisis, what do church testers, including this one, seek out: overadjusted YMCA secretaries, or at least caricatures of these much-maligned men. The atypical man—perhaps like the candidate who scored as "compulsive, undiplomatic, and rebellious"—may be the very minister needed to save his church from vitiation.

Testing abuse in the ministry is partially the result of an obsession among the more liberal northern and eastern sects, Presbyterian, United Lutheran, etc., to scrupulously avoid the recruiting of Elmer Gantry-like ministers, religious "fanatics" and fundamentalist preachers who see damnation in all modern mores. Says one Presbyterian official involved in a minister brain watch: "We are looking for men with the proper motivation. Some say a minister has to have a 'calling from the Holy Spirit.' As soon as we get over that nonsense, we will be all right."

A man's "calling" for the ministry, and whether it comes from the Spirit above, or a spirit within him, is ostensibly measured by a new ministerial test, the "Theological Inventory," developed by Reverend F. Kling, a psychologist-clergyman working with the Educational Testing Service on a research program in collaboration with the National Council of Churches. The test attempts to measure a man's motivation for the ministry in two basic terms: special leading, the traditional "call;" and natural leading, the modern viewpoint of the ministry as a profession that deals with people, and with God, as part of all humanity. As Kling states it: "In the conception of the person looking for special leading, God enters directly into human affairs, and causes His works and His will to be unmistakenly evident to the believer . . ." To the natural leader, however, he says: "God's role in human affairs is more indirect, His works indistinguishable from natural causes and effects . . ."

The test favors no one type over the other, but most liberal denominations make it clear that they prefer to avoid the old-fashioned "special leader" type. There is considerable disagreement in Protestantism whether Kling has isolated the basic "personality" factor of the ministry. Meanwhile, the test has been given to incoming students (not used for selection) at twenty-three seminaries in a dozen Protestant denominations, and these future ministers, and their Kling scores, will be followed up for some time to come.

Even the Catholic Church is yielding to the tester's blandishments. Two years ago, two Catholic seminaries in New York, Cathedral College and St. Joseph's, adopted personality testing for seminarians, and are presently "watching it" to see if the program proves of value. A local clinical psychologist who has been engaged jointly by the seminaries gives applicants for the priesthood a full battery of tests— IQ, MMPI, Figure Drawing Test—plus a depth interview. According to one seminary director, not all applicants "rejected" by the tester are turned away from the priesthood. "In some cases we give the lad the benefit of the doubt," he states, pointing out that this provides a chance to check the performance of some tester "rejects" against the "recommended" students. Although far from a scientific control, the possibility that the rejects will prove to be able priests may provide the ancient church with a relatively inexpensive lesson in modern brain watching.

Despite Protestantism's heavy flirtation with testing, not everyone in the ministry agrees that personality tests can help in the search for dedication to God. Although many applicants to the nondenominational Union Theological Seminary in New York do have MMPI scores—given by local church groups—attached to their applications, Union does not take the test very seriously. "Within the range of MMPI scores that most applicants get it is impossible to make decisive judgments," says Dr. Donald Dawe (Th.D.), dean of students, who is equally skeptical about the Strong and Kling as minister-pickers. The admissions officer of Drew Theological, a Methodist institution in Madison, New Jersey shares his doubt. Says she: "There are no good personality indices being used in the selection of theological students." Both critics, however, constitute a minority of churchdom. Today, in few business houses of Mammon is brain watching as devoutly worshiped as in the schools of God.

The nation's law schools were almost struck with a similar test-blight not long ago, but were saved by a simple experiment conducted beforehand by the Law School Admission Test Committee and the Educational Testing Service. ETS constructed a sizable battery from ETS' own Personality Research Inventory, through tests for "tolerance of ambiguity" (a trait supposedly of value to lawyers), dogmatism, social aspirations, gregariousness, sentence completion, social conscience, and even a set of sixteen special Thematic Apperception pictures to measure "need for achievement" in social, economic, academic, and professional areas. (Economic achievement was measured by three pictures, including one of a man buying a camera on time payments.)

The tests were given to students in sixteen law schools throughout the nation and checked against the only available criteria, first-semester and first-year law school grades. "The results were very negative," candidly states an ETS spokesman. In fact, they did worse in predicting success in law school than the nonpersonality Law School Admission Test, the predictive value of which (.33 in nine schools measured) ETS had hoped to improve in the first place. The two-year experiment having been conducted with restraint and careful validation, personality testing for lawyers was struck from the record.

The personality of the American physician is a heavily discussed backyard and parlor topic, much of which would undoubtedly sound unflattering to the doctor's ears. Although what many believe is a deteriorating human situation in the medical profession cannot wholly be blamed on the testers, there has been an increasing emphasis on the personality testing of medical school applicants during the past half-generation.

The American Psychiatric Association has stated: "We do not yet know what special qualities make a good medical school student or proficient physician." Nor has anyone developed the personality pattern for the "ideal" doctor. But despite this, according to a survey published in the *Journal of Medical Education*, 15 of our medical schools are using personality tests in processing applicants. Of the 15, 4 report that they use the Strong "doctor" key (how your prejudices compare with those of a group of successful doctors); 7 use the MMPI; 2 the Rorschach; and 2 the Kuder Preference Record. Recently the Strong has even developed several "specialist" keys for closer checking of group biases.

Testing is in flux in the medical community. Eleven other medical schools state they plan to adopt it, while 16 more have tried and discarded the technique, ostensibly as worthless. One of the disenchanted is the State University of New York College of Medicine in Brooklyn (formerly Long Island College of Medicine), which for six years recently gave applicants to the school a figure drawing test. After the hopeful young doctors had drawn their sketches, they were evaluated by a staff psychologist, who asked in a recent report: "Are there indications that he has sufficient resources to stand up under the inevitable stresses of medical school, or would his sensitiveness and human insecurities be too heavily taxed? Is there evidence of bizarre thinking or of deviant personality reactions?"

The "indications" in artless drawings of unclothed females may have stifled an occasional Schweitzer, but the threat at this medical school, at least, has been removed by "administrative policy."

The pervading influence of the brain watcher on our students, from elementary grades to graduate school, should create a sizable blip on our personal radar screens. Allowing ourselves to be catalogued for economic survival is not notable, but perhaps defensible in industries where personal courage is rewarded with career oblivion. But the ease with which we have ceded our youngsters' minds to the tester's harsh experiments has been an invitation for him to expand his activities and, as we have seen, to have the schools—like industry—enforce his will. Whatever else we do about it from here on, we must credit the brain watcher with a spectacular and virtually bloodless initial victory.

8 SO YOU WANT TO BE AN EXECUTIVE?

"What is a good executive? Well, first of all, he's scintillating, brilliant, extremely analytical, a man who thinks spontaneously on his feet, and is aware of every facet of business."

This response from a New York management consultant is probably the most innocent description extant in the field. No one, surely few of us, could fear such a cataloguing of the intelligent competent male, and surely few corporations could resist hiring him. The unfortunate truth, however, is that many testers (and the clients who pay the $100 to $250 per executive probe) do not agree that this uncommonly brilliant individual is necessarily what the corporation needs or, more explicitly, what they have ordered.

The tester has in fact developed an exquisitely elaborate set of criteria for the executive, from the shadings of his political opinions to the emotional stability of his overweight wife. As many successful management men have learned, survival depends more on the mastery, either intuitive or learned, of these traits than the "scintillation" or "spontaneity" described by the well-meaning management consultant.

Various parts of this volume have been implicit primers and the savvy corporate male has naturally absorbed many of the test-taking hints while contemplating conquest of the brain watcher, for thrill and profit. Parts of all testing techniques have meaning for the executive or the aspiring member of the management class. However, the proper study of the tester-executive relationship, and how to emerge grinning on top of it, requires a detailed compendium of executive traits and tests used to measure them. In this chapter we expect to explain these in some depth, hopeful that men of scintillation and good will who will lead the next generation of American industry can always use additional Freudian armament in their struggle upwards. Here then is a modern executive's guide to "personal image building."

POLITICAL AND ECONOMIC OPINIONS

A psychologist-tester at the Manhattan management counseling firm of George Fry ripped away at the coyness usually put up around this subject: "Most all good executives are conservative Republicans," he says candidly. "They are not striving to have any radical change made in the political and social philosophy. One of the things we look for in the good executive is the desire to identify with the haves instead of the have-nots."

In the past decade especially, the Corporation has been heavily influenced by the Liberal Ethic and its ramifications, by the aggressive humanism of the multibillion-dollar foundations they spawned, and the necessity of projecting a liberal and progressive image in their corporate advertising and public relations. In the public and political arena, industrialists such as Paul Hoffman and Nelson Rockefeller have wrapped themselves in liberal glory, while enlightened business leaders such as Thomas Watson, Jr. have even invited larger corporate taxes, if necessary, for better government. In the welfare area, the corporation rivals the government as a patron of collectivism, outpacing the government as a dispenser of such "liberal" panaceas as prepaid health insurance, sick benefits, and the sharing by workers and executives—over and above their wages—in the profits of industry.

The executive tester, however, has never been told, and he still operates in the backwash of a disappearing tenet in which the word "liberal" is an anathema. He is convinced that he best serves the corporation by populating it with unreconstructed reactionaries. How is allegiance to the Grand Old Party and nineteenth-century economic intransigency spotted by the tester? Often he simply asks a man about his attitudes, directly or indirectly, during the depth interview. If not, he has a choice of several paper-and-pencil tests with scales keyed to identify the secret liberal.

The Minnesota Personality Scale, for example, has an entire section—Part V, Economic Conservatism—devoted to identification of woolyheads, Democrats, and even advocates of "cooperative housing." Sample questions from the conservative scale are a reasonable guide to whether your political-economic attitudes need a retrogressive revamping: The MPS asks whether you, for example, Strongly Agree, Agree, are Undecided, Disagree, or Strongly Disagree, with the following?

People should not patronize stores that are being picketed by labor unions.

The government ought to guarantee a living to those who can't find work.

Most great fortunes are made honestly.

The executive receives five points for each strongly conservative answer on the scoring sheet. The suitable executive is antilabor, and against cooperatives and public housing, even though all are supported in the national platform of the Republican Party. If you agree with the first two questions and disagree with the last—feel intuitively that there is a touch of larceny connected with every great fortune—you may be happier elsewhere than in an executive suite.

While it is essential to appear conservative, it is equally unwise to "strongly agree" with all paleozoic viewpoints and look, as says the test author, like "someone with reactionary viewpoints which exclude the absorption of new material in some social sciences." Moderation on the side of conservative Republicanism (avoiding the native social radicalism of the late Senator Taft) is the key.

Several other tests pursue the same dogged liberal. Personnel Institute's popular "Ess-ay Inventory" poses a set of twenty-five socioeconomic-political queries to be answered through a range from CT (Certainly True) to CF (Certainly False). Try these three as a gauge of which side of center you test out on:

The Chinese should be granted the same opportunity for citizenship that we grant to Europeans.

The things that wealthy businessmen want the government to do are usually good for the country as a whole.

Our country should use armed force if necessary to protect the property of its citizens in Latin American countries.

The obvious answers—against Chinese citizenship, in favor of armed support for economic investments, and a general belief that the attitudes of the business community always promote the general welfare—mark you as a fit and trusted management man.

Although the tester welcomes it, a conservative approach is not the only requirement in the economic realm. He wants to feel secure that things "economic" permeate your being, and that money—in the general scheme of life, as a symbol of status and accomplishment—and the necessity to accumulate it are your prime movers. Even though this attitude need not be learned today, when our lives seem dominated by money, the tester has set a trap for the *nouveau* materialist whose heart is not properly ensconced in his wallet.

As we have seen (in Chapter II: The Big Quiz) the widely used Study of Values attempts to isolate this economic drive in contrast to other life values: the religious, political, theoretical, social, aesthetic. According to most test users, the true executive should always score highest on "economic," and generally next highest on "political" drives, with low scores on "aesthetic" and "religious." Unless the work touches on research, he should score only average in "theoretical," or scientific, values.

As an example of this proper economic, money-pragmatic drive, the SOV poses this true-false dilemma: "The main object of scientific research should be the discovery of truth rather than its practical application." The skilled (or schooled) executive knows that the answer is "false."

To impress the tester on the Study of Values it might help to memorize this little testing ode, composed by the author, in halting meter, from the essence of the test:

> Art is ridiculous,
> Music a bore,
> The classics meaningless
> To the man who wants more.

Science has its place,
Technology's fine,
But no thrill compared
To multiplying what's mine.

Napoleon and Caesar
Served reasonable careers,
But what a pity men like Galileo
Have business fears.

I'll take a sales manager to a clergyman
Every time.
Ah, but Henry Ford and his Flivver A—
That's civilization sublime.

The political and economic mind check is reserved not only for corporate brass, but often for the executive trainee, and even the foreman, who is also expected to think "management." One tester recalls such a politicoeconomic borderline case. "A young fellow was being considered for the job of foreman of a printing plant," the tester explained. "For a number of years he had been a union officer and we were concerned about his personal views. However, after testing him I could see that he had been in a struggle with himself, and that now he could consider himself a member of management."

The hopeful, or advancing, executive who is driven by liberal thoughts and unconvinced that business activity is an end meant to dominate our civilization can, like the young foreman, engage himself in a private struggle—a tussle of passion in which the tester hopes the liberal will be destroyed and the management man will emerge victorious. Of course, should the executive become sufficiently successful, and independently wealthy, to approach the brain watcher on equal terms, he might, like Secretary of Defense McNamara (formerly of Ford), label himself an "Independent," especially during a Democratic administration when the euphemism is still well right of current center. However, for most of us, it is simpler merely to "pass" as a mild conservative, using our knowledge of the tester to provide a realistic camouflage.

SCORED BIOGRAPHIES

Since childhood we have been ingrained with the concept that having humble or comfortable beginnings, what we did with our spare time when still fourteen, or whether Papa was a Brahmin Yankee or a second-generation Armenian had nothing to do with eventual success—that the silver ring could be snatched by anyone agile and competent enough. Now, the tester tells us, it was all a sweet but painful hoax. Our origins and the biographical data accumulated on the way up, he says, are the true criteria of our worth. And, naturally, he can measure it, with a scored life history test. Of all the excesses from the brain watcher's black grab bag, this one is possibly the most damaging in a democratic society.

A successful executive being groomed by an executive talent scout for a $40,000-a-year vice-presidency, was asked to fill out a Biographical Inventory. Although not unlike the usual application blank, it was more detailed in its inquisition. How many brothers and sisters? How large was your home town? Were you an officer of your senior class in high school? Incredibly, the application blank had the information neatly outlined in multiple-choice questions such as: "How far did your mother go in school?", with five choices ranging from "She didn't complete grammar school" to "She is a college graduate."

Whether the vice president gets the job will depend on how well his own life history, from birth to yesterday, matches the biography of the company's "successful" men. If coming from a large family rather than being an only child, for example, seems to predominate in the firm, it does you—a lone sibling—little good to argue that this is not a crucial work factor. *It is,* says the biographical personality tester.

The scored biography is making joining the corporation analogous to certain country club memberships: you must first provide background credentials. To find the proper credentials, we need only study a typical scored biography, such as one used by Richardson, Bellows, Henry & Company, New York management consultants through whose offices many of our leading executives are funneled.

RBH use a 52-question, multiple-choice scored biography entitled "Individual Background Survey." Their key is naturally not public information, but much of it can be easily deduced. For example: What was the economic level of the neighborhood in which you grew up? (A) High; (B) Above Average; (C) Average; (D) Below Average; (E) Poor. Despite tycoons such as Floyd Odlum, who once rode the back of a swift ostrich in a rodeo for fifty cents, the biography testers are convinced that good executives come from "stable middle-class homes," and neither the affluent nor the poor have the proper birthright for the corporation.

The range of RBH's scored biography, like most, is personally kaleidoscopic. It covers your education, your parents' education, your father's national origin, number of children in the family while growing up, your family's economic and social vintage, whether you loafed or worked as a teen-ager, your extracurricular activities in school, how many people are now dependent on your support, armed forces service and rank, how often you have been a leader of community or school activities, the kind of leisure you shared with papa, your standing in class, marital happiness, and even how many times you changed schools before the age of sixteen.

To put your best "life" forward, we can safely deduce that it is best to have native-born, high school- or college-educated parents, spring from a middle-class background, and be one of several rather than an only child. You worked as a youngster whether you needed the income or not, served in the armed forces, preferably as a commissioned or noncommissioned officer, shared hunting and athletic pursuits with dad, graduated in the upper quarter of your class, lived and studied in the same community throughout your childhood, have three or four dependent on your livelihood, and, naturally, are a perennial PTA and Community Chest mogul.

The partially published key of the American Chamber of Commerce's scored biographical inventory supports this approach. (With the help of a Florida tester, the Chamber claims to have developed a biography that ostensibly differentiates 71 percent of its staff executives from the inferior Chamber men throughout the country.)

What are the application-blank essentials of the Chamber executive, a job that commands considerably less pay than a similar responsible job in industry? Many of the answers, none of them surprising, are provided in a report in the *Journal of American Chamber of Commerce Executives*. "He typically was drawn from the middle-class socioeconomic background. His childhood was spent in a happy, stable family life," says the *Journal* article. "The majority either had to help their families financially while growing up or worked because they wanted to. Any similarity here between the future Chamber chief executive and the familiar Horatio Alger story apparently is not coincidental!" The analogy is interesting especially since Horatio Alger's heroes —who rose from poverty and near-homelessness to achieve riches and honor—could never have passed the Chamber's middle-class-oriented inventory.

The executive is a lifelong leader, and he is constantly involved in extracurricular activities, generally in a top slot, the Chamber report indicates. In fact, in the first group of forty-seven executives studied, says the report, "41 percent had been president of their high school class!" He was also a debater, a participant in school plays, and an editor of his school paper or annual. He takes an active interest in sports, and his reading preferences are magazines, newspapers, and material on business and commerce. "A hard worker," says a *Nation's Business* article on the Chamber study, "he puts in 58 hours a week on the job. He appears to place more emphasis on his career than anything else."

The accuracy of these biographical studies is doubtful for, as we shall see, statistical generalizations make individual evaluations virtually meaningless. The biographical inventory measures only the differentiation between the applicant and the mean successful man. Furthermore, even these claims admit sizable error, variances which are probably several times as great in reality. The Chamber's scored biography, for example, using its suggested critical score of 41 (so many points for each favorable item) would not only eliminate 66 percent of the below-average group, but would force the expulsion of 29 percent of the superior men. And, if their figures have statistical sense, approximately half their average producers would also be turned away.

What does it mean for the man who may one day have to submit to the scored biography? Plainly it is not wise, or feasible, to concoct an entirely new life history; your imaginative tale might be checked. However, one of the reasons why many "successful" men score higher may be that the same self-protective attitudes that shape their daily lives have helped them shape their biographies. Without fabricating entirely, the prudent executive, born and raised in a fading, small industrial Ohio town where his working-class father rented the upstairs of a then thirty-year-old Victorian Gothic with peeled shingles, could—with only the slight strain implicit in a common American facility for glorifying our past—visualize the homestead as at least "average" or possibly "above average" without injuring anyone, and possibly adding to the ancestral village's pride. As for Dad, who came from Ireland or Czechoslovakia at the age of five: how easy to remember only his dedicated patriotism, and check him off an "American-born." He worked hard "toward" that high school diploma until he had to be apprenticed at the machine shop at fifteen to help out at home. Why not an honorary high school diploma, much like the ones granted many World War II veterans—especially since it was his concern for then-unattainable education that insured your college degree? Strain further: surely during his forty-five years at the lathe, at one time he served as a shop foreman, a fellow member of the management team.

Common sense, the hints implicit in the multiple choices, and a scrupulous eye for the future rather than the past will generally insure a passing executive grade. Keep in mind that if the tester has decided to unmake the American dream, we may be duty-bound to make it vibrant again, even if it requires a hyperbole or two in the common good.

The morality of such an approach is decidedly on the side of the employee. When seeking a job, we offer dedication to the position but make no claims of ethnic or communal superiority, or grant the tester (or the corporation) the right to deride our beginnings for his profit. If it were not an abused notion, we might say it was un-American.

RELIGION

Religious devotion and the corporation do not blend well. The corporation will not openly tolerate freethinkers or even agnostics, but it—or at least its brain watchers—distrusts the soul who offers true piety to any God except business. If they spot him, say on the religious scale of the Study of Values, or in a depth interview, he may be counseled to enter the ministry, but leave production to the harder-headed. That the spiritual (the tester generally prefers to call it the "mystical") conflicts with the pragmatism of modern business is one of the brain watcher's fervent beliefs. On the religious scale of the Study of Values, on which, says one tester, "successful people score low," is this spiritual trap: "Would you consider it important for your child to secure training in: (a) Religion; (b) Athletics." Despite your own convictions, it is wiser to evidence more interest in the Little League than in Leviticus.

However, the executive is expected to be a churchgoer and, if he likes, even a pillar of the vestry. Says one tester, summing up many brain watchers' attitudes toward the proper relationship between the executive and his Maker: "Good executives are generally churchgoers but not pious people. They buy church and religion as something that is sociologically worthwhile."

CONFIDENCE

Dr. Theodore A. Jackson (Ph.D.), head of psychological services for Stevenson, Jordan & Harrison, Inc., management consultants, explained the unique importance of executive self-confidence with the help of an impressive mimeographed chart entitled "Psychological Foundations for General Competence." At the top of his chart, Dr. Jackson has written a tester's imitation of Dr. Einstein's formula for the conversion of mass and energy, $E = MC^2$. In its new form it reads: GC (General Competence) = I (Intelligence) $\times$ D (Drive) $\times$ C^2 (Confidence). "The good executive," he says in explanation of his symbolism, "need not be the brightest one, but he must be one of the most confident. Even a Phi Beta man with low confidence is of little practical value to most corporations."

The relative unimportance of intelligence compared to confidence in Jackson's formula is easily visualized by checking it against his model, Einstein's equation, in which "M," the mass, occupies the same relative position as "Intelligence." The tremendous bang over Alamogordo verified Einstein's equation: the "E," for energy, exploded out of a comparatively small mass (since made smaller) and only achieved its cataclysmic proportions because of the immensity of C^2, the speed of light squared. Similarly, executive confidence —guts, balls, moxie, self-assurance, ascendancy, or what have you—taken to the second power is the equational factor that really makes the executive suite secure.

Dr. Jackson's magic formula and its emphasis on confidence is a mathematical synthesis of much opinion in the testing field. Controlled confidence, rather than brilliance, is truly the hallmark of the modern executive. Nevertheless, many testers do give a typical IQ test (Wechsler, Otis) and expect you to score at least around the 110–120 level. Although far from a genius score (most college students do as well), it is a reasonable performance, assuring the tester that he is not recommending a backward adult born with masterful assurance.

The factor of confidence is measured on almost every popular personality test, often with the same, slightly altered, or borrowed questions, and it is not too difficult for a man to present himself as having as much confidence as Stalin at Yalta. The confident executive is expected to score somewhere between the seventy-fifth and ninetieth percentile of the general population, scrupulously avoiding the top few percent as carefully as he does the spineless three-fourths of the general population.

On the Bernreuter, self-confidence is measured on scale F1-C, which, peculiarly enough, is called "self-confidence." Confidence questions on the Bernreuter are of the "leadership" and "shyness" type and are not difficult to anticipate. For example: "At a reception or tea, do you feel reluctant to meet the most important person present?" As a mental key to confidence on the Bernreuter, keep in mind that you are seldom reluctant, you lead, you are impervious, you bluff—you are human steel, coated with unpitted chromium plate.

The Thurstone Temperament Schedule has a somewhat similar scale called "Dominant," which asks such questions as: "Are you likely to take charge in case of an accident?" If you had not noticed, the executive does. The forced-choice Gordon Personal Profile labels executive upper lip as "ascendancy," and measures it with sets of four statements, each of which relates to a person's Ascendancy, Responsibility, Emotional Stability, and Sociability. The testee is asked to mark which of the four is "most like" him, and which is "least like" him. For example:

> Free from worry or care.
> Lacks a sense of responsibility.
> Not interested in mixing with the opposite sex.
> Skillful in handling other people.

The properly *ascendant* executive is most skillful in handling people.

However, mastery of the question form is not full executive protection. The projective tester has a deeper view of self-confidence, which, as we have seen, he probes with inkblots and other paraphernalia of his art. To the Rorschach man, confidence is more accurately a man's "self-concept," or "what he thinks of himself way down." Here, we can mainly recapitulate general advice given in Chapter III: The Clinical Testers; the confident executive handles his inkblots masterfully, populating them with humans in action. If he does see animals, they are invariably large snarling beasts, generally bears or lions. The man who conjures up small animals and humans in ethereal smiling poses is obviously too unsure of himself to handle a corporate credit card.

EXECUTIVE OVERDRIVE

Do not make the error, however, of thinking that corporate confidence, as valuable as it is, was ever meant to include chestiness, or distaste for organizational discipline or authority. "Men love to follow the decisions of superiors whose competence they respect. But decisiveness is not obstinacy or bullheadedness," warns a spokesman of Rohrer, Hibler & Replogle in an article in *Modern Industry*.

William E. Henry, who has been associated with Social Research, Inc. of Chicago, in a paper entitled "The Business Executive: A Study in the Psychodynamics of a Social Role," pointed out the inherent danger of ever becoming so inflated that you consider yourself superior to, or outside the control of, the corporation. Says he:

> The successful executive posits authority as a controlling but helpful relationship to superiors. He looks to his superiors as persons of more advanced training and experience whom he can consult on special problems and who issue to him certain guiding directives. He does not see the authority figures in his environment as destructive or prohibiting forces. In contrast a few executives of the "Self-made," driving type characteristic of the past of business enterprise maintain a specific concept of authority with regard to Self. They are the men who most always forge their own frontiers, who are unable to operate within anyone else's framework, to whom cooperation and teamwork are foreign concepts.

One of these vibrant nonteamers of the type who built America and his inevitable failure in the sloggish corporate environment was described by Dr. Burleigh Gardner, executive director of Social Research, Inc. in an article in *Advanced Management*.

A 2,000-employee firm was looking for a new personnel director, and a young man of thirty, who had a brilliant record with a management consulting firm in setting up personnel systems, was being considered. "This man not only had the technical knowledge, but he was very intelligent and energetic. He made a good impression and was obviously a man who was headed for a top position," says Gardner. However, he was put through a test battery which quickly ended the romance. According to the testers, he was an overdominant executive. States Gardner: "(a) He was a young man in a hurry to gain recognition and responsibility; (b) He tended to impose his ideas on the organization and would subordinate everyone else in his desire to get things done his way; (c) When he met opposition he would ride roughshod over anyone in his way; (d) He couldn't work well as a member of a team if he had to give way to others. . . . Needless to say, the company selected a less brilliant but more cooperative man for the job."

The moral: In handling a test situation of confidence or dominance, it is best to make like a grizzly. But be a bear with more growl than incisors, with a big brown coat of fear born of seeing other fierce colleagues like yourself mortally wounded by unsentimental hunters—the tester and the corporation.

OTHER TRAITS

Sympathy is usually not considered an executive asset. "Most good executives do not identify with people in difficulty. They are not softhearted and not very sympathetic. Sympathetic people identify with the underdog and are generally insecure," one tester explains. Sympathy as a trait is specifically measured on one test, the Washburne S-A Inventory. ("If you had a free trip to go see a murderer hung, would you go?") Curbing excessive softheadedness—without taking it to the extreme of insensitivity—can be essential.

Emotional stability, as we have seen repeatedly throughout, is a must for the successful executive. Fortunately, these are the simplest items to identify and answer correctly on personality quiz tests. Almost all "neuroticism" questions are either direct ("Do you experience many pleasant or unpleasant moods?") or the hypochondriacal type ("Do you sneeze very much?") discussed in Chapter V: Sick, Sick, Sick. Avoiding frankness is essential here, for the immature tester has confused neuroticism with candor. Most important, keep in mind that you are being statistically compared with a generation of liars before you. Job-hunting is hardly the time to upset your career, and the tester's norms, with honest neurotic replies.

Cultural interests. "Many executives have a strong interest in literature, and a wide variance in their cultural interests. Why, I recently had lunch with the chairman of the board of an advertising agency who is interested in archaeology. Another fellow is running a symphony orchestra in Cleveland, and a vice president at Olin is a buff on modern art. Other good executives, on the other hand, have no cultural interests at all. It is not necessarily a distinctive executive characteristic."

This commentary by a sophisticated tester is interesting, *but do not be sucked in* by this solitary tolerance of the cultured businessman. By and large, as we have seen, testers consider all cultural interests suspect, and even the sign of a disoriented executive. On tests such as the Kuder Preference, the Strong Vocational Interest, the Study of Values, and others with literary or other cultural scales, *it is always safer to play the boor.* To most testers, the good executive has little or no interest in the arts, except possibly in the old masters and French impressionists as a sound business growth investment.

For example, given the choice on the Kuder to:

a. Visit a fine art museum
b. Visit a recreation center for people in the slums
c. Visit a famous medical research laboratory

it is wisest to visit the laboratory. Although this is the prudent answer, a sizable percentage of executives—if granted a brain-watching moratorium—would undoubtedly prefer to browse in the Louvre. In fact, as we have seen, on several tests, "culture" has been made an internal part of Masculinity-Femininity scales, and excessive curiosity about poetry and other obscure arts can be embarrassing to the well-functioning male.

WIVES

Occasionally, the executive will find that he is being tested in tandem. Although only a small percentage of executive wives have yet to meet the tester formally (many have been surreptitiously surveyed by psychologists during home visits: see Chapter IV: Testing Men on the Job), the incidence of wife-testing is increasing. John A. Patton, a Chicago management engineer, recently commented: "It has reached the stage where many companies will not hire or promote an executive without taking a good look at his wife."

Questions about the testing and evaluation of executive wives are generally met with embarrassed glances or shy feignings in the test industry, but a few testers have found the work sufficiently routine to discuss it openly. What do testers look for in a spouse? Must she match her husband's brilliance and executive demeanor? One psychologist, a staff member of a Park Avenue consulting firm, summed up much of the testing opinion on the subject. "I approve of the testing of wives in certain instances," he says. "It is a messy thing, but it can give you an insight not only into the wife, but her husband as well. What do I look for? Most important, does she supply her husband with things that he needs? She may not have social graces. In fact, she may be a passive, dependent, fat, stupid slob, but if he likes to sleep with her, she's a good wife. On the other hand, a fashionable attractive woman with too much drive may be bad for an executive. I am having dinner with a man and his wife when they come to New York. My client wants to find out whether his wife is pushing him to unrealistic ambitions. If I find it is true, I will counsel her to stop driving him toward a nervous breakdown."

Executive wives have taken formal personality test batteries and had all their traits checked out at several testing firms including Richardson, Bellows, Henry & Company and BFS Psychological Associates of New York, both of whom test executive wives preparing to go overseas with their husbands for a corporate tour of duty. RBH gives a $500 one-and-a-half-day test-for-two to couples contemplating going to Chile for a mining company that has extensive copper deposits there.

They put the woman through the same testing regimen as her husband—including the Kuder, the Sentence Completion, the inkblots, a depth interview, the Study of Values—from which, among other things, they hope to extract her attitudes toward making this giant move. "We try to find out if she is interested in her husband's career through thick and thin. We also look for women who can get along with the nationals. We would not want biased individuals."

BFS, which has basically the same test battery plus a few of its own, tests wives of engineers, accountants, and teachers who are about to take overseas assignments. They were happy to elaborate further on the executive wife overseas. "What do we look for? Well, it should be a happy marriage," says a BFS spokesman, "and we want to be sure that the wife is not being pulled overseas. If she is unhappy there, it will prevent her husband from doing a good job. These people generally go into small towns. The wife should not be a gossip, nor should she be hoity-toity either."

How does the average woman face a battery of psychological tests? "Wives do well on the tests," BFS points out, "but actually they don't have to be geniuses, just indicate that they are good helpmates."

Should your wife receive the nod, you can coach her in outwitting the tester. Remind her that (at least in front of the brain watcher) your career and your welfare are her major concerns. She should not, however, give the impression that you are horse-collared and that she is driving you on to a faster and faster pace.

The idea of testing executive wives so impressed one client that he sent his consultant a young woman to check. "It turned out that it wasn't his wife," the psychologist recalled, "but a young lady he was contemplating marrying. He wanted us to test her out first."

OEDIPUS NIX

The possibility of an unresolved Oedipus complex beneath the well-suited exterior of a seemingly adjusted executive rankles some apprehensive testers, who are afraid that not even the corporation can compete with Mom. (See Chapter III: The Clinical Testers.) Knowing this, the good executive will keep his Freudian cues in reserve ready for instant use during a depth interview or on projective tests. On the Thematic Apperception Test, for example, avoid creating stories in which you might be construed as either a dependent child, or even an adult who still needs, or desperately loves, Mom. You are permitted somewhat stronger ties to Dad, as long as they are not restraining. The corporation reserves that position for itself.

Do not make the error, however, of ignoring the importance of Mom and Dad during your childhood, when a good relationship between parents and child is expected. If you and Dad were not close, they are afraid you will be a psychological weakling. The tester also warns that a strained relationship with Mom during the formative years might make for promiscuity. If a man was not reasonably close to his mother, without being overprotected as a child, he generally ends up chasing women. Explains the tester: "If he had no affection from his mother, he actively seeks it wherever he can get it, which can sometimes get a man in trouble."

ACHIEVEMENT

Almost all testers are convinced that the good executive has a strong desire for "achievement," and although they would be the last to admit it, conceive of him as a man with a *neurotic* drive for accomplishment as a goal in itself. ("They conceive of themselves as hard-working and achieving people who must accomplish in order to be happy," says W. E. Henry, formerly of Social Research, Inc., who ostensibly unearthed this trait during a study of 100 successful executives.) In fact, the good executive, say many testers, is more interested in the "stimulation" of accomplishment than in the finished product, the rewards, glory, or prestige, although he does value all these to some extent.

To tap your "achieving" desires, probably the most popular executive test today is the Edwards Personal Preference Schedule, which has a scale appropriately called "Achievement." If you work more for the rewards (an even chance to meet your mortgage payments) than the necessity to achieve, be especially careful on the Edwards.

The Edwards pits you against two statements that are supposedly equal in social desirability (see Chapter XI: Brain Watching: Science or Cult?), and asks you to choose. For a superior score, it is best to choose the "achievement" half in most of the couplets in which it appears—as in this Edwards teaser:

A. I like to help my friends when they are in trouble.
B. I like to do my very best in whatever I undertake.

The true achiever answers "B."

DEPTH INTERVIEW

Most executive appraisals include a depth interview. As we have seen (Chapter IV: Testing Men on the Job), the interview is a significant moment in corporate life, a battle of wills between the psychologist intent on making you relaxed—in fact, psychologically supine—and you. He hopes that your inherent defenses against such intrusions will be paralyzed by his "sincerity," leaving you unguarded, even if only for a telling instant.

Your proper role in this newly-traditional duel is to reverse the cast of characters: to appear ingenuous and to *relax the tester* by feeding him what he wants to hear—your good family relations, your disciplined life, your solid good health, agreement with corporate aims and philosophy, confidence that good work and cooperation will bring you along to the top—without appearing to be forcing it down his gullet. Through a conjured-up image, rather than your true self (unless you happen to be as "square" a character as I have presented), and subtle parries of his thrusts, you can successfully move the depth interviewer into a defensive posture. It can and is being done every day by successful executives, almost all of whom share our common neuroses and instability, but never during a depth interview. The cardinal rule: never trust the depth interviewer. As one prominent non-brain-watching psychologist (see Chapter IV: Testing Men on the Job) has implied, he is not motivated by your mental well-being.

EXECUTIVE LOCATORS

The traditional brown-desk-and-linoleum employment agency, where personality testing would be as conspicuous as an abstract Miro mural, is being phased out of much medium- and high-level executive placement work. Increasingly it is being replaced by the modern "executive locator," "recruiter," or "developer," who, like the management consulting firms which dabble in the same field, has gauzed his work with a film of professionalism.

The interesting aspect of these new specialists is that, by and large, they are helpmates of the brain watchers, and usually pretest executive applicants before the corporation gets to them. (Testing by recruiters is not universal: the head of Bernard Haldane Associates, Executive Development Consultants, for example, thinks it is meaningless in his hunt for "excellence.") A typical recruiters' testing program is operated by the highly reputed executive placement firm of James C. Sinnigen & Company, which does not handle applicants unable to command at least $12,000 a year.

Sinnigen does a "complete appraisal" of a man's "personality, strengths and weaknesses" by having him tested by John H. Cornehlsen, a Manhattan psychological consultant. The results of the tests go to the Sinnigen people, who give a detailed playback to the executive hopeful. A "case history" on the man is then circularized among hundreds of corporations to whet their interest in this pretested, almost hothouse management orchid. But here this recruiter, at least, parts company with the zealous brain watcher: the report only includes a personality profile if the man's test report was *positive*. The corporation is left guessing about the other ones.

Since the recruiter gets paid not just for finding executive talent, but for consummated deals in which his clients, the executive and the corporation, come to terms, he has a proprietary interest in having his job seekers show the best side of their personality. Openly or subconsciously, he is then operating a beat-the-testers cram course. "Sometimes companies will accept our personality evaluations, but most clients retest our men," says one recruiter. "Our tests are sort of a rehearsal for him, and he understands them better the next time."

Another Manhattan recruiter permits his flunkers to take their tests over a second time. "If a man can correct his personality traits once he learns about them, and come back and pass the second time," he says, "it's perfectly all right with me."

Moral: Although the executive recruiter is close to management, he is equally concerned with more and better placement fees. By taking a personality battery at the recruiter's office and getting a candid playback on your scores, you have a practical lesson in test-taking. In addition, if the recruiter will give you a second chance to take the test, you will have an opportunity to show him your swift response to his excellent psychotherapy. Avail yourself of any rehearsal offered: the corporate brain watcher doesn't believe in second chances.

NEW OBSTACLES

In the *Harvard Business Review*, Robert N. McMurry, who operates a sizable testing operation, makes a frightening proposal for the evaluation of key executives—an idea that is best revealed by directly quoting the source. "Where the candidate is over thirty-five," says McMurry, "whether he is being brought in from the outside or upgraded from within, it is also desirable that a measure be obtained of his biological intelligence, using a test such as that developed by Ward C. Halstead of the University of Chicago. This is designed to detect physiological changes that may have affected the structure of the brain. A condition which contributes to the development of executive neurosis is physiological deterioration of the prefrontal lobes of the brain, and to a lesser extent, of the entire cerebral cortex."

The Halstead Battery is no outlandish Aldous Huxley prognostication. Ward Halstead, a professor of psychology, claims that his "neuropsychological" measurements made mainly from "motor" reactions to stimuli can compute what he calls "brainpower" or "biological intelligence," which he profiles into ten parts including "memory," "mental power," "judgment," etc. Our brains, he claims, have an age that may be entirely divergent from our chronological age, and he states that his console-controlled tests can determine if "brain deterioration" has aged, and therefore slowed, our mental functions.

In a question-and-answer article in *Nation's Business* Dr. Halstead explains the commercial testing use of his "brainpower" measurements. "Experts have described the tests as helpful in strengthening a business organization, as yielding information that can be useful in selecting, placing, promoting, and assigning key management individuals," he says. In answer to the question: "Could you give an example of how the Halstead Battery has been used in this way?" the psychologist answers with a case history taken from his neuropsychological files:

There was a case of three vice presidents of a large Chicago company, with assets of more than $50 million, from whom a new president was to be chosen.

Their ages, experience, records with the company, social backgrounds, ambitions and other outward factors made them about equal candidates. The board of directors wanted to do more than pick the best of the three for the top job; it wanted also to be sure the other two would give the new president their wholehearted support.

The board chose Mr. A. to be president because our test revealed that, although, at 51, he was the oldest of the three according to the calendar, Mr. A. had in fact the youngest, most efficient brain. The chairman had made the brainpower of the candidates the prime test for the selection.

The laboratory findings on the Halstead Battery revealed that Mr. B., at 45, "was a considerably older man than his years," while Mr. C., at 48, was beginning to show the signs of wear and tear.

Mr. A.'s brainpower and efficiency are young, flexible and adaptable in the patterns most commonly found in men under 35. Somehow, Mr. A. has cheated the calendar.

Individual discussion of these facts with the other two candidates led them to go along with the selection of Mr. A. and to pledge their support to him as a natural for the presidency.

This "natural" was the choice of a highly controversial technique. Critics consider it highly debatable that Dr. Halstead's test can actually determine "brainpower" or "biological intelligence" or that these factors even exist in the terms expressed. (See Chapter X: Once Upon a Mind, on the failure of physiological measurements of intelligence half a century ago.) Dr. William M. Thetford, a faculty member of Columbia College of Physicians and Surgeons, who has worked on the Halstead Battery, states "grave reservations" about the accuracy of claims that the test measures culture-free "biological intelligence" or can, except in extreme cases, determine the so-called "biological" age of the brain.

"I believe that standard individual intelligence tests such as the Wechsler-Bellevue are more appropriate for this task," says Thetford. "A man's manipulative skills and motor reflexes, which play an important part in the Halstead test, can be poor, yet he may still be a man of great intelligence. As to its use in executive selection, I believe that except in cases of severe damage to the brain, the battery cannot discriminate closely between individuals. I believe that its use in this area is being oversold by its developers and I would not consider it an appropriate test for the selection of executives in industry."

Meanwhile, the individual is hopelessly at bay in this situation, in his inability to check out his own prefrontal lobes. But of course, any job-searching executive who would submit to such a supposed probe of the deterioration of his cerebral cortex would probably deserve the unholy news that his gray matter is older than he is.

Personal image building for the modern executive is not a

simple delineated program, a condensed "pony" that can be corralled for any test situation. However, the advice, either specific or implied, in this chapter and throughout the book should make the job of reassuring even the most insecure brain watcher considerably easier. If most of the trait requirements outlined fit your personality as is, the advice is superfluous for the brain watcher is already *simpatico*. If not, the application of many years of persistence and luck, *or* a few minutes of perjury, are the alternatives for a successful, fruitful executive career.

9 SO YOU WANT TO BE A SALESMAN?

Testing and its potent effect on a man's career is not news to the average company salesman, who has been weaned on test batteries the way his father was toasted into the business with a colloquy of off-color gags. The art of brain watching was born in the 1930's to evaluate the hard-fisted depression salesman, and today, partly because of the considerably smaller price tag ($20–$35 to test salesmen vs. $100 or more for executives), more salesmen are personality tested than men in any other single occupation.

The price has also made individual attention economically unfeasible and it is unlikely that most salesmen will ever be confronted by a live psychologist or a depth interview. Typically, the salesman is interviewed by a company personnel man, then either given a package of quiz tests to take at home and send in to a mail-order testing outfit, or perhaps told to visit a blind projective house where a clerk administers the pseudo-Freudian battery to a large group of salesmen at a time.

SENSE OF HUMOR

Among the test batteries designed for salesmen, one quiz appears with amazing regularity: the "Sense of Humor Test," which is actually Part V of the popular George Washington University "Social Intelligence Test." The image of the gregarious traveling peddler is still very much part of the tester's consciousness. Whether or not the marketing field has changed, he still insists that no sales novice be allowed to pack a sample case and join our growing number of salesmen (now over 2,775,000 men according to the Bureau of Labor Statistics) without first being able to handle at least twenty vintage jokes, from the close-pursed Scotsman to the pre-vaudeville Rastus dialect gags—the spinning of which today would probably lose more sales than it would clinch.

The composition of comedy and what makes people laugh is a debated subject, for individuals, regions, and generations vary in their approach to humor. The tester, however, has settled the debate by resurrecting some very poor jokes, many in bad taste, and giving the applicant an opportunity to choose one out of four punch lines as the proper socko ending. Even though the humor is uniformly weak, the droll lines do stand out, if not as humor, at least in contrast to the other three alternatives.

Try this "salesman's friend":

"So you want a divorce, Rastus?" "Yes, suh; Ah sho'ly does. 'Count ob my wife making an ironical remark." "An ironical remark?"

Reply: (A) "Yes suh, she says I'se black as de ace ob spades."

           (B) "Yes suh; she says if you don't go to work, I'll hit you in yo' face wid di iron."

           (C) "She says I have a very delapidated character."

           (D) "Yes, suh, she says I'se to come home and not see dat other gal."

At the risk of draining the enjoyment of this aged gasser, the correct answer is B. The remainder of the test poses similar gags, involving a lady in a lower berth, another Rastus gag (this one about desertion), a supposedly sexy play on the word "virtuoso," and even a house painter making a speech in the House of Representatives ("My place is on the scaffold"). Few of the jokes are amusing, but more important from the applicant's point of view, they are obvious. Answering at least 18 of the 20 correctly is enough to convince most managements that you are sufficiently hail-fellow to sell their machine parts.

SOCIAL INTELLIGENCE

Every salesman, says the tester, should have a large reposi-
tory of "social intelligence." There is no arguing with this
positive encompassing idea, but a closer look at what he
means by it is less assuring. Social Intelligence, as defined
by the George Washington University testers, includes Sense
of Humor, as we have seen, and four other components:
Judgment in Social Situations, Recognition of the Mental
State of the Speaker, Memory for Names and Faces, and Observation of Human Behavior. All but the last, which is a
true-or-false test, consist of multiple-choice questions.

Judgment in Social Situations is a test that invites platitudinous answers to unimportant questions. One example
may be helpful in understanding the test author's prejudices
(the best guide to passing any personality test) about "judgment." Try your social intelligence on this one:

Assume that you are a professor of economics in a large
university, and Smith, one of your students, complains
that Jones, another student, is a Communist. You should:

(A) Send for Jones and tell him that Smith has complained about his Communistic belief.
(B) Ask some of the students to try to convince Jones
of his error.
(C) Call Jones and prove to him that Communism
won't work.
(D) Tell Smith to pay no attention to Jones' talking.

The correct answer is D. One of the themes of the test is
that true judgment is actually caution, and avoidance of
confrontation. If you meet someone actually weeping, you
pretend not to notice; a businesswoman who is meeting a
schoolteacher for lunch does not discuss her own work or
educational tendencies, but "some current topic of general
interest." Similarly, an accusation of Communism is to be
ignored. If caution and avoidance fail, a platitude may succeed: If a man of sixty is complaining about the difficulty of
his job, you "lighten his work," a noble opinion shared by
few in industry.

The Memory of Names and Faces—a test in which you are
to mate names and one-inch portraits studied at the beginning of the test—is a throwback to the concept that any salesman and/or successful politician who fails to recall an ac-

quaintance of few minutes' standing is flirting with occupational disaster. Test Four, Observation of Human Behavior,
is a fifty-question quiz, which attempts to codify human attitudes into a simple true-false test. Surprisingly, in this
part, the tester has brought at least a veneer of sophistication to his concepts. For example: "In business success, in-
fluential friends are often as important as hard work." Amazingly, he agrees with you. The correct answer is "True."

The total possible score on the Social Intelligence Test,
including the Sense of Humor section (one point for each
punch line), is 160 points. Employers prefer men in the top
quarter, making a score of 130–150 a prerequisite for many
a sales job.

EXTROVERSION

The good salesman is naturally "extroverted," says the tester.
In fact, he should surpass at least four-fifths of the population in his optimistic, outgoing nature, and score between
the eightieth and ninety-fifth percentile on this trait. One
company profile graph describes the presence of "extroversion" as evidence of "staying power" and ability to "bounce
back" after sales turn-downs, and the absence of it as a
sign of being "worrisome, moody and easily discouraged."

Fielding the extroverted questions on the typical quiz
test is as simple as selling air-conditioned cars to Persian
Gulf sheiks:

Are you more concerned about sports than things intel-
lectual?
Are you considered to be "shy"?
Do you feel ill at ease when in a group of people?
Do you try to stay out of the spotlight at social func-
tions?

The obvious answers (Yes, No, No, No) will satisfy the
tester. Since salesmen's extroversion is allowed to soar to as
high as the ninety-fifth percentile, be as near perfect as possible, begrudgingly allowing few or no admissions of loneli-
ness or sensitivity.

DOMINANCE AND SELF-CONFIDENCE

"Can he take the lead in social and/or sales situations with drive and aggressiveness? Or is he unaggressive, inclined to let others take the lead, and disinclined to 'fight?' " asks one sales test. Naturally, the salesman is a fighter, in the best un-Willy Loman-like tradition. The properly aggressive salesman scores as well in dominance as in extroversion and again a near-perfect score is essential for survival.

For example:

When you are served badly at a restaurant, do you complain to the manager?

Do you insist on putting over your ideas even if you have to fight for them?

Are you self-conscious about returning purchases to the store?

Does the presence of people in superior positions in the business world make you feel less important?

If you are truly a salesman, you "bitch," you fight, you couldn't care less about exchanging, and no large cheese, boss or otherwise, makes you feel schoolboyish.

Expectations of your self-confidence are similar, if a little less stringent (seventy-fifth to ninetieth percentile). One big point-loser here is answering key questions incorrectly. For example: "Do you usually work things out for yourself rather than get someone to show you?" (Yes.)

SOCIABILITY

The true salesman must show the tester that people, rather than ideas, nourish his soul, and that gratification comes only in groups. The properly social-dependent salesman is playful, talkative, lonely with himself and with books, and would not be unhappy with a hand-buzzer at a Legion convention. Some sample social questions and answers are:

Do you talk a lot at parties? (Yes)

Do you find reading books more enjoyable than being with friends? (No)

Does life seem livelier when you are with a group of people? (Yes)

Do you prefer a Broadway drama to a dance? (No)

SALES INTEREST

A pervading interest in *persuading* people, says the tester, is the sign of the successful salesman. He attempts to measure this with two personality tests, the Kuder Preference Record and the Strong Vocational Interest Blank, which are as common in the business as Fort Lauderdale sales conventions.

The Kuder taps the selling applicant on his "Persuasive Interest"—supposedly some kind of elemental instinct common to lawyers, writers, and salesmen—by asking embarrassingly transparent questions that provide no threat. For example, which of these three do you like the most, the Kuder asks.

> Sell vegetables?
> Be an organist?
> Raise vegetables?

Even the magazine space salesman (many have been through the Kuder) who raises vegetables in his exurban garden—and *gives* them away—has the common sense to check "selling vegetables" as an indication of his unquenchable persuasive drive. Similarly, every question on the Kuder or Strong that features the word "sell" or "advertise" is to be checked indiscriminately. The *interested* salesman, says the brain watcher, in effect, is interested in little else.

ADJECTIVES AND SUCCESSFUL SELLING

At the big 3M, the Minnesota Mining and Manufacturing Company, personnel men not long ago asked 600 of the firm's salesmen to fill out an "Adjective Checklist," one of the tests then being used to select sales personnel. The test consists of thirty-six groups of five adjectives (Sturdy, Handsome, Tidy, Intelligent, Cheerful) and the salesman is asked to check the adjective in the group that is "most descriptive" and that which is "least descriptive" of himself. The Minnesota testers, writing in *Personnel* magazine, boast of their choice of the adjective test because it can "minimize faking." Since each adjective in the group is supposedly equally desirable socially, the choice of adjective is considered "objective."

Actually, of course, this type of test is eminently fakeable.

Obviously, being either "tidy" or "sturdy" never won a sales competition. From the answers of these corporate experimental hamsters, Minnesota Mining has compiled the adjectives that supposedly differentiate their "top-notch" from their "less effective" Scotch-tape pushers. The good salesman is successful, uninhibited, persistent, outspoken, persuasive, sociable, wordy, thorough, active, confident, daring, and excitable. The 3M failure, on the other hand is, more apt to be scientific, original, inventive, reflective, sentimental, self-denying, tactful, curious, artistic, and reasonable. "From these findings," the 3M authors state profoundly, "we might form the hypothesis that better salesmen actually tend to see themselves as salesmen, whereas less effective salesmen do not."

The 3M test shares the adjective in common with the Activity Vector Analysis. Describing yourself as a "salesman" on the AVA is not considerably more difficult. Although there are eighty-one adjectives (and four personality vectors) on the test, Vector 2—"Social-Ability"—is the most significant for the salesman. He scores high on this by checking off the friendliest adjectives he can find on the AVA list —words such as "enthusiastic, attractive, persuasive."

The AVA profile of the "good outside salesman," for example, is not impossible to duplicate. It shows our man to be quite aggressive and—surprisingly realistic—to have *low* emotional control, a reflection on his impatience, restlessness, and dislike of a confined position. He tends not to conform, but above all, his "social-ability" surpasses that of almost all 64,000,000 other wage earners.

SALESMEN AND FREUD

To the projective tester, the salesman is a psychological ne'er-do-well, a mass of unfulfilled drives. The square, straightforward image he portrays on the quiz tests is considered an amusing surface portrait of the psychological storm actually raging inside the American salesman. Rather than an upright, stable, friendly, confident individual concerned with selling as some abstract persuasive art, the projective tester sees the salesman as a money-hungry, frustrated entrepreneur who dislikes control and likes people only well enough to exploit them for his own gain.

In a *Sales Management* article, the sales manager of a firm which employs a projective tester for salesman selection talks openly about the makings of a salesman for the highly-competitive ladies'-wear field. "The first question I want answered about a candidate for our sales force is: What is his basic motivation? Why does he want to sell? . . . And if I get such answers as 'I like selling because I like people,' or 'I like travel and the challenge of new places, faces, problems,' or 'I want comfort and security,' I am immediately uninterested. I am, however, interested in men who say, 'I want more money. I think I can make more money selling than anything else I can do!' "

He presents seven characteristics of the competitive sales builder: acquisitiveness, selfishness, aggressiveness, persistence, shrewdness, verbal skills, independence, much of which adds up to an unattractive, grubby, but supposedly profitable portrait. The ideal salesmen, says this sales manager, are men for whom money-hunger is more important than security, prestige, or social respectability; men who put their own interests above anyone else's; men who don't really care whether people like them or not but who can affect enough "interest" in others to get their job done smoothly; men who have a flair for getting people to do what they want them to do, without their realizing or resenting it; men who know how and when to play on emotions or stick to facts; men who want to run their own show and dislike being supervised.

The projective tester claims that he has no difficulty identifying these skillful manipulators. "If a sales applicant does too well in arithmetic and detail, we get worried," a Ph.D. blind projective tester who processes several thousand men such as this a year confided. "Most good salesmen are sloppy and impatient and should do poorly on anything that requires planning. On interest tests, he generally scores poorly on the mechanical and clerical scales. On the Draw-A-Figure test, his sketch should be poor and without much detail. We don't want a man who is too self-revealing on the tests. This is a bad trait for a salesman. It would put him at a disadvantage with a potential buyer. We find this in the sentence completion. The good man covers up and tells us very little. He feels independent and doesn't like supervision. How do we learn that? Well, on a Thematic Appercception, for example, he might tell a story in which an employee (a salesman) and his superiors are arguing. The employee becomes annoyed and takes his case right over his superior's head, to the big boss. This is the kind of man who will do a good tough competitive sales job."

Count ten, however, before rushing headlong to complete your next set of projective tests in the unorganized and secretive manner recommended by this tester. The money-hungry operator is the ideal salesman only for those firms and industries where competition is rough (and somewhat tumble), and a salesman must psychologically rough up his customers a little for bigger and better commissions. But remember that corporations and sales policies vary, and that the "friendly" salesman with a pleasant, semimanagement attitude is often preferable in certain jobs.

The two breeds of salesmen, and how they coexist in the very same industry, were described by one tester, whose clients include two whiskey makers with sales policies poles apart. One of them, Brown-Forman, thrives on repeat orders, and seeks salesmen who will build solid, long-range good will among package-store owners. The other distillery carries a large line, including some avidly sought brands, and others that accumulate dust on liquor-store shelves. "This company needs salesmen who will almost hold up the liquor-store man to get him to buy the less popular brands along with the leaders," says the tester. "This takes a hard-shelled, highly-competitive, almost paranoid type, who doesn't enjoy taking no for an answer."

The projective moral: The clinical tester is convinced that by and large good connivers make good salesmen. Present yourself on the projectives only as square and cooperative as the company is reputed for its good manners. Otherwise, feed him the fleet-footed huckster he expects.

THE SALES EXECUTIVE

"The distributive executive is likely to be a salesman at heart, with administrative abilities in addition."

This obvious comment by Harriet Bruce Moore of Social Research, Inc. sums up, actually, the personality requirements of the sales executive, a business phenomenon who has risen to spectacular heights of power in the corporation since World War II, and is now in management control of sizable firms that once considered the sales manager a playful and necessary eccentric who was liable to show up at an annual meeting wearing brown and white shoes.

A full description of this management salesman, taken from Thematic Apperception cards, was presented by Miss Moore at the Civil Service Assembly Annual Conference. An excerpt from this involved treatise gives some idea of how the tester views him: as a cross of the true management man and the salesman, a business hybrid somehow psychologically crippled by his salesman background and skills.

"He [the sales executive] usually comes to the conclusion that a great part of executive work lies in making decisions. This activity is inflated in his eyes, and he is likely to make a decision at the drop of a hat," says Miss Moore. "Assertiveness, leadership, salesmanship, and decisiveness are all rolled up into one neat package, often called the 'positive approach.' Our Thematic tests suggest that the distributor's very high esteem for decisiveness stems from a deep-lying and unconscious fear that things undecided are lost, that failure arises from not being sure. It is of course also quite true that the desire to compete successfully and to influence other people continually, arises from belief that one's 'true weaknesses' will come to the fore if things take their natural course. People might not agree, they might not buy, they might not believe."

Moral: Don't worry about such neo-Freudian chatter. To present yourself as a fit sales executive, merely temper your sales presentation on the test with an equal sprinkling of management executive traits. In the quiz tests, you generally score with the salesman but have less need for people and constant human contact. In the projectives, you still have the salesman's flair, but show considerably more organization, detail, and respect for authority and supervision. The IBM data-computer salesman, for example, who must score high on both management values and sales interest on the Strong test to have a shot at management at the electronic giant (see Chapter II: The Big Quiz) is a case of proper "sales executive" orientation.

Looking at the increasing volume of our imports, the widespread use of cheaper overseas manufacturing facilities by our large corporations, and the decline in the ranks of the factory working man through automation, someone recently predicted that within a generation America would become a nation of salesmen. The prediction may be exaggerated, but there is little doubt that the brain watcher-salesman battle is a reality, and who emerges from it victorious will become increasingly important to more and more wage earners every year.

PART THREE

Probing The Brain Watcher

10 *ONCE UPON A MIND*

Many a man bogged in the obvious complexities of our civilization who has had a personality test battery suddenly forced at him which may change his arduously carved niche in society has undoubtedly asked himself: "How in the hell did this all begin?"

The history of brain watching is the story of man's inherent and pervading curiosity about his fellow man. The testing of man to measure his capacity or his personality, or to predict what he will do tomorrow (and why) is as old as man himself. Ancient Chinese supposedly placed delicately carved symbols of various occupations before an infant boy and glowed as he "chose" his future life's work. This same civilization is credited with the first extensive testing system, a ninth-century civil service examination not unlike the voluminous ones we give today.

Historic civilizations also devised the trial by fire or sword, "situational tests" which the Office of Strategic Services tried to resurrect and adapt during World War II as predictors of the success of Allied bridge-blowers and spies. Plato suggested that a soldier's bravery could best be measured by facing him with some frightening adversary beforehand and gauging his fear. Some oriental religious sects practiced a situational test of clerical devotion—a willing and attractive female placed temptingly before an ascetic monk.

The modern history of testing begins in two separate directions in the nineteenth century, in both the attempts to measure man's intelligence and in the early work on the mentally disturbed. In fact, much of the confused use and misuse of personality testing today stems from this unfortunate coincidence of development. The power of the individual brain—how intelligent a given person is—fascinated early researchers as much as it does us. As early as 1838 a French researcher, Esquirol, concluded that a child's command of his native language was the key to his intelligence, a concept still woven into modern I.Q. measurements. With this idea, Esquirol developed a workable test to distinguish between subnormal children by dividing them into levels of imbecility and idiocy.

His ideas escaped later researchers and in the "scientific" orgy of the later 1880's the emerging discipline of psychology became convinced that the answer to the riddle "how smart" could only be found in a man's measurable *physiological* body functions. The new scientists rashly broke out an era of premature intelligence testing that in some ways is a tintype of the massive personality testing situation today. Enthusiastic psychologists, biologists, and uncatalogued researchers brandished calipers to measure a subject's skull size, fingered head-bumps, hammered knees for quickness of reflexes, and made elaborate measurements of keenness of vision and hearing. They were religious in the belief that the sum of the strange arithmetic was somehow man's "native intelligence."

The fashion became so respectable that the renowned English biologist Sir Francis Galton measured fellow Londoners' intelligence for pennies a head in his South Kensington Laboratory with intricate tests of vision and mechanical reaction time. At the Columbian exhibition in 1893, Americans and tourists had a chance to do the same, and not only self-test their sensory and motor reactions but—as in personality quizzes today—check them out against "intelligence" norms graciously provided by the exhibitors. After a decade of self-delusion, the failure of physiology as a measuring tool (except, as it took fifty years to prove, for airplane pilots) became obvious. A more reasonable approach—what testers lovingly call "the breakthrough"—came along unexpectedly in 1904 in a simple, apparently nonscientific scheme.

Alfred Binet, the father of modern testing, and then a professor at the Sorbonne, had been chairman of a committee to investigate the education of subnormal children in the Paris school system. Before he could continue, he realized it was essential to first have some measure of the unfortunate children's learning potential, as meager as it was. Like Esquirol seventy years before him, he decided that the child's verbal and cultural level was the best available indicator of intelligence.

The result was a thirty-question verbal test, the Binet-Simon Scale, which asked the children direct questions beginning at elemental queries on whether it was "morning" or "night" up through knowing which way was "left" or "right," to more complex ones. By grading the questions according to those that almost all normal children of that age could answer, Binet produced the first "mental age" scale for intelligence. The child's mental age was determined simply by the highest group of questions he could answer in full.

The American psychologist L. M. Terman of Stanford University later revised the test as the Stanford-Binet and developed the now-familiar I.Q. or Intelligence Quotient— the ratio of a child's mental age to his chronological age— an overworked and sometimes overvalued number ranging anywhere from virtually 0 up through 100 (mean) to 175 or more that has thrilled and chagrined American parents for the last forty years.

Although most psychologists admit that I.Q. tests measure cultural level rather than pure capacity, the blissful fact that the test "worked" at all has given modern psychometric psychology a foundation on which to stand and sometimes even crow. The reputation of I.Q. tests, even though they are graying (see Chapter VII: The Three R's Through Graduate School), has given some brain watchers the spine needed to bluff through their other tests, especially in the unchartered fields of personality.

The other world from which testing evolved was the Freudian, from work with the disturbed, and the clinicians' hope that some objective measurement of psychosis could be developed. Two German researchers, Ebbinghaus and Kraepelin, experimented on psychiatric patients with a variety of tests, including arithmetic computations and memory measurements. The most satisfactory was free association, the ancestor of projective testing. Kraepelin asked his abnormal subjects to call out the first word that came into their mind from a given stimulus, while Ebbinghaus refined the technique into the sentence completion test similar to the ones in use today.

Like so many other technologies, personality testing was galvanized by the two large wars of this century. Each of them left its indelible and hasty mark on brain watching, creating a commercial hydra-head out of what was once a gentle research animal. In 1917 the American Psychological Association was called in as a consultant to the Army and, under Robert M. Yerkes, developed the famous Alpha test, an intelligence instrument given to 4,000,000 draftees.

By this time the influence of psychiatry had advanced sufficiently for the Army to want to screen out "psychoneurotics" in advance, and the job was given to medical men, who handled it on an interview basis as they also did in World War II. A prominent psychologist, R. S. Woodworth, decided to help out by constructing an interview guide— the Woodworth Personal Data Sheet—composed of some 200 questions he had dragged out of the psychiatric and clinical literature. It then occurred to him (the Newton's apple of testing) that if it could be made into a questionnaire it could be a simple, scorable psychoneurotic-spotter.

He tested the questions on students at Columbia University, where he taught, and discarded those questions that 25 percent or more of the students answered in the suspected psychotic way. The remaining questions were given to both unselected draftees and psychotic servicemen, and refined to a 116-question inventory, the first modern personality test. These questions, which have since spawned hundreds of grandchildren in the testing world, were thrown at unknowing World War I draftees. A score of 10 was considered normal, while a score of 30–40 supposedly indicated a psychoneurotic personality. The forty-five-year-old sample seems strangely familiar:

1. Do your eyes often pain you?
2. Did you ever make love to a girl?
3. Can you stand the sight of blood?
4. Are you afraid of responsibility?
5. Do you get rattled easily?

The Woodworth was a failure. It did not satisfactorily select the psychoneurotics from the good trench material among World War I dogfaces. However, here the early personality tester first showed the flaw that runs through the

entire history of his "science." Instead of the disappointment of mass failure forcing him to seek the truth in another direction, he was so overjoyed at having a psychoneurotic tool—even one that didn't work—that he enthusiastically threw all his energies into its use and development. Ever since, independent proof of each personality test's
inability to do what it was constructed to do has provoked
the same strange response from the brain watcher.

After the War, the Woodworth Personal Data Sheet was
published in a civilian edition. During the next decade a
host of similar tests, with questions frankly stolen from
each other, made their appearance. In 1925, it was the
Colgate Mental Hygiene Test. In 1928 Allport put out the
popular Ascendance-Submission Reaction Test which he developed by giving sample questions to 400 students at Dart-
mouth and 200 women at Goucher, Wellesley, and Radcliffe.

About the same time Louis L. Thurstone dipped into the
central mixing pot of personality questions and pulled out
600 from the Woodworth, the Colgate, the A-S Reaction,
and elsewhere. The result, after he had whittled the test
down, was the Thurstone Personality Schedule. The following year, Donald Bell gave the Thurstone to students at
Chico State College, California, and found it wanting. Using
his student interviews as a guide, he revised it into the
Bell Adjustment Inventory. Three years later, in 1933,
Bernreuter developed the Bernreuter Test of Self-Sufficiency
with Washington University students. Then, two years later,
he amalgamated, sifted, and correlated four personality tests,
including his own, into the prominent Bernreuter "Personality Inventory," probably the first test to attempt to measure
a variety of traits.

This breathless march ended with approximately the same
test it had started with some eighteen years before. But
the sheer motion of the activity had stimulated interest in
these paper-and-pencil analyses.

How did the tests make the significant leap from the
psychologist's university laboratory into the hot hands of
personnel men? Several stories are told, but the link was
probably provided by two men: Professor Samuel Stevens
of Northwestern University and the late Jack Klein, a forceful Chicago salesman-advertising-promotion man who had
been operating sales clinics to teach salesmen "how to work."
According to Klein, a chance conversation on a plane trip
led him to Stevens, who had tested thousands of students
with the new personality tests as part of vocational guidance

work. Klein and Stevens formed the nation's first personality testing company in 1938, but industry was still not
attuned to mind-probing, and the alliance of promoter and
scientist collapsed in four months.

Klein was determined to break through, however, and,
as he once recalled, he scoured the libraries for mention of
psychological tests, studying and buying every one that was
mentioned at least twice. He had written an article for
Sales Management Magazine, "How to Keep the Lemons
Out of Your Sales Staff," and in the late 1930's, when the
sales manager of Bauer & Black, manufacturers of surgical
dressings, approached *Sales Management* for advice on selection, they sent him to see Klein.

Klein realized the opportunity and set up an "experiment" with the Editorial Board of *Sales Management* as
judges. The Bauer & Black sales manager placed the names
and ratings of 15 of his firm's salesmen in a sealed envelope. Klein tested the same 15 men, dispensing with the
psychologist's indispensable scoring key, and instead read the
test answers "like a narrative." When the confidential envelope
was opened, Klein's ratings coincided with the Bauer & Black
sales manager's 13 out of 15 times. At that instant, one
man's masterful instinct had given birth to personality testing
for hire.

The new industry had its adolescent stirrings in the era
just before World War II. A handful of testing companies,
charging as little as $7.50 per head, began operating; new
tests like the MMPI and the early projectives first came
into commercial use; and a sprinkling of corporations began
experimenting with internal testing systems.

The story of personality testing during World War II
is much like that of the previous war—a series of stark,
striking failures. At the outbreak of war, hundreds of psychologists were recruited for selection, classification, and
morale work, much of which appears to have been of substantial value. Fourteen million servicemen took their
AGCT (Army General Classification Test) and similar aptitude tests which helped grease the cranky job of classification.

Under Dr. John C. Flanagan, now head of the American
Institute for Research in Pittsburgh, a huge team of Army
Air Corps psychologists developed a battery of mental and
motor tests—from map-reading to reaction-time tests involving blinking red and green lights—for the selection of aviation cadets. The results proved reasonably valuable (.63 cor-

relation) in predicting which cadets would graduate and which would wash out. The value of this nonpersonality screening, at least in extreme scores, was shown by the fact that over 70 percent of those with a 9 score graduated while less than 10 percent of those with a 2 won their wings. (A recent thirteen-year follow-up study, "10,000 Careers," by prominent psychologist Robert L. Thorndike, showed, however, that the tests failed to predict the success of these same cadets in civilian life.)

With such a mass of unwilling guinea pigs on tap, it was inevitable that psychologists in every cranny of the services would yield to the itchy desire to pull out the personality tests. They did, but despite years of activity and research, all of them failed. The same aviation cadets were given the Rorschach inkblots, the Kuder Preference Record, and other personality probes with negative results. The Navy, too, tried painfully to retrace the work of Woodworth, adding the more modern concept of asking the sick questions in a forced-choice inventory. With it they developed a psycho scale, the Personal Inventory, which was supposed to predict which sailors would eventually be labeled as "Section Eights," but this too failed. (In fact, had the Navy's PI been used as a general screening device for all services, it would have proudly served the Axis powers by mislabeling 930,000 perfectly normal servicemen—some fifty divisions—as hopeless psychotics, without detecting 48 percent of the relatively small number of true psychotics.)

The grand attempt in World War II brain watching was conducted at a top-secret rolling-country estate, "Station S," near Fairfax, Virginia, forty minutes outside Washington, D. C. It was one of the training stations of the Office of Strategic Services, the hazardous undercover branch headed by Brigadier General "Wild Bill" Donovan. A team of psychologists, psychiatrists, and sociologists were gathered here to assess new OSS recruits and predict which men were best equipped to carry off the organization's cloak-and-dagger tasks—assignment to the Yugoslav Communist underground, parachuting into France and outfoxing the Gestapo, to spying in Calcutta or Prague.

By the time the Assessment Branch of the OSS had finished testing 5,391 recruits in the two war years between 1943 and 1945, it had evolved as the most complex and time consuming personality check ever made in history. Assessment at "Station S" took a full three days. Colonels removed their eagles, sergeants took off their stripes, civilians discarded mufti and spent a crowded seventy-two hours together in unmarked Army fatigues. The testers paid scrupulous attention to details, including the manufacture of what they considered the trappings of a proper cloak-and-dagger atmosphere. Each man was told to forget his true name, occupation, and home town. He had to invent a "student name" and a "cover story" with which he would live for the three full days. He was to be prepared to be challenged and to defend his concocted tale at all times. Only if authorities pulled him aside and whispered that "X" conditions were in effect was he to tell the truth. To heighten the drama and keep prying civilians away, the OSS spread the rumor that "S" was actually a camp for mentally ill servicemen.

Testing went on twenty-four hours a day. In the report on the program, *Assessment of Men*, the authors point out that everything was "grist for the assessment mill." Testers watched and meticulously noted the way men shook hands, their chitchat during the midnight snack, "wisecracks overheard in the hall," "the gesture with which a man reacted to defeat in a game of bridge," and even the ring of their fictitious names as they answered roll call. States the OSS report: "There were those who spoke their names as though they were their own, loudly and confidently, those who spoke them softly and with guilt as though telling a lie, those who became blocked, unable to speak any name."

No attempt was made to gauge specific OSS skills: how well a parachutist leaped or landed, how skillfully a man could cut a Nazi's jugular from behind or pose as a Romanian with the appropriate regional accent. Instead the men were put through a giant personality watch, including a battery of conventional personality tests and specially developed situational ones. They filled out a personal history form ("At what age did you stop wetting the bed?"), went through a depth interview, took slews of paper-and-pencil personality tests ("What would you most like people to say of you after you have lived your life?"), projective tests, an intelligence test, a health questionnaire, the McFarland Psycho-Somatic Inventory to weed out hypochondriacs, and a 100-item sentence completion test.

The situational tests were the OSS's *metier* and have since become legendary in the testing community. Recruits were asked to scale two 10-feet-high walls spaced 8 feet apart without dropping into a simulated 200-feet-deep "canyon" between; solve a murder mystery about a psychologist having an extramarital affair with someone involved with spies; build

a man-sized Tinkertoy with the "help" of two associates—
Kippy and Buster—who were actually OSS stooges trying to
frustrate the recruit. The most famous of all was the "Brook"
leadership test in which a group of men had to transport a
rock (percussion caps) and a log (super-secret range finder)
across an eight-foot brook with only a bottomless barrel,
some rope and a pulley, and short boards.

OSS psychologists watched the three-day dramatic pro-
ceedings from close in, and scored each recruit on the traits
they *thought* would best suit a modern conspirator. After assessment, each recruit was described in an 800-word personality sketch, doubled-checked by several staff members,
and given a composite score ranging from 5 for "outstanding" down to 0 for totally "unsatisfactory."

Two years later, when the war was over, the results of the
assessment came in. The most pertinent was the OSS man's
rating by his theatre commander on the work he actually
accomplished, whether in a Washington laboratory or a
Greek partisan camp. When compared with the predictions,
the vaunted OSS assessment program *proved to be a total
flop*. As the OSS itself puts it: "None of our statistical computations demonstrates that our system of assessment was of
great value."

Their admission is actually an understatement. Many
men judged outstanding did unsatisfactory jobs and vice
versa. The correlation between the prediction and performance was a worthless coefficient of .23, while others, like
"emotional stability" came out a low .08, approximately the
same as if OSS recruits were chosen by the spin of a roulette
wheel instead of this extravagant brain watch. The results
would have been even worse, except for the intelligence
test, which—although still not a worthwhile predictor—
did twice as well as the best personality test. Obviously the
test of cruel war proved more challenging than the psychological cover games played on the rolling Virginia estate.

One reason for the failure appears to be the traditional
superconventionality that the tester brought to his OSS work
despite his flimflam pose of a flamboyant cloak-and-dagger
tester. The model OSS man, the testers had theorized, should
not only be intelligent but be "a good team-player," and a
"man of good will" as well—a job description that seems
better tailored for a complying junior executive or a depart-
ment-store floorwalker than the lone black-faced parachutist
loaded with lariat strangler and plastic explosives assigned
to blow up a bridge and possibly endanger the lives of inno-

cent civilians in occupied France. Perhaps the Fairfax testers would have done as well (or as badly) by seeking out highly neurotic GI's anxious to fulfill their boyhood dreams of playing "spy." The intrusion of the tester undoubtedly altered the vital work of the OSS in World War II, with absolutely no evidence that it was for the better.

The mere existence of a highly developed OSS program was an exhilarating experience for the psychologists who participated. Most of them could not wait after World War II to bring their disproven techniques into industry. They were quickly joined by hundreds of other psychologists who had been given virtual control over the service careers of millions of men, by part-time professors seeking new sources of income, and more recent psychology graduates turned testers. Faced with this onslaught of professional experts loudly proclaiming their skills, industry, which had once fended off early testers, now willingly capitulated to the blandishments that personality testing "could do the same" for them. The testing orgy of the 1950's—and, as it appears, the 1960's—was in full strident swing.

11 BRAIN WATCHING: SCIENCE OR CULT?

"Personality tests are of little, if any, value in employment."

The author of this startling comment on the inaccuracy of the whole personality test blight is no bastion of anti-science. Not only is he an eminent psychologist (former president of the New York State Psychological Association), but currently he heads an organization that is one of the nation's leading personality test distributors. What appears to be a strange schism between philosophy and the cash register is explained readily by the courageous spokesman, Dr. George K. Bennett, president of the $2,000,000-a-year The Psychological Corporation. According to Bennett, his company will not sell personality tests to such unqualified practitioners as employment managers and nonpsychologist personnel men. It will, however, sell them to psychologists, who ostensibly have the good sense to use them for guidance and research, not the popular and profitable culling of employees for industry.

Dr. Bennett's doubts about personality testing in industry could hardly be called a crusade, but neither is it a lonely voice in the psychological dusk. Many psychologists, most of them a reasonable academic distance removed from the testing marketplace, have gratuitously expressed the opinion that there is more sell than science in personality testing, and that much of the work being done today is unsound (and dangerous) as pre-Repeal aged-in-the-bathtub gin. In fact, not only academic psychologists, but many brain watchers themselves are equally skeptical—if only about the other fellow's test practices.

The most surprising insight into this discord and fratricidal back-biting can be found in the *Mental Measurements Yearbook,* a tester's bible where colleagues get the rare professional opportunity to dissect each other's test inventions within the secure bounds of a review not unlike the familiar ones in the Sunday book section. A study of the *Yearbook* (which has had five editions in a generation) is an eye-opener for the uninitiated skeptic. If some of the articles were put into the framework of a science, say chemistry, they would read like works of professional chemists wrangling over whether valences and elements exist and whether compounds can actually be created in a test tube.

Although the Edwards Personal Preference Schedule, for example, is currently a brisk bestseller in employment testing, the review of it in the latest edition, the *Fifth Mental Measurements Yearbook* is considerably less enthusiastic than test-buyers. "Judging from the literature on the PPS at this date," says a review by Frank Barron, research psychologist, University of California, "the verdict of caution should be that the test is not yet ready for use in counseling or personnel selection."

Benno G. Fricke of the Evaluation and Exams Division of the University of Michigan reviews another currently popular test, the Gordon Personal Inventory, in a similar doubting tone. He says: "But frankly, and in summary, the reviewer at this time can see no good reason why a test user should want to obtain the Gordon Personal Inventory scores." Albert Ellis, the prominent New York consulting psychologist, says of the highly touted MMPI: ". . . the efficiency of its use for individual diagnosis still remains to be proved."

The brilliantly marketed AVA test system, which transforms underappreciated personnel men into blue-ribboned analysts in three weeks, is equally mauled in the *Fifth Mental Measurements Yearbook.* One reviewer, Brent Baxter of Prudential Insurance, after lampooning its brief training course, questions AVA as a whole. "A few studies made by independent research men have not shown the test to be effective in sorting out the more and less successful men on a given job," says Baxter. In the same volume Dr. Bennett, of The Psychological Corporation, interrupts another highly negative review of the AVA to make a sweeping condemnation of all personality inventories used for selection work. "Over the past forty years a great number of self-descriptive inventories have been constructed and tried out," he says. *"This reviewer is unable to recall a well-established instance of useful validity for this class of questionnaire against a criterion of occupational success."* (Italics mine.)

The various editions of the *Mental Measurements Yearbook* are also punctuated with skeptical reviews on the supposedly "established" tests. "Claims made for the instrument go beyond the data," is the verdict on the Adams-Lepley Personal Audit. The Allport Ascendance-Submission Test comes off little better: "Very doubtful that the scale can be employed without verification. . . ." The Bernreuter is summarily dismissed with the comment, "No convincing evidence of validity."

Although the annoyance of reviewers occasionally peeks through, most of them exercise admirable self-control. Occasionally a sensitive psychologist does feel compelled to use the *Mental Measurements Yearbook* as an acceptable outlet for his outrage, to lament the injury to the reputation of practicing psychology which some feel has been committed by the personality test operation. In the *Fourth Yearbook,* for example, a reviewer discussing the "Life Adjustment Inventory" could no longer contain himself, and used the unfortunate test as a prop for his anger. "Perhaps the inventories will find their best use in bonfires celebrating our emergence from the ruts that the personality and adjustment testers, ably abetted by high pressure salesmen, have carved out for us," he wrote.

Even the awesome inkblots, whose amorphic forms loom like granite Rorschach monuments to the uncritical, have come under strong anti-brain-watch fire. In a *Fifth Mental Measurements Yearbook* review, the famed Dr. H. J. Eysenck, director of the Psychological Laboratories of the Institute of Psychiatry, University of London, delivers a lengthy devastation of the test—comments previously only hinted at in closeted tones in the typically less than candid psychological circles. "On all the usual criteria, therefore, it must be concluded that the Rorschach has failed to establist its scientific or practical value," says Eysenck forthrightly. "This is becoming more recognized, largely as a consequence of the improved standards of Rorschach research in recent years, which has given rise to many well-controlled and well-analyzed studies, the results of which have been uniformly negative."

Next to the blots, the test with the most sanctified reputation is the drawing-like Thematic Apperception, for which the reviewers have reserved similar comment. Says one devastating TAT critique: "Various studies indicate that the TAT has little if any validity as a clinical test."

The succession of surprisingly bad reviews of personality tests, in both the *Mental Measurements Yearbooks* and the professional journals, is lively, if endless, reading. What brings the reader up sharply is how these same derided instruments could be the heart of a giant that judges over a million of us each year and sharpens its psychological appetite annually.

How did the emerging science of psychology become such a pliant tool for brain watching? The laxity of scientific discipline, salesmanship, naïveté of businessmen, and our culturally conditioned reflex to respect any findings labeled as "scientific," are all part of the answer. But the core of much of this scientism of testing has been the adroit use of statistics—numbers that can and do lie—to create an aura of scientific precision that in fact does not exist.

To make the gibberish of psychometrics digestible, it is first important to understand a few key statistical terms used to evaluate a test. Most of these words, like "reliability" and "validity," are powerful images, and are often misused, deliberately or otherwise, by testers. Both have the sonorous ring of *science*, but the unfortunate truth is that an adroit brain watcher can skillfully manipulate these terms and present a test with a relatively high "reliability" and "validity"—of say .90—that has never tapped, and could never tap, the recesses of anyone's personality. Although it is seldom advertised by test designers and their marketing adjuncts, both glamour terms often refer to the internal mathematics within a test—correlations between different tests, other traits, and other trade paraphernalia—and almost never to the true relationship between a test score and human behavior.

"Reliability" is a key word in testing. Although it does not pretend to tell how well a personality test, for example, succeeds (predicts), it is, at least, a key to whether there are extravagant errors in measurement—errors based on ambiguous questions, faulty test construction, lack of comprehension of test rules. It should also include the concept that you might have shone on Tuesday and flunked on Monday when a weekend hangover clouded your personality. Reliability comes before validity, for a test score must be a reasonably *true* score before it can be used for any decisions, even bad ones. "If our measuring instrument is unreliable," points out the Test Service Bulletin of The Psychological Corporation, "any judgments based on it are necessarily of doubtful worth. No one would consider relying on a thermometer which gave readings varying from 96 to 104 for persons known to have a normal temperature."

Reliability can be measured in many ways, including comparing the scores on two halves of the same test (Split-Half Reliability), comparing scores on two forms of the same test, or the more rigorous trial of giving the test twice to the same group a week or two apart, a system called "test-retest reliability."

Surprisingly, many personality tests are bad thermometers, and scores on such tests must be taken with a large, educated granule of salt. Reliability is never perfect (1.0) but some intelligence tests, like the Stanford-Binet, have high reliabilities (over .9) even though their validity is considerably lower. Psychologists vary in their opinion of how low reliability can go before a test, or a scale, should be discounted. Depending on test faith, this generally ranges from .8 to .7. When a test score reliability gets as low as .6, for example, an applicant taking the same test twice might emerge—say on its "sociability" scale—as both a retiring introvert and a glad-hander, with no clue as to which, if either, is his true score. Furthermore, as reliability decreases so does the *theoretical limit* of a test's validity. Expressed in a formula, a test's maximum validity is the square root of its reliability.

The manual of the Thurstone Temperament Schedule, for example, lists the reliability of its seven traits (Stable, Vigorous, etc.) on samples taken at the University of Chicago. Although the test has been the bulwark of several elaborate corporate testing empires, its reliability was shown to be quite low, averaging in one trait (Active) as low as .48, and only .64 on all seven.

Such chinks in the tester's armor are seldom advertised. Many tests list relatively high reliabilities in their manuals but independent checks—using the more rigorous test-retest technique—often emerge with less than complimentary statistics. One researcher put the highly touted MMPI through such a test-retest regimen and found two of its psychotic-spotting scales, Depression and Paranoia, registering as low as .66 and .56 reliabilities. Translating the blood-less numbers into case histories could mean that a sus-piciously deep-set paranoic tendency pinpointed by the MMPI may be treated easily. The therapy is simple: just wait seven days and give the test again to the suspected paranoic. There is an excellent chance that his suspiciously high score—and with it his psychosis—will simply fade away.

Another test-retest debacle, this time on the Thematic Ap-perception Test, was described in the *Journal of Consulting Psychology*. The TAT was first given to a group, then after a nine-week hiatus, administered again. The result, even for test critics inured to low reliabilities, was astounding. The reliability correlation between the two sets of scores was a ridiculous .26, indicating, as many have suspected all along, that as an objective measurer of personality, the TAT is virtually worthless.

Validity is the other half of the statistical coin. Validity, in general, means how well a given test measures what it says it measures. For test buyers, and their unwilling sub-jects, this should mean how well predictions based on per-sonality test scores check out with a man's performance on the job. This is the conclusion the corporation has paid handsomely for.

The better intelligence tests for children, for example, generally have a validity coefficient of .50 when measured against their criterion—the prediction of school grades. In validity measurement, 1.0 stands for a perfect prediction record, .00 for simple chance prediction that could be ac-complished with a two-sided coin, and −1.0 for an inverse relationship.

Validity coefficients, however, are a misleading statistical trap for the uninformed. Although .5 sounds quite respecta-ble and seems like a 50 percent prediction rate (a common misinterpretation that undoubtedly pleases educators anxious to impress parents with the accuracy of IQ measurements), it is actually *less than a 15 percent improvement over a chance guess* about how well Johnny will do as a student. Whether predicting personality, intelligence, aptitude, or what-ever, the validity coefficient must be quite high before it can do even reasonably better than chance. When "predic-tive efficiency" is plotted against the "validity coefficient" it produces a very shallow graph that only starts to rise sharp-ly just before perfect validity. To make the 50 percent im-provement over chance would take a rare validity coefficient of .866, for example. In many tests, because of low reliability, such a score is even *theoretically impossible*.

Measures of *true*, or predictive, validity are virtually non-existent in personality tests in industry, mainly because virtually no experimenters ever dip down into the unemployment slag heap to follow up the poor scorers who have been summarily rejected, but without whom a proper validity study is impossible. (Erwin K. Taylor and Edwin C. Nevis stress this in the *Annual Review of Psychology*. "There appears to be a real need for studies that follow up rejected job applicants and compare their fate with that of matched samples or equally qualified but selected applicants," they state.) Because of this essential failing, testers constantly retreat back to other types of internal measurements and comparisons that are called "validity" only because of semantic accident.

Unfortunately, some clever test designers and their selling allies have successfully passed off these internal mathematics of personality tests as "validity" to unsophisticated personnel men and other buyers. A Test Service Bulletin of The Psychological Corporation points up this testing gamesmanship. "A published 'validity' coefficient based on the sample which contributed to the selection of the items and the making of the key (in the case of personality and interest inventories) is misleading," says the Bulletin. "Coefficients so described should be unambiguously described. They are *not* validity coefficients which tell the practical user what he may expect if he uses the test or inventory."

The lack of validity proof has not curbed the hawker instinct in test makers and sellers, and puffed claims about a test's value in selection are common despite lack of real statistical proof. In the *Annual Review of Psychology, 1961,* the section on Personnel Selection, written by Taylor and Nevis, lambastes the trumpeting of one personality test. "Such claims, without any basis in empirically established validity, are not unique to this instrument," they say. "They are, unfortunately, the rule rather than the exception."

A classic caricature of how handsome validity statistics can be distilled from raw nothings by the clever use of internal mathematics was described in *Educational and Psychological Measurement* by Edward E. Cureton of the University of Tennessee in a playful article, "Validity, Reliability, and Baloney."

Cureton first gave a vocabulary test to 29 of his students, then readministered it two weeks later. The test proved to have a reliability of .90 and a correlation between scores and school grades of .23. Hoping to improve the validity— relationship between test scores and grades—he developed his own 85-item test, which he called "Projective Psychokinesis Test." After the 29 students took the new test, he checked to see if those students who had better school grades had favored certain test items. He picked these out and weighted them *plus one* on his scoring key. If those students who had bad grades favored another item, he weighted that item *minus one*. When he had finished "refining" his new test, he had winnowed it down to a 24-item test with a startling validity: .82 correlation with scholarship, sufficient to make any admissions dean's mouth salivate.

What was this startlingly accurate test? Merely a simple game of brain-watching chug-a-lug. Metal discs with the numbers 1 to 85 were placed in a cocktail shaker. The "test" was agitated, and the discs thrown out onto the table. The discs that came out "numbers up" were scored plus, and those "face down" were scored minus.

"The moral of this story, I think, is clear," says the article's author. "When a validity coefficient is computed from the same data used in making an item analysis, this coefficient cannot be interpreted uncritically. And contrary to many statements in the literature, it cannot be interpreted 'with caution' either. There is one clear interpretation for all such validity coefficients. This interpretation is—'BALONEY.' "

One of the major barriers that exclude brain watchery from even a cousin-kinship with science is the almost complete neglect of *cross-validation*, which lies at the basis of scientific verification. You observe initially, perhaps construct a theory, equation, serum, then cross-validate by trying it out—under strict discipline—with an outside control to see if it has objective validity. The Salk polio vaccine, for example, even though successful in the laboratory trials, first had to be tried out on a tremendous sample—and comparative control group—before claims could be made for its efficiency. In the cross-validation experiment, the vaccine was given to 440,000 children, while 210,000 children received a worthless placebo, an experiment that verified its effectiveness against paralytic polio as 80 to 90 percent.

Let's compare this with a typical personality "validity" study in a corporation, an exercise in suspended scientific judgment which many personnel people and company testers have confused with the scientific method. A test or battery is first given to the organization or division en masse. The testees are then divided into groups of "better" and "worse" performers based on some criteria such as sales volume or, in the case of executives, their supervisors' ratings. The battery scores, the test scores, the scores on single traits, and then even responses to individual questions are analyzed scrupulously in the hope of finding any subscore—no matter how unrelated to the job performance—that seems to differentiate the good men from the bad. This test, scale, or handful of questions is then elevated as the corporate scoring key, a Merlinesque arrangement of Yes's and No's that will supposedly predict future good employees for Corporation X.

The American Management Association text *Selection of Management Personnel* details one such ridiculous "research" program which found that "better" gas and electric district foremen at Consolidated Edison in New York scored more "self-sufficient" and less "sociable" on the Bernreuter than their "indifferent" counterparts. Rather than chalk up this tidbit as a probably meaningless and possibly chance statistic that would need years of research to validate with a control group, the enthusiastic testers naïvely enshrined it as part of a selection key. Advancing the test cult another notch, they pompously suggest it be used for "Sifting Out Unlikely Candidates or Arranging the Candidates in the Order of Probable Success."

In this typical corporate hodgepodge of scientism, the tester often finds that the key that served so well for years now no longer seems to work. He concludes that it needs some "refining," and he makes minor "adjustments" to account for new people whose performance did not exactly match the anticipated. As the years go on, questions are discarded, new ones adopted, the key changed imperceptibly, keeping it always current, always "valid," and never checked.

This technique—sometimes falsely dignified with the name "empirical" by status-pushing brain watchers—bears no relation to scientific cross-validation. The key developed under this common industry technique opens nothing except the corporate cash box on behalf of the testing industry. Firstly, as we have seen, the simple act of not following up bad scorers destroys the most important part of the sample.

Furthermore, the whole scientific basis of cross-validation requires the initial experiment to be unchanged during its check. When the key is altered, no matter how slightly, the whole validation trial must be started over again. In its Test

Service Bulletin on "Cross-Validation," The Psychological Corporation warns against this type of faulty experimentation: "We do not have cross-validation data until we administer the tests without change, without further revision or refinement, to an entirely new and independent set of criterion groups."

The ignorance (or Machiavellian stupidity) of testers can be compared to what this author would call the "Retroactive Roulette System." Addicted gamblers sometimes use the fortunate chance run of a roulette wheel of a few hundred turns to work out elaborate "red-black" betting systems. When cross-validated at the casino, however, they almost invariably fail. Rather than abandon the "system," it is altered to account for that new chance situation, and so on. Similarly, brain watchers are sustained in their unchecked systems because statistically, the different answers of two groups on 15 scattered personality questions could only happen by chance, say, 1 in 1000 times. This "proof" is the same kind that makes 10 reds in a row at the roulette table—a chance occurrence that also happens approximately once in a thousand times—the statistical springboard for lost fortunes at Monte Carlo.

One test critic recently pointed out that personality testing keys seem almost uniformly unstable, and that "results of one study frequently break and disappear under reapplication." One reason (there are many) was suggested by the Test Service Bulletin. "Chance is the gremlin," says the Bulletin. "The larger the number of predictors—be they tests, items, or pennies—the more careful we must be to guard against being fooled by chance results that may 'look' meaningful."

The statistical validity of personality tests rests on a foundation of quicksand and can be easily interred by any thoughtful critic. This, however, is far from its only sin of scientism. There is considerable doubt that the whole *theory* of personality testing can be proven, or is even tenable. Academic psychologists are candid in their lack of agreement on human personality, its components, or even its description. For example, in *Psychology of Personality*, edited by J. L. McCary, six authors present varied views of the human personality, from Margaret Mead's "cross-cultural" approach, through Gestalt psychology, cybernetics, and ethnology, to Leopold Bellak's directly "psychoanalytic theory of personality."

Some sophisticated testers admit the deficiency in grounded

theory, but as one tester-psychologist-professor who operates a Park Avenue test house states it half-embarrassedly: "We don't really know what human personality is. But I'm hopeful that with the large test battery we use—both projectives and inventories—we are measuring at least part of it."

Most question-and-answer testers, however, are unconcerned about the controversy. They have already decided that the human personality is composed of individual traits which, when measured, then placed together in a profile, constitute the true human personality. What are these traits? Simply those a particular test author has named or, more precisely, *invented* for his questionnaire. Some believe the human psyche must be cut at least sixteen ways (Cattell), while seven suffices for others (Thurstone), and a mere four for Bernreuter and the AVA. The quiz man's only ponderous problem seems to be: "Is the human personality really one-seventh Dominance or is it better described as one-fourth Sit-ability?"

This trait theory of personality has been examined by many researchers and found heavily wanting. Since these tests depend on questions and answers, they measure "aggressiveness" by asking how aggressive you are. This is similar in validity, as one critic commented, "to an IQ test that measures intelligence by asking the subject how smart he is." Lee J. Cronbach, professor of psychology, University of Illinois, deflated this tester myth by pointing out that a high score on what a test author may call "persistence" means only that the subject has a "tendency to claim to be persistent."

The quality of test questions and their nonsensical interpretations are fair game for outspoken psychologists including consultant Albert Ellis of New York. In the *Fourth Mental Measurements Yearbook*, Ellis toys with a popular test which asks: "Do you wish you were more attractive?" and then grants a point for "stability" for those who answer "No." "[This] means," says Ellis, "that only those who lie to themselves or to others are considered to be well adjusted in our society."

The inventory tester is quite satisfied with simple "Yes," "No," and possibly "?" answers to his questions. At least one researcher, however, has investigated the common-sense critique that such questions are often ambiguous, that people not only interpret them differently, but mean different things when they answer. Further, there is little opportunity to explain in detail to an unsympathetic graphite-oriented IBM machine.

To check out this theory, a skeptical researcher, P. Eisenberg—who reported his findings in the *Journal of General Psychology*—first administered a series of personality test questions to 219 college students, then asked them to explain why they had answered the way they did. One of the questions was the perennial: "Do you like to be alone?" Of the 219 students, 55 answered in writing that they *did like to be alone when they had work to do*. The 55 were unanimous in what they meant; however, in answering the skimpily worded question, they had interpreted its *meaning* differently. Eighteen had answered "Yes"; seventeen had marked "No"; and twenty had circled the question mark. In effect, the 55 had received different test scores for the same answer.

Since questions of this type describe "vigor" or "sociability" only because the test author says they do, Illinois' Lee Cronbach, among others, has stated categorically: "The names given to traits by test authors cannot be trusted." Testers seldom agree on the meaning of identical trait names, and in fact, testers' definitions of their traits often do not agree with the dictionary definitions of the word. The definition of "neuroticism," as a tester uses it, may exist only in his own mind, making it a highly subjective measure.

The author of the Edwards Personal Preference, for example, includes lengthy definitions of his fifteen traits in his test manual. A comparison of his definitions and those in the *Oxford Universal Dictionary*, however, creates a great semantic gulf, possibly the deep waters of psychological fantasy. In the *Oxford*, his trait "autonomy" is described as: *Personal freedom; Freedom (of the will); the Kantian doctrine of the self-determination of the will, apart from any object willed; opposite to heteronomy*. Edwards' definition concurs in part, but then he expands freely on the English language in a new psychological slang. "Autonomy," according to him, also includes "to do things that are unconventional," "to criticize those in positions of authority," and amazingly, "to avoid responsibilities and obligations."

The most classic case of trait names that cannot be trusted is the MMPI, whose scales are still awesomely labeled Schizophrenia, Paranoia, Hypomania, even though the weight of research indicates the scales do not specifically measure these traits or tendencies. The authors of the MMPI have since reportedly stated that it would probably have been better if initially, instead of naming their scales, they had merely numbered them!

In one interesting experiment on the reliability of trait names, reported in the *Journal of Abnormal Psychology*, 172 college students took a series of personality tests. When the scores were compared, researchers discovered an amazing fact: the collegians labeled "introverts" on the Bernreuter Introversion-Extroversion scale had scored as "extroverts" on another quiz test. Another researcher, George N. Graine, in the *Journal of Consulting Psychology*, compared scores on Autonomy on the Edwards Personal Preference Schedule with its supposedly opposite trait, Group Conformity, on the Rosenzweig Picture Frustration Test. Surprisingly, he found a "positive" correlation between the two instead of a negative one, raising doubt about all the applicants rejected by corporations for showing fearless individuality as measured by the Edwards—men who actually may have been the very conformists they seek, or vice versa, or even somewhere in between.

The amusing possibilities of this type of research have titillated skeptical psychologists. At Northwestern, A. R. Gilliand did a comparison of the similarly named scales of the MMPI and a test popular in Los Angeles, the Humm-Wadsworth, matching up such similar "traits" as Hysteroid on the Humm with Psychopathic on the MMPI; Mania and Hypomania; Autistic and Schizoid; Paranoia and Depression. His findings: "No general agreement between scores on the two tests could be found."

Even the "interest tests," with their lucid-sounding scales, fail to correlate with those on their sister tests. A thorough research study by Dr. Wallace Gobetz of New York University indicates that the famed Kuder and Strong tests are talking about different things even though they bear almost the same labels. His results, for example, show only a .45 correlation between "art" interest on the Kuder and the "artist" scale on the Strong; and only .50 correlation between Strong's "business detail" and Kuder's "computational" scales. "Social service" interest, being labeled the same on both, should—if the English language is to hold up—have close to a perfect 1.0 correlation. The result: a bare .39, indicating that Strong and Kuder do not agree on what "social service" interest is, adding an insurmountable test burden to trusting corporations and counselors.

The fallacy of personality inventories appears to be deep-seated. In addition to the conclusion that trait names are meaningless, there is doubt that traits such as "honesty" or "sociability" are consistent enough in most people to be measured with these simplistic tools. People can be very sociable at parties, less with neighbors, and perhaps not at all in a corporate locale. Others are superficially sociable but shy away from friendships, and perhaps do not really enjoy the company of others. Honesty is a perfect example of the elusive multidimensional trait: Honest with one's wife? Honest with the government on a tax return? Honest with a freely offered expense account?

Two researchers—Herbert H. Meyer and Joseph M. Bertotti of General Electric—writing in *Personnel*, stress this point. "One reason why personality tests often fail to provide valid predictions is probably that personality 'traits' themselves are not always highly consistent. Our personalities vary somewhat with the situations in which we are placed. We are all 'retiring' in some situations and 'aggressive' in others. We may show great 'perseverance' in one kind of activity and little in another."

If the tests are this faulty, what do the scores mean? If not personality, what is being measured? Psychologist Albert Ellis makes a stab at this dilemma and comes to the conclusion that personality test scores are really measuring several outside factors: intelligence, motivation, psychological sophistication, psychological defenses, tendency to lie. His attitude toward their ability to measure *personality*, however, is indicated in a summing-up piece of recent research on personality tests. Says Ellis: "It was especially found that in none of the areas in which they are commonly employed do personality inventories consistently show significant group discriminations."

The testers are self-conscious about the skeptical eyes raised at their work, but have cleverly turned some criticism around to make it work for them. Agreed: tests are not all they're cracked up to be, say the brain watchers. But the skill is in the tester, not the test. That's why we need the "professional" interpretation of a trained tester, who can use "caution" in evaluating these raw numbers which might admittedly be a syrupy siren call for the uninitiated.

This vociferous peddling of "caution" as an antidote for bad tests passes the bounds of reason. The testers would have us believe that "professional skill" can make black into white: that misleading test scores can be alloyed into worthwhile personality indicators if left to the hands of a "trained" tester.

This propaganda has been known to turn even the heads of the skeptical. One giant electrical firm which is no proponent of personality testing (although it has had its share of naïve adventures) published a volume titled *The Selection Testing Program*. After discussing the limitations of personality tests, the booklet comments, in effect, that the observed scores are often *the reverse of the truth*, and must therefore be viewed with "care"! Says the industrial giant's strange testing guide:

"Unfortunately, the results of validation studies connected with interest and personality tests often give misleading results. For example, in some studies a negative relationship has been found between scores on a personality inventory and a criterion of on-the-job success. This is probably due to the fact that the high-rated people are more secure persons, who are inclined to be more honest and straightforward in answering questions. On the other hand, the low-rated persons are likely to be more insecure and defensive and therefore they may be more inclined to falsify their answers in order to get the highest score possible. Consequently the interpretation of results on tests in the interest and personality area must be made *with a great deal of care*." (Italics mine.)

It would be interesting to learn how "care" and "professionalism" can salvage hopeless validation studies, such as one conducted at the University of Minnesota. The Bell Adjustment Inventory was given to 800 students, and the scores put away temporarily. Meanwhile the same students were interviewed regularly during the college year by the campus guidance officer for any indications of home or emotional problems. The long-range interviewing results were then compared with the personality tests scores. The results? The Bell had falsely labeled 73 happy collegians as youngsters with pressing home problems, had failed to identify 40 who actually had these problems, and had chosen only 40 others correctly. Using all the "care" possible in the scoring and evaluation, the box score on "emotional adjustment" was even lower: the Bell had 32 hits, 75 misses, and 42 false identifications.

The fakeability of personality quizzes is a constant brain watcher's migraine. It has accounted for the recent popularity of the forced-choice tests, including the Gordon and Edwards, in which the applicant cannot answer "Yes" or "No," but must make a choice between alternatives, each of which is supposed to be equally "socially acceptable." The stymied applicant, unable, according to the theory, to pick out the favored item, then answers truthfully despite himself.

In the past year critics have taken a seasoned second look at forced-choice tests and their supposed unfakeability and value. Edwards originally tested the social desirability of his items on college students at the University of Washington, matching up those the students judged as equally desirable as the couplets in his test. Other studies, however, indicate that not everyone goes to the U. of W.—or any college— and that opinion on what constitutes "status" or "social desirability" varies greatly from group to group, and from person to person.

A study on the Edwards in the *Journal of Consulting Psychology* turned up highly significant differences of opinion on the "desirability" of 30 pairs of statements, a point substantiated by Samuel Messick of the Educational Testing Service. Without such *equal* couplets the entire theory of the forced-choice personality test is meaningless, for it is not only fakeable like its predecessors, but grounded on a false premise.

The sledge-hammer criticism that has been leveled against personality questionnaires has, ironically enough, given heart to other testers—the projective people, who are waging an intent battle for recognition and even superiority. Despite their admittedly impressive front, they are meeting with equal skepticism from unimpressed critics. The psychological literature abounds with rechecks of claims made for projective tests—from the Rorschach to the sentence completion tests —with the general conclusion that many of the initial studies were propelled by sheer enthusiasm, and little else.

We have already seen several projective studies end abjectly (Chapter III: The Clinical Testers), and there are hundreds more available if space permitted. Human figure drawing tests, for one, abound, as do their debunkers. In the *Psychological Bulletin*, one of these, Y. C. Swensen, examined a famous drawing test in depth and concluded: "Personality factors revealed through the test do not conform to Machover's hypothesis." Another figure drawing study (Silverstein and Robinson, *Annual Review of Psychology*) produced the same denouement. Working with children, these researchers showed that a group of experienced psychologists *could not* use the "55 scoring signs" to match up the figure drawings of normal and emotionally disabled youngsters.

There is a current cliché in projective testing that a person's "creativity"—the trait that has eluded and frustrated testers who know its twenty-four-carat market value—can be spotted in the movement visualized in projective tests. That the person who "sees" more movement in the stimuli is the one with a "feel" for the "original" is a favorite comment of projective testers. To check this off-the-skull theorizing, one researcher (D. P. Griffin, *Journal of Consulting Psychology*) asked the department heads of a college to select youngsters who had exhibited creativity in their work and those who had not. Griffin administered the Levy Movement Blots, a projective supposedly valuable for this esoteric function, to both groups. The result was simple failure. Neither the creators nor the noncreators had any more "movement"—at least in their blots.

The TAT and Rorschach are also mercilessly pilloried. The critiques range from doubt to denunciations that should make every inkblot practitioner blanch every time he asks an unknowing subject what he makes of one of the neat Swiss blots. In the *Revue de Psychologie Appliquée*, R. W. Payne states: "There is no evidence that the Rorschach can be used to assess whether or not individuals are well or poorly adjusted. . . . There is no evidence that the test is of any practical use at the moment, either for describing personality or predicting behavior."

Blind brain watching, in which the tester confronts a man's responses, rather than the man himself, accounts for a sizable percentage of the test industry's gross. Yet, judging from comments from many testers (not from blind firms), it is viciously attacked as an inferior art. Sidney Koran, a Long Island tester, for one, refuses to defend competitors who process only bloodless test forms. "I will not eliminate the interview," he says, "mainly because I am dealing with individuals and not with test scores as revealed in paper-and-pencil tests." Richardson, Bellows, Henry also find testing in absentia inexcusable. "I don't believe in blind psychological assessment," says a spokesman. "I think it's a game. You are asking the instruments to do something they are not designed for."

The projective brain watchers have assumed the attitude of a psychological élan that is designed to disarm the critic and awe the competition. Despite the bold pose, however, critical psychologists are convinced that projective testing is probably the furthest removed from science—that it is actually a personal art or talent, much like that of an abstract painter. "One of the problems with projective testing," says

Dr. Benjamin Shimberg of the Educational Testing Service in Princeton, "is that clinically oriented tests are being administered by clinically oriented people. How much is psychological technique and how much is art? Actually these people are applying years of training and experience, but they can't expand or really train other people to do it the way they do, because it is so personal."

An *art* that depends on some flash of intuitive powers is hardly the definition of science, and aware psychologists are the first to admit it. Probably the most devastating indictment of the projective artistry in testing was delivered recently by Professor Hans Eysenck of the Institute of Psychiatry of London in the *Fifth Mental Measurements Yearbook*. Eysenck outlined a definitive ten-point antiprojective brief in language fierce enough to convey his concern over a spreading cultism. Here are a few of his candid points, the guts of an historic psychological manifesto:

1. There is no consistent meaningful and testable theory underlying modern projective devices.

2. There is no evidence for the great majority of the postulated relationships between projective test indicators and personality tests.

3. There is no evidence for the predictive power of projective techniques with respect to success and failure in a wide variety of fields where personality qualities play an important part.

4. There is no evidence that conscious or unconscious conflicts, attitudes, fears or fantasies in patients can be diagnosed by means of projective techniques in such a way as to give congruent results with assessments made by psychiatrists independently.

We have already seen several testing fallacies at work. You cannot assume that a trait on a quiz personality test measures "neuroticism" because the test author calls it that; also whatever the test is measuring, it is generally doing it badly. Similarly, the projective tester has invented a scoring discipline for your reactions that has meaning only in his brain, if there. Few of these fallacies, however, would have a chance to dominate us without the cooperation of the businessman, who instinctively helps establish the criteria for his hired testers. If the tester presents a scale labeled "neurotic," the businessman immediately makes it quite obvious that he does not want anyone in his plant who scores high on such a nefarious measure.

This question of criteria—of what makes a good anything—is the largest unsolved riddle in human measurement. It makes little sense to catalogue opinions on a man's "sociability" if we have no idea how large a dose of it is necessary or preferable in society, the PTA, or the executive suite. The simple truth about criteria is that having tried to formalize them, we know no more about the subject now than before, and perhaps less.

Theories on the criteria of "executive personality" abound, for example, but most of them turn up with suspiciously positive, socially blessed traits. One psychologist, writing in *Personnel,* described the perfect executive criteria as the property of a man who is a black-and-white-thinker, an optimist, a self-confident, personable, practical individual who is predictable in words and action. And even an enormous extrovert. Others doubt that corporate personality is that easily defined. An IBM psychologist recently stated it this way: "In my observation, some good managers are sociable, some are not, some are religious, others are not, some delegate their work, others do not. Some are easy to work for, others are not." In the 1960 *Annual Review of Psychology,* B. von Haller Gilmer of Carnegie Tech puts this lack of intelligent criteria at the crux of the testing dilemma. "Progress in scientific prediction of executive success is severely hampered by inability to solve the criterion problem."

If most organizations and testers were candid, the truth would reveal that almost all criteria for job slots today are monumental hunches, prejudices about professional and occupational attributes garnered from such knowledgeable fountainheads as Sunday cartoons, Hollywood films, novels, and old corporate tales. On closer examination most of these industrial folktales turn out to be the fiction we always suspected.

As everybody who has ever viewed the pince-nezed bank tellers in films knows, clerks are not very aggressive. In fact, there is something in the very quietude of the clerk's psyche and his unaggressive bearing of cool, if not inspired, efficiency that engenders trust. Salesmen, on the other hand, as everyone also knows, are aggressive, often to a pushy fault.

These two "established" criteria were investigated by two researchers, who examined the personnel of a loan office of the Household Finance Corporation with astounding results. Says the report on HFC published in a National Industrial Conference Board publication: "In the case of many of the purchasable personality tests, results were obtained which ran counter to expectations. Clerical workers seemed to be more aggressive than salesmen, sales clerks were higher than managers."

The subjectivity of job criteria, and its relation to the prejudices of the man who establishes them for a firm—whether its psychologist, tester, or board chairman—was illustrated in an experiment conducted for the Adjutant General's Office of the U. S. Army. One hundred infantry company commanders were asked how they visualized their job. The responses differed broadly, with those of narrow outlook making such statements as "to follow orders." Others stated the broad approach: to "look after and protect the welfare of my men." Next, the superior officers were asked to rate the effectiveness of these same 100 company commanders, and also define their criteria for the job. The result was obvious: whether a company commander was rated effective generally depended on whether his concept of the job criteria agreed with his superior officer's.

The author of the article "The Riddle of Executive Criteria" in *Personnel* Magazine which described this study adds his own comment: "Industry, unfortunately, has not always appreciated the complexity of the questions to which it is seeking answers. Companies for the most part have wanted neatly packaged programs, not research."

Criticism of the lack of corporate research on criteria—of the habit of testing men for a job before knowing what one should be looking for—has partially penetrated through to a portion of the industrial community. Fourteen firms, including Bell, IBM, and Westinghouse, have financed an Executive Study under the research auspices of the Educational Testing Service. "We don't know what makes a good executive, but we are attempting an independent new look at the situation," says an ETS spokesman in Princeton, New Jersey. "Before we can assay a man, we have to learn more about job performance. We are doing this with an in-basket technique in which we simulate the executive's job, in this case the head of a large community fund. Through letters and memos he indicates what he plans to do. We believe this approach is better than seeking specific traits, which is probably meaningless in many executives."

This ETS research is undoubtedly noteworthy, but as in

all such programs, there is often a near-fatal shortcut between the simulated test situation and reality, a gap that
casts doubt even on such better researched studies in the
personality field. In the ETS Executive Study, for example,
it is "impractical" (too expensive) to provide the men with
secretaries. Instead, all work is done in longhand by the
executives themselves. Anyone who has worked as an executive can readily assess the difference in his efficiency, and
temperament, if he had to use foolscap and pencil to write
out all the decisions he wanted transformed into action. As
one ETS spokesman candidly comments: "Of course we don't
know if a guy who is decisive on the in-basket will be
decisive on the job, and vice versa."

The feeling that corporations do not really have a valid
idea of what they are searching for is indicated by the
constant reports of perspicacious test takers who not only
fake their way to valedictorian scores but also succeed ad-
mirably on the job. If testers' theories on job criteria held
water, the faker who temporarily mesmerizes psychologists
with a borrowed psychological profile would be unmasked
as soon as he exhibited his true personality on the job—a
personality which should be in conflict with the established
corporate criteria. As the less sophisticated personnel men
state it: "The people who fake are fooling no one but themselves."

The truth, however, is that since the personality criteria
are so unrelated to corporate reality, those who squeeze
through the initial testing mesh are quite safe if they simply
do what is expected of them—their job. An intimate demon-
stration of this, in which this author played an active "scientific" role, bore out the truth of the unlimited value of
faking, and the dearth of post-hiring personality requirements
with which to tangle.

A friend, an intelligent thirty-year-old with a *cum laude*
degree from a large eastern university, had been unemployed
for several months. He became jubilant when a billion-dollar
corporation answered his situation-wanted ad, but was
equally depressed at the request that he submit to a battery
of personality tests. He confided his problem, and when he
mentioned the firm name, this author realized that he had
interviewed its testing director and knew its test battery
intimately.

The night before his encounter, we sat resolutely at his
dining room table preparing for the grand experiment. The
major test was the Edwards Personal Preference, a forced-

choice test specifically designed to thwart such perverse attempts at image building. First he took the test honestly, without any help or extra instructions. The result was grizzly: a friendly (very high "nurturance"), lively (high "change"), self-thinking (high "autonomy") individual with absolutely no desire to manipulate the puppet strings of destiny (low "dominance" or "leadership"). This might be the profile performance of an ideal citizen of a better (simpler, less demanding) civilization, but his test scores were hopelessly askew from the obvious criteria demanded by the corporate empire he was determined to join.

The next task was imagining the corporation's executive criteria, actually projecting the Edwards profile into the company environment. For survival's sake, we performed an elaborate, intuitive brain watch on the corporation—an old-line, conservative outfit—and came up with their ideal man on the Edwards. Of the test's fifteen traits, we concluded he would have to score quite high on Achievement, Order, Affiliation, Endurance, and not as high—but still quite above average—in Dominance and Heterosexuality. On scales such as Nurturance, Exhibition, and Change, we concluded that scores near the norm would be safe enough. The good executive in this company, we were convinced (*a priori or hunch technique*) would score low in such uncorporate traits as Autonomy (to feel free to do what one wants), Intraception (to analyze one's motives), Succorance (to have a fuss made over one when hurt), Abasement (to feel inferior to others in most respects), and, naturally, Aggression (to get revenge for insults).

Having plotted the profile, we could have adjourned the session, hoping that the firmly implanted criteria would have correctly influenced his test answers the following morning. Instead, until four in the morning we painstakingly charted each of the test's 225 questions, working and reworking the forced-choice answers ("Choose one: I like to be able to do things better than other people can; I like to eat in new and strange restaurants") until we had *exactly* duplicated our estimate of the corporate ideal.

The following morning, after only three hours' sleep, the subject took his personality test for his intended corporation. The following week he was called in and congratulated by personnel on the fact that his test results were "exceptional." In light of his performance, they indicated, they expected good things of him. Today, a year since the great rehearsal, he is still with the firm, has received a promotion and a raise, and numerous plaudits for his labors. Yet today, if he were to retake the Edwards *honestly* (no kamikaze, he), he would still undoubtedly show that same undominant, autonomous, lively profile so fervently despised by his corporation and its testers.

The experience of testing the testers is an exhilarating one. The success of the first experiment led to the inevitable idea of choosing a subject and having him submit to a large number of personality tests, so that the results on each could be compared. Is a neurotic on one test invariably the same on another widely distributed national personality quiz? Are the maladjusted, the malcontents spotted equally well on all corporate personality quizzes? If the measurements are meaningful, as test authors claim, shouldn't they agree?

The most readily available and cooperative subject was the author himself. More than half a dozen major tests and their scoring keys were collected. Allowing a few days between tests to insure that boredom or ennui of a testing siege wouldn't influence the results, all the elite were taken —first the Bernreuter, then the Thurstone, the Edwards, the Washburne, the Gordon, the Minnesota Personality Scale, the Study of Values, the Kuder, the Strong, the MMPI, and even—with the assistance of an "analyst"— the multiadjective AVA. The attitude toward the questions would be the same in each case: reasonably honest without excessive introspection or flagellation. Even though it could hardly qualify as a perfectly controlled study, the results were anxiously awaited.

The tests agreed only on disagreeing. On the Bernreuter Inventory, the author emerged as a Gibraltar of Adjustment: emotional stability in the top 10 percent; self-confidence in the top 3 percent; and sociability in the top 8 percent—a cheery, assured, mature individual. The Minnesota Personality Scale, however, emerged with an entirely different man, one of only average stability and morale with a low social adjustment—in fact a somewhat troubled and morose man in the bottom 25 percent of the population. The clinical MMPI score was quite routine (near norm), while the Washburne was exultant: an ideal employee in the top 5 percent of the population: happy, nonalienated, with high purpose, good control, judgment, and even truthfulness.

While sociability was quite high on the Bernreuter, it was reasonably low on the Gordon Personal Profile, in fact, the lowest of its four measured traits. Stability and self-confidence on the Gordon were not as high as Bernreuter's, but responsibility zoomed to the ninety-fourth percentile. The AVA Analyst, however, doubted this "responsibility," at least in the corporate sense, for his verdict was that the respondent—whose vigor, or AVA "life force," was among the highest—would do better administering his own corporation.

The tests of interest showed no greater unanimity. On the Strong, the magic A (agreement with professionals in the field 69 percent of the time) came up strongly for "physician." But on the Kuder, the scientific interest was only average. On the Kuder, literary interest soared to the ninety-sixth percentile, but the "aesthetic" scale on the Study of Values failed to respond in turn. The low point on the Kuder was struck in "persuasive" interest (fifteenth percentile), but the AVA foresaw a fortune in life insurance selling. Although computational interest was reasonably powerful on the Kuder (sixty-fifth percentile), the Strong delivered discouraging C's for all the computational arts, from CPA to bookkeeper.

When digested, with consummate professional "caution," what could it all tally? Obviously, an extroverted hermit, both morose and happy, an unemployable who responds beautifully to corporate life, the average pedestrian soul who stands head-and-ego above the crowd, in a spectacularly adjusted, but highly neurotic way.

If personality testing is such an unholy intellectual waif, how, we might ask, has it managed to have itself adopted so eagerly, and by such well-heeled parents? One answer, of course, is the lack of *scientific* understanding among the businessmen-customers and their personnel managers who support it in such style. Dr. R. Stagner, writing in *Personnel Psychology,* elaborates this lapse of pragmatic sense among businessmen. "In the field of engineering, chemistry, power sources and raw material supply, the average businessman has learned to think realistically and to demand quantitative evidence concerning the value of an item before buying it," he says. "In the novel field of psychological measurement, on the other hand, many executives are still amazingly gullible. They often purchase expensive 'employee selection' programs with no scientific evidence that the service offered has any value whatsoever."

Another stimulant to test acceptance has been a series of well-circulated but groundless rumors on the spectacular success of such programs as the OSS World War II testing program and the Life Insurance Agency Management Association personality tests. As we have seen, the OSS was a monumental flop, and the LIAMA personality sections had a temporary, possibly chance validity that has long since vanished. But opportunist brain watchers, capitalizing on the uninformed, have continued to peddle the value of these supposedly impressive experiments. In fact, one large testing house in New York, with over 100 prominent industrial clients, claims to use part of an outdated LIAMA personality record and promotes it to clients as "one of the only validated personality tests."

Another common myth about personality prediction has been the "feeling" that the vast psychological screening program carried on in the armed forces during World War II saved the government money and catastrophe by weeding out personality risks beforehand and exempting them from military service before they could crack. Several years ago Professor Eli Ginzberg of Columbia University began an exhaustive study underwritten by fifteen industrial firms and the Ford Foundation, which was recently published in three-volume form under the title *The Ineffective Soldier, Lessons For Management and the Nation.* In the volume *The Lost Divisions,* Ginzberg relates how our psychological pre-screening activity eliminated 1,000,000 men—or 55 divisions —from military service, many of them inaccurately. "Our appraisal of psychiatric screening in World War II points to two conclusions: the screen was not very effective and it had little predictive value," he says.

The establishment of the testing empire demanded this gullible audience, but it also required enthusiastic proponents to do the selling, preferably practicing psychologists. In addition to the test firms and these men who became their consultants, there are also the academic men who author tests, the royalties of which can exceed their university stipends. What of their intellectual excellence, their scientific discipline, their professional integrity? Has it been lost in the melee of brain watchery?

The simple fact of the field is that personality "results" heralded by one experimenter fail to stand up under closer examination by a second. Charlatanism is seldom, if ever, at the core. The actual reasons are many, but one youthful psychologist, Dr. Robert Rosenthal, who recently won the $1,000 Socio-Psychological Prize of the American Association for the Advancement of Science, offers one possible explanation: unconscious bias. Calling it "The Phenomenon of Experimenter Bias," Rosenthal believes that results in social science experiments can be unconsciously altered by the personality and expectations of the one who conducts the experiment. Often the experimenter ends up not with the objective truth—but with the results he hopes for, and expects.

In this study, experimenters exhibited magazine photographs to students and asked them to judge whether the person pictured had been experiencing success or failure. He found, surprisingly enough, that subjects could be made to tend to agree with the experimenters' own ratings of the photographs through subtle unconscious gestures, manner, and tone of communication. The results of experiments can also be strongly influenced by the researchers' "ambitions," says Dr. Rosenthal, as in a study conducted for a Ph.D. or to prove a preconceived scholarly notion. (Or, equally, we might conjecture, to create a salable personality test.)

To fully understand the personality test debacle, we must also consider that it has been nurtured in the permissive, relatively undisciplined climate of psychology, a field that has yet to provide adequate controls on excessive claims and promotion of unsubstantiated research findings. Added to this is the psychologists' reluctance to wash any of their dirty linen in public and thus risk chipping the profession's not oversturdy image. The result, a plethora of extravagant claims of knowledge we do not have, and instruments that will not do what they state, has been the additional component needed to crystallize the "nonscience" of commercial personality testing.

To some sensitive psychologists, the din of testers is a revolting cacophony, but they feel relatively helpless against the slickly organized onslaught. One psychologist, W. H. Holtzman, writing in the *American Psychologist*, registered personal outrage at excessive claims made in test manuals on a basis of ethics—professional values which, he states, exist on paper but are seldom enforced. Holtzman makes his case around the American Psychological Association's Code of Ethics (paragraph B, Principle 15) relating to excessive claims—a brief that should be a rallying call for similarly distressed colleagues. "When taken very seriously, I dare say that this principle is violated more flagrantly than any other in our Code of Ethics," he states. "The enthusiastic author and obliging publisher cannot resist the temptation to sell the test as the latest word, the answer to

every eager personnel executive's problem. In glancing casually through some of the blurbs currently in circulation,
I have been greatly disturbed by the rather cavalier treatment of the fundamental issue by some publishers and their
authors. And yet no one seems to be doing much about it,
probably because in most cases there is not much that can
be done. Such promotional activities rarely seem outrageous
enough to goad someone into pressing charges of unethical
conduct."

The reticence of these scientist-psychologists has been ably
mated to the huzzas and profitable hoopla of their brain-
watching colleagues and the slothful ignorance of industry
—into a formidable cult that operates only through the
grace of many who should know considerably better.

12 CONCLUSION: MORALITY AND THE MEAN

Not long ago, in response to an article the author had written, an irate woman reader wrote that encouraging people, especially youngsters, to "cheat" on personality tests was an irresponsible act of immorality in a day when it needed little assistance. Instead of evoking dismay, the response was welcome, for she had inadvertently crystallized the argument against personality testing as one of modern morality.

Our elaborate system of law is designed to protect the individual against encroachment by the state, or by false witness. In return for veracity demanded in our courts we have provided the safeguards of law of evidence, impartial jury, and habeas corpus. During periods of nonlaw, however, when these safeguards are absent under tyranny, the history of morality shows that the individual has always been encouraged to resist with all human guile, including conspiracy, rebellion, and even terror.

While the dangers of nonlaw are fully understood and the responses to them condoned, we have yet to tangle with the implications of a *nonscience*—such as personality testing—and the individual's moral responsibility against such a threat. Although few in the corporate ranks will ever find themselves tested in courts of law, millions have seen their lives altered with the nonscience of personality testing without even a presumption of individual guilt. The moral implications of personality testing lie not only in its inaccuracy (which, by analogy, would mean filling our jails with the innocent) but its approach to group statistical guilt. A man is accused and convicted not for any unsocial act or behavior, but for his *variance,* either from a norm or a projective tester's highly imaginative criteria.

In this nonscience of group likelihood of criminality, just as in nonlaw, there are no specific safeguards, no psychological habeas corpus, no impartial judge or unanimous jury to review, rebuke, or even find in scientific contempt. Although society has not yet outlined the suitable defenses against nonscience, we should assume that they are quite the same as those needed to curb nonlaw.

In his pioneer work *The Organization Man,* William H. Whyte, Jr. has called personality tests the "Tests of Conformity." His observation is trenchant, but we might extend it further to describe them as the "Tests of Mundanity." The brain watcher, in his servile attempts to assuage management and live off its largesse, has grasped the current inadequacies and foibles of each occupation he is called upon to test and has used them as his solemn criteria. The personality and prejudices of the mean working doctor, journalist, sales manager—rather than the ideal—are his guidelines.

We have instinctively assumed that morality and the ideal have a spiritual kinship; that no matter how efficiently life squeezes us into compromise, the goal of human behavior is *not the pragmatic* that appears to work, but the contemplation of principles and the exceptional men who emulate them. However, tests such as the Strong Vocational Interest, for example, measure adaptability for a profession, not in terms of a person's relation to the ideals of the profession, but to the mean prejudices of the "average" men who people it. Few of us would want our future physicians, politicians, scientists, or even salesmen sculptured in the personality of the current practitioners, as satisfied or dissatisfied as we may be with their performance. We argue and educate to escape the limitations of our mundanity, yet we have allowed—in fact subsidized—the brain watcher to bring us sharply back toward it.

The importance of impartiality of judgment is another caisson in the framework of our morality, and the partiality of much in personality testing has been questioned. Because the tester's judgments flatter, appease, comfort, or convince the corporation which pays, and are in their joint vested interest, we must assume his operation is not impartial. Dr. Lawrence S. Kubie, Associate in Neurology at the Columbia College of Physicians and Surgeons, makes this point strongly in a booklet, "Psychiatry and Industry," published by the National Committee for Mental Health. "In the first place it is clearly essential that the representatives of the psychological sciences should be in a position the impartiality of which can never be questioned," says Dr. Kubie. "They must be like the expert who is retained by a court, rather than the expert whose testimony is hired by one side of a legal controversy. *Therefore they should never be employed by labor or by management*." (Italics mine.)

Dr. Jay L. Otis of Western Reserve, former president of the Division of Consulting Psychology of the American Psychological Association, coined the phrase "psychological espionage" (see Chapter IV: Testing Men on the Job) to describe some aspects of corporate testing. He too raises the point of impartiality and the moral and ethical role of psychologists, especially when wielding test instruments of which the subject is ignorant.

"Again we find that many persons referred to the professional psychologists are there because they were sent, not because of any desire on their part," Otis says. "Some are in legal trouble, some are victims of job maladjustment, some are applicants, some are being considered for promotion, and some for possible transfer or discharge. What role does the psychologist assume? Does he represent society or the criminal, the company or the incumbent, the employment manager or the applicant, the manager or the failure? The examinee is on safe grounds during the examination until he is faced with certain psychological measures he does not understand. Without telling him the ultimate implications of his remarks we show him some inkblots and proceed to help or harm him by interpreting such remarks as cat, insides of person, branches, sweet peas, sunset and crab in terms of introversion-extroversion, inferiority and insecurity. I merely raise the question, do we as psychologists have the right to subject a captive examinee to an examination without a full explanation of what the real purpose of that examination is? Certainly this form of study comes under our definition of psychological espionage."

Dr. Otis' incisive comments raise many points, all touching on the morality of the brain watch: the tester's espionage; the moral implications of using disguised tests; the captive examinee; and the violation of personal privacy. Dr. Harry

Levinson, director of the Division of Industrial Mental Health of the Menninger Foundation, speaking before the American Psychological Association, denounced current personality test policies which violate personal privacy and warned of public arousement. "Failure to reach policies more sound than those which are presently being employed," he said, "will bring down upon the heads of the psychologists the same appellations which for a long time were thrown at industrial physicians who, because they were regarded as company spies, became anathema to employees."

The obeisance of the tester to management, and his compulsion to protect what he thinks are the best interests of the corporation rather than the individual, lie at the core of his partiality. In his volume *The Servants of Power*, Loren Baritz tells the fifty-year history of the strange alliance of management and the social scientists, in which the sociologist, the psychologist—and the tester—who work for industry have each become just another "animated tool," more than anxious to serve power on the corporation's—rather than his own professional—standard. Of them all, the personality tester has sold his birthright of impartiality the most willingly.

To take a full look at the brain watcher, we should also consider the morality of prediction. Firstly, the immorality of false prediction is obvious. The child labeled a "delinquent" who proves to be a thoughtful teenager and a healthy adult, the executive shunted aside as a predicted "failure" who proves successful in a firm that eschews predictions, are obviously victims of an unholy conspiracy. We have seen enough of this false prediction in brain watchery (including the hundreds of hopeful young advertising men who fooled the 4A tester's dire predictions) to conclude that this aspect of it is clearly immoral.

Many doubt the existence of *any* valid prediction by personality testers, even on a broad group basis. But, for the sake of this discussion *only*, we will entertain the thesis that some testers have achieved broad *group distinctions*, significant in testing terms of perhaps a 10 percent improvement on chance. What is the morality of predictions that are "psychologically significant," yet wrong almost half the time? Obviously, assessing men by group averages violates our concept that the group, or society, operates only to serve the individual, not the reverse as in other societies.

We should, perhaps, extend the argument one niche further: that the *mere attempt* to predict the behavior of individual men is a violation of personal destiny. The prediction, and the undue value placed upon it, influences the destiny—and therefore the behavior—of the man *without his consent*, and is therefore intrinsically immoral. There is something unspoken but still clearly defined in Western idealism that revolts against the limiting of a man and his fate through predictive categorizing, false or otherwise.

The immorality of discrimination in employment seems to be well settled in our culture. Refusal to hire or promote a Slav, Negro, Italian, Jew, Puerto Rican, or whatever, because of his color, religion, or extraction, is still prevalent, but a vestige that we have clearly labeled as immoral and have been fighting with education and FEPC law.

But while the battle against obvious discrimination has been proceeding reasonably well, the new and more subtle discrimination of personality testing has assumed proportions at least equal to the "No Jews Need Apply" psychology of a half-century ago. In most states, it is illegal to ask a man to state his race on an application blank, yet there is no hesitancy in asking about his sex life on a personality test. We dictate that an airline must hire a Negro as a stewardess, yet we permit corporations to exclude certain "types" because they are "too liberal," or "too autonomous," or insufficiently or excessively "heterosexual," or handicapped with too much "dominance," or too little of it. Is it any less offensive to discriminate against an "Introvert" than an "Italian"?

The new discrimination of personality testing has been recognized by the administrator of one state's Fair Employment Practices Commission, but only, it is reported, on the usual grounds of religion. He has asked that offensive questions on religion be omitted from a test. A closer examination by FEPC groups will perhaps reveal the deeper extent of this new discrimination, for the criteria of race, color, and religion are only the traditionalist trappings of prejudice. We now have a host of new false symbols of separateness —from high neuroticism scores to noncreative inkblot responses—to contend with. They will require a more assiduous, and technically competent, FEPC if we are to properly tangle with this new barrier to equal opportunity.

Discrimination through testing occasionally goes further in its prejudicial base. The use of clinical group tests, such as the MMPI, to screen normal people for employment is a case in point. In fact, the moral and legal question of their use in employment screening has already been discussed by one large test distributor, The Psychological Corporation.

One of its Test Service Bulletins, entitled "Personnel Selection Tests and Fair Employment Practices," states: "Quite a few personality tests are designed for use in clinical diagnosis and personal counseling of individuals who are suspected of psychological maladjustment or who seek help on personal problems. *Even though the personnel officer would like to use them in the hiring process, there are several compelling scientific reasons why he should not—reasons as compelling as the legal question of their use.*" (Italics mine.)

The legality of the employment use of such "psychotic-hunters," with their mislabeled "schizophrenia" and "mania" scales, is not questioned often enough despite the fact that quasi-medical diagnoses are made from them, often by unqualified personnel. The potential danger of such practice is obvious, and one in which the public deserves the full protection of the law.

The sensitive psychologist who has turned to brain watching for its better income ("If the academic and business testing fields were equally lucrative I would prefer to do academic work," admits a Long Island "personnel consultant") may be intuitively aware of many of these arguments, and be desperately seeking a moral "out" for his behavior. He is reinforced by the fact that the psychological profession is currently timid about self-criticism and discipline of its members—whether they provide canned pseudo psychology on television or do errant personality testing. There is also the hopeful rationale that his personality testing, if not beneficial to individuals, has at least a salutary effect on the American corporation, and therefore our economy.

The idea that a moral argument for brain watching exists in a corporate sense is just as false as many other brain-watching premises. During the past decade, when testing has been most prevalent, the growth rate of our economy has declined. Although there is absolutely no evidence that one has caused the other, if we were to use the tester's own techniques, we might call it a "suspicious correlation" that should at least be investigated.

In actuality, the truth—thus far—is probably that although it has personally injured and threatened untold numbers of individual lives, testing has had only a slightly dragging, if any, effect on the economy. Some giant corporations who use testing flourish, as do those who violently refuse its intrusion. (I suspect that small companies seeking rapid growth suffer more from its excesses.) In a prosperous era, in an industrial empire that has already been established, only a rash and murderous personnel policy could destroy it, especially with the army of talented and well-educated youngsters who are anxious to enter the corporate cocoon. Whatever the criteria, some of these youngsters—through guile or chance—will inevitably match the tester's requirements and be accepted. The great gamble is the firm in a highly competitive industry which turns to personality testing to improve its relative position, perhaps to find that it has sapped some of the original strength that built it.

There are also those who believe that this corporate luxury of de-emphasizing the individual will eventually come home to roost during a crisis. Andrew Hacker, of the Department of Government of Cornell University, sees this stress on corporate adjustment rather than the raw nerve of the individual as a flirtation with disaster. Writing in *Commonweal*, Mr. Hacker—although not speaking specifically about testing—makes his point eloquently. "The corporation man is adjusted to be sure: but he is only adjusted to the needs of the present. The time will come, as it always has, when men will need new concepts, new institutions, and when crises now unheard of will have to be faced. The premium then will be on the force of the individual personality and an impatience with complacent schemes for social stability."

This de-emphasizing of the individual is foremost among the brain watchers' many sins. The necessity for a "safe" hiring policy that will not agitate the management who pays, has made the tester suspicious of the true individual. Using his averages as a guide, the tester rationalizes that the individual is more apt to rock than guide the boat. He knows that although evenness and constancy in men may not move civilizations, or corporations, forward, it is difficult to trace any slow, imperceptible backward movement when things appear so steady.

In actuality, in most situations of stress (or fierce competition) it is the individual who rallies the group, makes the unique contribution, extracts sense out of chaos. "Most great advances are made by individuals," agrees Professor Malcolm P. McNair of Harvard University. "Devoting too much time in business to trying to keep everybody happy results in conformity, in failure to build individuals," he writes in the *Harvard Business Review*. "It has become the fashion to decry friction, but friction has its uses. Without friction there are no sparks."

The tester's fight for "adjustment" has plainly been a fight for the status quo, and a fight against genius and its unpredictability. The dull business leader is usually willing to make this compromise in return for the tester's guarantees that his work force will be stable and tranquil. Slowly—although increasingly—leaders of the business community are grasping the fatal implication of such policies. Reed O. Hunt, president of the giant Crown Zellerbach Corporation, for example, recently asked for the complete elimination of personality tests as inconsistent with our desperate need for "individuals" who can create the "new products, processes, and technological improvement" needed for growth.

The testing blight has had another negative effect on corporate morality—namely, the disintegration of human values in the relationship between employer and employee, between supervisor and those he supervises. It has heightened the dehumanization that has always been latent in the corporate atmosphere. George Odiorne, director of the University of Michigan Bureau of Industrial Relations, for one, warned in a recent speech that the use of "forms and techniques adopted from those used by psychiatrists on emotionally disturbed patients" is helping to destroy the "human element" in industry.

"The most damning thing about appraisal interviews is that the human qualities of both individuals are set aside for its duration," Odiorne states. "After several sessions, you find two actors talking past each other at The Psychological Corporation. Take the common appraisal question which asks the subordinate to list his principal weaknesses for his boss. Who but a fool would hand his boss his real weaknesses on a silver platter? The question practically demands that anyone with his wits about him lie like Judas." Odiorne calls most appraisal systems "mechanical policing methods to create a deadening conformity within the organization," and suggests: "Perhaps the time is ripe to start again . . ."

The encroachment of personality testing has been felt by millions in industry and in our schools. However, it may be difficult for the bystander whose life has not yet been affected to wax overly moral about its implications. Each day the brain watcher extends his domain to include more and more of these innocents, and he is either inviting rebellion by extending the melee, or is successfully preparing for a situation of total puissance of the tester.

Some of his new adventures, like the Scientific Appointment Service, which uses personality tests to match prospective mates for a price, are droll. In fact, one psychologist, the late Professor Truman Lee Kelley of Harvard—coauthor of the Stanford Achievement Battery—recently made headlines when he bequeathed a small fortune to his sons under the condition that the wives they select first pass a series of mental and personality tests.

Other of the tester's encroachments have the more frightening implications of predictive "classification" that may one day touch every aspect of our lives and make the brain watcher's predictions more important than our actual behavior. At Columbia University Teachers College, for example, the Safety Education Institute has been studying—with the aid of personality tests—the supposed personality characteristics of frequent auto accident offenders. Their goal, according to a spokesman, is "to be able to classify individuals into driver types in advance, which should be of great help to licensing officials and insurance companies."

If "successful" (meaning that public officials will have joined the gullible ranks of industry), the availability of a driver's license and reasonable insurance rates will depend not on how many accidents you have caused—but on the tester's prediction of your personality and how it will supposedly affect your future safety record. Fortunately, at present, the Columbia researchers—despite publicized claims to the contrary—state that "there is now no reliable and valid test yet devised to do this job properly."

(The theory behind the study, that a small percentage of people are involved in many accidents and must therefore be "accident-prone" is debunked by a research paper, "Human Factors In Accidents," published by Dr. John Flanagan's American Institute for Research. The AIR points out that such a situation is in fact, a chance "mathematical necessity," and adds: "There does not seem to be any simple short-cut to identifying the accident-prone.")

Stimulated by this project to classify drivers in advance by personality testing, it should not be difficult for us to visualize a Central Personality Bureau of the near future, which will electronically store in each metropolitan area the personality and character traits of every resident. Like credit bureaus today, the record will be available to all interested parties—a man's employer or potential employer, his landlord, the state, his creditors, the criminal and civil courts, and perhaps his prospective bride, or her father—at a nominal fee ($10 or less). There might also be an opportunity every half-decade for an individual to "up psyche" himself by taking the Bureau's newest battery of tests and perhaps register the improvement that time—and the careful consideration of what society expects of him—has made in his personality.

The possibility of such a bureau, if it appears extreme, might seem less remote if we consider how easily we have seemingly relinquished our constitutional rights of protection against search and seizure when it applies to our minds instead of our properties. Apparently there is something more sacrosanct in the inviolability of our split-level castles than in the private nobility of our brains.

Brain watching today cannot be successfully minimized or dismissed. Man's curiosity to know more and more about his neighbor increases regularly, as does the volume, if not the quality, of the techniques for such study. Rather than wait and work patiently toward a better understanding of the problem, the brain watcher has decided to use the opportunity to earn rather than learn. If his powers continue to grow, we may find ourselves totally overwhelmed by this aggressive nonscience in this most scientific of ages. To surrender now to a twentieth-century mystique which many have confused with an inevitable touch of progress would indeed be a harsh irony.

Glossary of Testing Terminology

Activity Vector Analysis (AVA)	Prominent personality test system given and interpreted by laymen
Adams-Lepley Personal Audit	Common personality quiz
Adjective Checklists	Personality tests based on a subject's choice of adjectives that best describe him
Aesthetic Values	Non-corporate attributes
Alcadd Test	Quiz on drinking habits ostensibly used to predict alcoholism
Allport Ascendance-Submission Reaction Study	Common personality quiz
Alpha Test	World War I intelligence measurement
Aptitude Tests	Measures of potential ability rather than personality
Assembly-line Testers	Testers who evaluate subjects entirely by impersonal machine scoring
Assessment	Personality evaluation
Autonomy	Another non-corporate attribute
AVA Analyst	Company personnel man turned tester by a three-week cram seminar
Battery	A collection of specially

	chosen tests generally given to a subject during a single session
Bell Adjustment Inventory	Common personality quiz
Bernreuter Personality Inventory	Exceptionally popular personality quiz
Biographical Inventory	Evaluation technique that scores your life history as a test
Biological Intelligence	Current attempts to measure intelligence physiologically
Blacky Pictures	A Freudian-based projective test using dog illustrations. Given by some school districts to gauge children's adjustment
Blind Testing	Personality assessments made without ever meeting the flesh and blood subjects
California Test of Personality	Common personality test often given to junior high and high school students
Cheat-proof Tests	New clinical tests that supposedly thwart subjects who lie on personality quizzes
Clinical Testers	Testers who administer "advanced" tests, such as the Rorschach Inkblots, to measure the personality of normal people
Color Charts	Corporate organizational charts color-keyed by psychologist-testers to indicate an employee's probable future in the company
Corporate Scoring Key	Personality scores established as the model for people applying for jobs, or up for promotion, in the corporation

Corporate Testers	Psychologists employed full time by a company to test applicants and employees
Correlation	The statistical relationship between two testing factors: i.e., prediction of job success and actual job success. Usually expressed in decimal figures
Counseling Tests	Personality tests given to school children in many districts by guidance people and school psychologists
Cross-Validation	Seldom-used testing technique of independently checking unchanged test research with outside control group
Cut-off Score	Score set by tester below which applicants are rejected
Depth Interview	Psychologically-contrived job interview designed to plumb depths of human psyche
Draw-A-Man Tests	Popular method of personality evaluation based on a subject's drawings of the human figure
Edwards Personal Preference Schedule	Currently popular personality test that offers a choice of alternate statements instead of seeking "Yes" or "No" answers to questions. (See "Forced Choice")
Empirical Testing	Evaluating personnel by comparing their scores with supposedly successful subjects. The empirical tester eschews psychological theory
Executive Locators and/or Recruiters	Modern employment agencies, some of which use personality testing to screen applicants

False Positives	Men falsely labeled as misfits or psychotics through statistical testing error
Forced Choice Tests	Tests such as the Edwards Schedule that force the subjects to choose between two alternate statements
George Washington Social Intelligence Test	Test commonly used in the selection of salesmen
Guilford-Zimmerman Temperament Survey	Popular personality quiz
Halstead Battery	Battery of neurological tests, named after its developer, which supposedly measures executive capabilities
Human Inventory	A massive personality assessment of the management of an entire corporation often accomplished in a single brain watch
Humm-Wadsworth Temperament Scale	A clinically-oriented personality test developed and in use in the Los Angeles area
Hypomania	Mild psychosis supposedly measured by certain personality tests
Instrument	A test
Interest Tests	Quizzes that supposedly measure job suitability by gauging a person's interests
Job Criteria	Testing theories on what attributes are essential for any given job
Kling Theological Inventory	Experimental test to determine suitability for the calling of minister
Kuder Preference Record	A test of job interest much used in schools and industry

Levy Movement Blots	A Rorschach-like personality test that is used by some testers to measure a subject's "creativity"
Lie Scales	Series of "goody" questions inserted to trip subjects attempting to create near-perfect psychological impressions
Management Development	Tester jargon for a continuous executive brain watch
Manson Evaluation	Personality test that attempts to predict alcoholism
Mean	Average
Median	Mid-point of a group: 50 percent have higher scores and 50 percent have lower scores
Mental Measurements Yearbook	Authoritative reference book which includes collection of professional reviews of tests
Merton System	The evaluation of personality by studying bulges and ridges on face and skull. System has been used by several companies including The Budd Company in Philadelphia
Mf Scales	Measures of Masculinity and Femininity found in many personality quizzes. Sometimes used as clue to suspected homosexuality
MMPI (Minnesota Multiphasic Personality Inventory)	Extremely popular quiz that attempts a clinical diagnosis of personality (i.e., Schizophrenia Scale)
Non-Cognitive	Factors other than intellectual, such as personality
Norm	Average, mean (May also be Median)

On-the-Job Testing	Personality evaluation of men already employed. Often a key to their corporate future
Percentile	Statistical measure of where an individual scores in relation to the total population of a group or a sample
Personal Image Building	Cheating on personality tests
Personality Inventory	Question and answer tests
Predictive Efficiency	How well, or badly, a test actually predicts what it claims to, measured in percentage above or below simple chance
Problem Checklist	Psychological test given to school children (in many districts) in which they are asked to unburden themselves
Profile	A subject's psychological make-up, sometimes indicated on a graph
Project Talent	Mass testing of high school students (including personality tests) sponsored by the Department of Health, Education and Welfare
Projective Application Blank	Surreptitious use of a subject's job application blank to measure his personality rather than check his education and work history
Projective Tests	Armament of clinical testers. Tests, such as Rorschach Inkblots and Figure Drawing, seek unstructured responses to varied stimuli
Psychological Contamination	Testing jargon for a subject's work experience or

	background which might conflict with "pure" personality test results
Psychometrics	The use of statistical techniques in psychological measurement
Psychometrist	One who uses psychometrics
Red Downgrading	Term used by color-charting on-the-job testers to describe men recommended for dismissal because of psychological failings
Reliability	How well a test score compares with the "true" score. Measurement of the error involved in the test-taking process
Rorschach Test	Popular clinical inkblot test developed in Switzerland in 1921 and now used extensively in corporate personality testing
Scale	Part of a test that ostensibly measures a particular aspect of the whole: i.e., "neurotic" scale on a personality test
Scientific Selection	Brain-watching jargon for personality testing
Scoring Key	Supposedly non-existent "right" answers to personality tests provided with every test manual
Sense of Humor Test	Series of outdated jokes used to select salesmen. Part of the George Washington Social Intelligence Test
Sentence Completion Test	Projective test in which subject fills in endings to unfinished sentences using "free association"

Significant Item	Test question whose responses appear to statistically distinguish one group of subjects from another
Situational Tests	Modern variety of trial by fire or sword. Personality measured under actual or simulated conditions such as the OSS' unsuccessful attempts during World War II
Social Desirability	Theory behind forced-choice tests. Alternate statements are supposedly equal in status value
Sociogram	A classroom personality test in which students brain watch each other at teacher's behest
Statistical Correlation	The same as Correlation. Number is expressed in decimals from −1.00 to + 1.00
Strong Vocational Interest Blank	Popular testing tool that scores a subject's supposed adaptability for 45 occupations and professions by comparing his interests and prejudices with those of people already in the field
Study of Values	A test based on Eduard Spranger's research on "Types of Men." The SOV divides human personality values into six areas: aesthetic, religious, economic, political, theoretical, and social
Thematic Apperception Test	Much-used projective instrument that probes personality by interpreting what a subject thinks is taking place in a series of illustrations

Thurstone Temperament Schedule	Common personality quiz
Trait	A quiz tester's subdivision of human personality; i.e., introversion, sociability, etc.
Validity	Measure of how well a test actually performs; whether it describes or predicts what it claims to. Validity is usually expressed as a statistical correlation
Washburne S-A Inventory	A popular personality quiz which employs a surreptitious "lie" scale
Weighting	Assigning special statistical emphasis to different parts of a test in order to make it, or make it appear, to perform better
Woodworth Personal Data Sheet	The precursor of all modern personality quizzes. Developed during World War I as a psychological screen for servicemen

THE CORPORATE ADJUSTMENT INVENTORY*

Answer the following questions (1–15) by circling either Yes or No.

1. Is your sex life satisfactory? — Yes No
2. Are you talkative at social gatherings? — Yes No
3. Did you ever take anything that belonged to someone else? — Yes No
4. Do you tend to be unconventional in your social or religious beliefs? — Yes No
5. Do you enjoy spending an evening alone? — Yes No
6. Do you always tell the truth? — Yes No
7. Would you like a job such as a forest ranger's that kept you away for a few years? — Yes No
8. Did you ever greedily take more than you should? — Yes No
9. Can you express yourself better writing than talking? — Yes No
10. Do ideas run thrugh your head that keep you awake? — Yes No
11. Have you ever kept anybody waiting for an appointment? — Yes No
12. Do you lose your appetite when you get upset? — Yes No
13. Does it bother you to have people watch you work? — Yes No

* By Martin L. Gross. "The Corporate Adjustment Inventory" is based on current question-and-answer personality test theories, but has been developed solely as illustrative material for the testee. It is not available for research studies or sale to testers, test distributors, or corporations. No claims of any kind are made for normative data, reliability, and especially, validity.

14. Are you considered a little indifferent to the opposite sex? Yes No
15. Did you ever want to get even with somebody? Yes No

Answer the following questions (16–28) by circling either A or B.
16. When I am late for a public meeting, I prefer
    A. To stand in the rear   B. To take a seat up front
17. When doing my work, I generally
    A. Plan far ahead   B. Concentrate on the immediate
18. Life is
    A. Wonderful   B. Too much trouble
19. Are you more interested in reading about
    A. Julius Caesar   B. Aristotle
20. The main objective of scientific research is
    A. Practical application.   B. Discovery of truth
21. In regard to the AFL-CIO, workers should be encouraged to
    A. Join   B. Stay out if they want to
22. Which society represents the higher degree of civilization?
    A. Modern industrial society   B. Ancient Greeks
23. Which makes you feel better?
    A. Admiration   B. Achievement
24. Which would you rather have?
    A. A good friend   B. $500
25. Which would you read first in the New York *Times?*
    A. Stock market reports   B. Drama section
26. Which activity interests you more?
    A. Athletics   B. Intellectual affairs
27. Which would you prefer?
    A. A hard, interesting job   B. An easy, uninteresting job
28. Which would you prefer?
    A. $20,000 in 1973   B. One new car and its upkeep

The following questions (29–64) are a test of your interests. Next to each, mark whether you like (L), dislike (D) or are indifferent (I) to the item or activity.

29. Boxing matches
30. Repairing a jet engine
31. Beautiful scenery
32. Smokers
33. *Ladies' Home Journal*
34. Looking in store windows
35. Shooting a machine gun
36. Snakes
37. Engineering
38. *Mademoiselle*
39. Writing letters to friends
40. Hunting
41. Buying furniture
42. Going to auctions
43. Teaching school children
44. Running a crane

45. Football
46. Seeing scientific exhibits
47. Art galleries
48. "Blue" movies
49. Bridge
50. Racing a sports car
51. Raising flowers
52. Poker
53. Long walks
54. Croquet
55. Formal dress affairs
56. Bosomy girls
57. Being a frogman
58. Sporting pages of newspapers
59. *House and Garden*
60. Professional hunter
61. Burlesque
62. Fixing things around the house
63. Running a lathe
64. Cooking

Decide quickly whether the statement (65–79) is True (T) or False (F) and mark each one appropriately.

65. I often get athlete's foot, especially in the summertime.
66. Most attorneys are honest.
67. There are too many frills in modern education.
68. Almost anything can be fixed up in the courts if you have enough money.
69. I like mannish women.
70. I get angry when I run out of whisky when the store is closed.
71. People should not patronize stores that are on strike.
72. I have used alcohol excessively.
73. Taxes on large incomes are too high.
74. I am interested in accumulating a substantial amount of money.
75. Manners are an essential aspect of life.
76. I believe in God but I think some people make too much of a fuss over religion.
77. We should encourage public housing projects for poorer people.
78. I would rather look at scientific apparatus than at new products of industry.
79. There is something wrong with my mind.

Mark to what degree the following questions (80–103) apply to you. (A) Almost Always (B) Frequently (C) Rarely D Almost Never

80. Do people regard you as queer?   ( )
81. Do you find it difficult to start conversations with people of the opposite sex?   ( )
82. Are you at ease with older people?   ( )
83. Do you catch cold?   ( )
84. Are you critical of the American way of life?   ( )
85. Do you cry?   ( )
86. Do you feel that people are watching you on the street?   ( )
87. Do you feel ill at ease at a party when you are dressed more informally than others?   ( )

88. Are books more entertaining than companions?   ( )

89. Do you find it hard to brush off salesmen?   ( )

90. Do you object verbally when a person steps in front of you in a line?   ( )

91. Do you enjoy a good drink of whisky or a cocktail in the morning?   ( )

92. Do you have trouble making friends?   ( )

93. Do you try to persuade people to do things?   ( )

94. Does criticism bother you much?   ( )

95. Do your teeth need dental work?   ( )

96. Are you tired when you wake up in the morning?   ( )

97. Are you self-conscious in front of superiors in business or school?   ( )

98. Have you been a leader in groups or clubs?   ( )

99. Do you ignore feelings of other people when working for an important goal?

100. Do you think about possible misfortunes?   ( )

101. Do you feel inferior?   ( )

102. Do you get pimples, carbuncles, or boils?   ( )

103. When you get hungry, do the pangs come on quickly?   ( )

Sense-of-humor test. Read the following jokes (104–106) and choose the punch line you believe is funniest.

104. Two men and a well-shaped blonde are flying in a small airplane when the engine conks out and they decide to jump. The men grab the only two chutes. Says one man to the other: "What about her?" The second man answers: "We'll have to scratch her." Surprised, the first man asks:

   A. "Think we have time?"
   B. "Wasn't she a good kid?"
   C. "Why did it happen to her?"
   D. "Will you promise to bring three chutes next time?"

105. Politician speaking to a farm crowd looks for a place to speak from. One farmer obligingly brings a manure spreader which the politician mounts. Says the politician as an opening remark:

   A. "I can see Indiana from here."
   B. "This is the first time I've ever stood on the opposition's platform."
   C. "Thank you for the best seat in the house."
   D. "Perhaps this will help fertilize my thoughts."

106. Scotsman whose large valise has just been thrown off a moving

   A. "You're a wee bit freshie, conductor."
   B. "Now see what you've done.

train because he refused
to pay the baggage fee:

My laddie will surely bump
himself when he hits the
ground."

C. "Conductor, you haven't the
soul of a Scotsman."

D. "You'll pay for this, conductor."

SCORING KEY FOR "THE CORPORATE ADJUSTMENT INVENTORY"

The questions were designed to test you for seven traits, plus possible clues to alcoholism. The traits are listed by the following
keys:

ES—Emotional Stability   M—Masculinity
 S—Sociability   SH—Sense of Humor
SC—Self-Confidence   T—Truthfulness
BV—Business Values

(Score the point values next to the trait indicated after each answer. The scores can be entered on a list of the seven traits.)

1–15. Yes or No questions. Score five points for each correct
answer.

1. Yes ES	6. No T	11. Yes T
2. Yes S	7. No S	12. No ES
3. Yes T	8. Yes T	13. No ES
4. No BV	9. No S	14. No M
5. No S	10. No ES	15. Yes T

16–28. A or B questions. Score five points for each correct answer.

16. B SC	20. A BV	24. A S
17. A BV	21. B BV	25. A BV
18. A ES	22. A BV	26. A S
19. A BV	23. B ES	27. A BV
		28. A BV

29–64. This was a test of your masculinity. The correct answers
are listed below. Score +2 for each correct answer. Score −2 for
each incorrect answer. Score 0 for each I (Indifferent) answer.

29. L	38. D	47. D	56. L
30. L	39. D	48. L	57. L
31. D	40. L	49. D	58. L
32. L	41. D	50. L	59. D
33. D	42. D	51. D	60. L
34. D	43. D	52. L	61. L
35. L	44. L	53. D	62. L
36. L	45. L	54. D	63. L
37. L	46. L	55. D	64. D

65–79. True or False questions. Score five points for each correct answer.

65. F	ES	70. F	ES	75. T	BV
66. T	BV	71. F	BV	76. T	BV
67. T	BV	72. F	ES	77. F	BV
68. F	BV	73. T	BV	78. F	BV
69. F	M	74. T	BV	79. F	ES

80–103. Choice of A, B, C, D questions. All correct A or D answers score five points. All correct B or C answers score two points. Incorrect answers receive no points.

80. C, D	ES	88. C, D	S	96. C, D	ES
81. C, D	SC	89. C, D	SC	97. C, D	SC
82. A, B	SC	90. A, B	SC	98. A, B	SC
83. C, D	ES	91. C, D	ES	99. C, D	S
84. C, D	BV	92. C, D	S	• 100. C, D	ES
85. C, D	ES	93. A, B	SC	101. C, D	SC
86. C, D	SC	94. C, D	ES	102. C, D	ES
87. C, D	SC	95. C, D	ES	103. C, D	ES

104–106. Score 10 points in Sense of Humor (SH) for each correct answer.

104. A	105. B	106. B

SCORING AND INTERPRETATIVE HINTS:

Emotional Stability (ES): Scores of 80–100 can be considered "high," while 0–40 are "low." Other scores are in the middle range. Almost without exception, high scores on ES are a prerequisite in industry.

Sociability (S): Scores of 30–45 are "high," while 15–30 are in the average range. Sociability is less essential to executive success, and average scores are generally desirable. Salesmen, however, are expected to score well on this trait. (See Chapter IX.)

Self-Confidence (SC): As indicated throughout the volume, SC is invaluable to corporate success. Scores of 40–50 may be considered sufficiently "high." A perfect score of 55 may be an indication of over-confidence. (See Chapter VIII.)

Business Values (BV): A BV score of 80–100 is an indication of proper management and conservative orientation. An average or low score may indicate too liberal, impractical, or aesthetic a viewpoint. (See Chapters II and VIII.)

Masculinity (M): A score of 55–82 indicates a sufficiently masculine, or non-cultural approach to convince the tester of your virility. (See Chapter V.)

Sense of Humor (SH): A score of twenty is sufficient for most management applicants, while the proper salesman should score well on all three questions (30).

Truthfulness (T): This typical "lie" scale rewards testees who score 20–25 on this trait. A score of 15 makes the tester somewhat suspicious. If your T score is 10 or less, throw away your test results: the tester has lost confidence in your candidness.

Alcoholism: Check numbers 70, 72 and 91. Two or more incorrect answers are ominous warnings.